Essential German

Edited by
Christopher Warnasch and Helga Schier, Ph.D.

Content in this program has been modified and enhanced from *Starting Out in German*, published in 2008.

Published in the United States by Living Language, an imprint of Random House, Inc.

www.livinglanguage.com

Editor: Christopher Warnasch
Production Editor: Carolyn Roth
Production Manager: Tom Marshall
Interior Design: Sophie Chin
Illustrations: Sophie Chin

First Edition

Library of Congress Cataloging-in-Publication Data

Essential German / edited by Christopher Warnasch and Helga Schier. — 1st ed.
    p. cm.
 ISBN 978-0-307-97159-3
 1. German language—Textbooks for foreign speakers—English. 2. German language—Grammar.
 3. German language—Spoken German. 4. German language—Self-instruction. I. Warnasch,
Christopher A. II. Schier, Helga.
 PF3129.E5E88 2011
 438.2'421—dc23
                              2011023728

This book is available at special discounts for bulk purchases for sales promotions or premiums.
Special editions, including personalized covers, excerpts of existing books, and corporate imprints,
can be created in large quantities for special needs. For more information, write to Special Markets/
Premium Sales, 1745 Broadway, MD 3-1, New York, New York 10019 or e-mail specialmarkets@
randomhouse.com.

PRINTED IN THE UNITED STATES OF AMERICA

10 9 8

Acknowledgments

Thanks to the Living Language team: Amanda D'Acierno, Christopher Warnasch, Suzanne McQuade, Laura Riggio, Erin Quirk, Amanda Munoz, Fabrizio LaRocca, Siobhan O'Hare, Sophie Chin, Sue Daulton, Alison Skrabek, Carolyn Roth, Ciara Robinson, and Tom Marshall.

How to Use This Course **6**

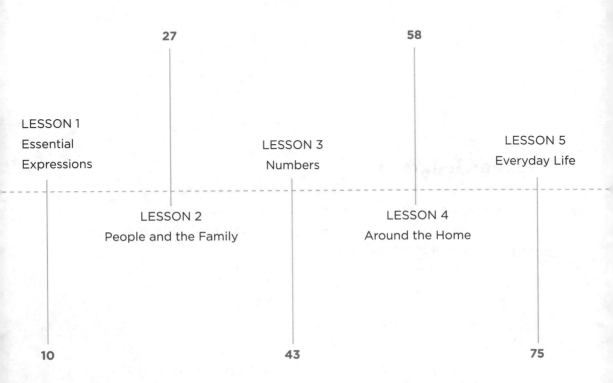
COURSE

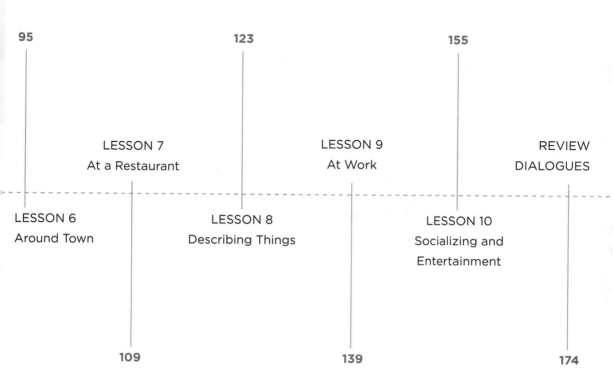
OUTLINE

How to Use This Course

Guten Tag!

Welcome to *Living Language Essential German*! Ready to learn how to speak, read, and write German?

Before we begin, let's go over what you''ll see in this course. It's very easy to use, but this section will help you get started.

PHONETICS

The first five lessons of this course contain phonetics (in other words, [owf VEE-der-zay-ehn] in addition to **auf Wiedersehen**) to help you get started with German pronunciation. However, please keep in mind that phonetics are not exact—they are just an approximation of German sounds using English (-like) spelling—so you should rely mostly on the audio, *not* the phonetics, to improve your pronunciation skills.

For a guide to our phonetics system, see the Pronunciation Guide at the end of the course.

LESSONS

There are 10 lessons in this course. Each lesson is divided into three parts and has the following components:

Welcome at the beginning outlining what you will cover in each of the three parts of the lesson.

PART 1

- **Vocabulary Builder 1** listing the key words and phrases for that lesson.

- **Vocabulary Practice 1** to practice what you learned in Vocabulary Builder 1.

- **Grammar Builder 1** to guide you through the structure of the German language (how to form sentences, questions, and so on).

PART 2

- **Vocabulary Builder 2** listing more key words and phrases.

- **Vocabulary Practice 2** to practice what you learned in Vocabulary Builder 2.

- **Grammar Builder 2** for more information on language structure.

- **Work Out 1** for a comprehensive practice of what you've learned so far.

PART 3

- **Bring It All Together** to put what you've learned in a conversational context through a dialogue, monologue, description, or other similar text.

- **Work Out 2** for another helpful practice exercise.

- **Drive It Home** to ingrain an important point of German structure for the long term.

- **Parting Words** outlining what you learned in the lesson.

TAKE IT FURTHER

- **Take It Further** sections are scattered throughout the lesson to provide extra information about the new vocabulary you've just seen, expand on some grammar points, or introduce additional words and phrases.

WORD RECALL

Word Recall sections appear in between lessons. They review important vocabulary and grammar from previous lessons, including the one you just finished. These sections will reinforce what you've learned so far in the course, and help you retain the information for the long term.

QUIZZES

This course contains two quizzes: **Quiz 1** is halfway through the course (after Lesson 5), and **Quiz 2** appears after the last lesson (Lesson 10). The quizzes are self-graded, so it's easy for you to test your progress and see if you should go back and review.

REVIEW DIALOGUES

There are five **Review Dialogues** at the end of the course, after Quiz 2. These everyday dialogues review what you learned in Lessons 1–10, introduce some new vocabulary and structures, and allow you to become more familiar with conversational German. Each dialogue is followed by comprehension questions that serve as the course's final review.

PROGRESS BAR

You will see a **Progress Bar** on almost every page that has course material. It indicates your current position in the course and lets you know how much progress you're making. Each line in the bar represents a lesson, with the final line representing the Review Dialogues.

AUDIO

Look for this symbol ⊙ to help guide you through the audio as you're reading the book. It will tell you which track to listen to for each section that has audio. When you see the symbol, select the indicated track and start listening! If you don't see the symbol, then there isn't any audio for that section. You'll also see ⦿, which will tell you where that track ends.

The audio can be used on its own—in other words, without the book—when you're on the go. Whether in your car or at the gym, you can listen to the audio to brush up on your pronunciation, review what you've learned in the book, or even use it as a stand-alone course.

PRONUNCIATION GUIDE, GRAMMAR SUMMARY, GLOSSARY

At the back of this book you will find a **Pronunciation Guide**, **Grammar Summary**, and **Glossary**. The Pronunciation Guide provides information on German pronunciation and the phonetics system used in this course. The Grammar Summary contains a helpful, brief overview of key points in the German grammar system. It also includes a **Grammar Index**, which lists the principal grammar topics covered in this course and where to find them in the book. The Glossary (German-English and English-German) includes all of the essential words from the ten lessons, as well as additional key vocabulary.

FREE ONLINE TOOLS

Go to **www.livinglanguage.com/languagelab** to access your free online tools. The tools are organized around the lessons in this course, with audiovisual flashcards, interactive games, and quizzes for each lesson. These tools will help you review and practice the vocabulary and grammar that you've seen in the lessons, as well provide some extra words and phrases related to the lesson's topic.

Lesson 1: Essential Expressions

Lektion eins: Wichtige Ausdrücke

lek-tsee-OHN īns: VIKH-tih-geh OWS-drew-keh

Willkommen! [vil-KOH-men] Welcome! In this first lesson, you'll learn some basic expressions and other useful words and phrases to get you started speaking German. You'll learn how to:

- ☐ Greet someone and ask how they're doing
- ☐ Use basic courtesy expressions
- ☐ Ask simple questions when you meet someone
- ☐ Use both formal and informal forms of address
- ☐ Put it all together in a simple conversation between two people meeting for the first time

But let's begin with some essential vocabulary. Ready?

Remember to look for this symbol ⊙ to help guide you through the audio as you're reading the book. It will tell you which track to listen to for each section that has audio. When you see the symbol, select the indicated track and start listening. If you don't see the symbol, then there isn't any audio for that section. You'll also see ⏸, which will tell you where the track ends. Finally, keep in mind that the audio can be used on its own for review and practice when you're on the go!

Vocabulary Builder 1

▶ 1B Vocabulary Builder 1 (CD 1, Track 2)

Hello./Good day.	**Guten Tag.**	GOO-ten tahk
Good morning.	**Guten Morgen.**	GOO-ten MOHR-gen
Good evening.	**Guten Abend.**	GOO-ten AH-bent
Hi.	**Hallo.**	HAH-loh
Welcome.	**Willkommen.**	vil-KOH-men
How are you?	**Wie geht's?**	vee gayts
Very well.	**Sehr gut.**	zayr goot
Thank you.	**Danke.**	DAHN-keh
Goodbye.	**Auf Wiedersehen.**	owf VEE-der-zay-ehn
Bye.	**Tschüss.**	chewss
See you soon.	**Bis bald.**	bis bahlt
Take care.	**Mach's gut.**	makhs goot

You'll see phonetics in the first five lessons of *Essential German* to help you get started reading. For a guide to the phonetic system used here, see the Pronunciation Guide at the end of the course. Take note of one important issue in written German. In the phrases **guten Tag** (*good day*), **guten Morgen** (*good morning*), and **guten Abend** (*good evening*), did you notice that the nouns **Tag** (*day*), **Morgen** (*morning*), and **Abend** (*evening*) are all capitalized? That's because all nouns, whether they're proper names or not, are capitalized in written German.

✎ Vocabulary Practice 1

Now let's practice what you've learned! Fill in the blanks with the correct German translations of the following phrases. If you don't remember some of them, that's fine. You can always go back over the vocabulary builder section and review.

1. *Good morning.* _____

2. *Thank you.* _____

3. *Bye.* _____

4. *Welcome.* _____

5. *Hello./Good day.* _____

6. *Good evening.* _____

7. *Hi.* _____

8. *Goodbye.* _____

9. *How are you?* _____

10. *Take care.* _____

11. *Very well.* _____

12. *See you soon.* _____

ANSWER KEY

1. **Guten Morgen**; 2. **Danke**; 3. **Tschüss**; 4. **Willkommen**; 5. **Guten Tag**; 6. **Guten Abend**; 7. **Hallo**; 8. **Auf Wiedersehen**; 9. **Wie geht's?** 10. **Mach's gut**; 11. **Sehr gut**; 12. **Bis bald**.

Grammar Builder 1

▶ 1C Grammar Builder 1 (CD 1, Track 3)

German has a few sounds that will be unfamiliar to an English speaker. Have you noticed the vowel sound **ü** in:

Tschüss.	chewss	*Bye.*

It's pronounced a little like *i* in *kiss*, but with the lips rounded as when you're pronouncing *oo* in *food*. Here it is again: **ü, ü**. For example, the German word for *to kiss* is **küssen**.

küssen	KEWS-sen	*to kiss*

Another unfamiliar sound is the sound **ch** in:

Mach's gut.	makhs goot	*Take care.*

It's a bit similar to the *k* sound in *luck*, but you need to keep pressing the air out, rather than stopping it abruptly. Try it again: **mach's gut … mach's gut …**

Okay, now let's go over the rest of what you've just learned. First note that there are different kinds of greetings in German depending on the time of day:

guten Morgen	GOO-ten MOHR-gen	*good morning*
guten Abend	GOO-ten AH-bent	*good evening*
guten Tag	GOO-ten tahk	*good day*

When you're choosing a greeting, you also need to consider whom you are talking to. If you're greeting someone you're friendly with, you may choose a less formal expression, like **Hallo** [HAH-loh] (*hi*).

The same is true for saying good-bye. If you're talking to someone you don't know well, you can say **Auf Wiedersehen** [owf VEE-der-zay-en] (*good-bye*). If the other person is a friend, you may want to say **tschüss** [chewss] (*bye*) and **mach's gut** [makhs goot] (*take care*). Now, let's continue with some more words and expressions.

Take It Further 1

▶ 1D Take It Further (CD 1, Track 4)

In these sections, we'll expand on what you've seen so far. We might break down some of the new sentences or phrases you've seen, look more closely at additional words that have been introduced, or expand on a grammatical point. For now, though, let's look at a few points of German spelling and pronunciation.

You've probably noticed by now that **w** is pronounced like English *v*. You saw this in:

| auf Wiedersehen | owf VEE-der-zay-ehn | *good-bye* |
| Willkommen | vil-KOH-men | *welcome* |

And of course we've already covered the pronunciation of **ch**, which is similar to a *k*, but pronounced with the tongue pulled further back in the throat, with a rasping sound. But note that the combination **tsch** sounds like the *ch* in *church*.

| Mach's gut. | makhs goot | *Take care.* |
| Tschüss. | chewss | *Bye.* |

That brings us to the sound of **ü**, which we've also already covered. The two dots above the **u** are called an **Umlaut** (OOM-lowt). They only appear over three letters: **ü**, **ä**, and **ö**. To make the **ü** sound, say something like the *i* in *kiss* or the *ee* as in *see*, but round your lips as if you were saying *oo* in *food*. We'll come back to **ä** and **ö** later. Keep in mind that in the transliteration, **ü** is represented as *ew*. But it's not the same *ew* as in *new* or *flew*! We don't have the **ü** sound in English, so *ew* is really just a shorthand.

A few other German vowel sounds are written with two letters. The important ones to remember are **au**, **ei**, and **ie**. The combination **au** is pronounced like *ow* in

owl or *ou* in *hour*, but it will be phonetically represented as *ow*. The combination **ei** is pronounced like the *i* in *price* or the *y* in *my*. It will be represented with the long i: ī. And the combination **ie** is pronounced like the *ee* in *see*, and it will be represented as *ee*.

Ausdrücke	OWS-drew-keh	*expressions*
auf Wiedersehen	owf VEE-der-zay-ehn	*good-bye*
eins	īns	*one*

Here's a tip for keeping **ei** and **ie** straight. The English name of the second letter of each combination gives you a clue about how to pronounce it: **ei** = i (ī), and **ie** = e (*ee*).

Vocabulary Builder 2

 1E Vocabulary Builder 2 (CD 1, Track 5)

Do you speak German?	**Sprechen Sie Deutsch?**	SHPREH-khen zee doytsh
Yes.	**Ja.**	yah
No.	**Nein.**	nīn
A little bit.	**Ein bisschen.**	īn BIS-khen
What's your name?	**Wie heißen Sie?**	vee HĪ-sen zee
My name is …	**Ich heiße …**	ikh HĪ-seh
Where are you from?	**Wo kommen Sie her?**	voh KOH-men zee hehr
I'm from Canada.	**Ich komme aus Kanada.**	ikh KOH-meh ows KAH-nah-dah
It's nice here.	**Es ist schön hier.**	ehs ist shu(r)n heer

✎ Vocabulary Practice 2

Find the translations of the following words below:

1. *German*
2. *nice*
3. *I*
4. *no*
5. *speak (as in Do you speak German?)*
6. *here*
7. *come (as in I come)*
8. *from (as in from Canada)*

N	S	K	O	M	M	E	D
E	P	S	C	D	E	U	T
I	R	N	N	E	I	N	A
N	E	S	P	U	I	C	H
I	C	K	R	T	Ä	D	H
N	H	A	U	S	U	E	I
I	E	H	Ö	C	S	U	E
N	N	S	C	H	Ö	N	R

ANSWER KEY

1. **Deutsch**; 2. **schön**; 3. **ich**; 4. **nein**; 5. **sprechen**; 6. **hier**; 7. **komme**; 8. **aus**

Grammar Builder 2

▶ 1F Grammar Builder 2 (CD 1, Track 6)

The phrases and expressions that you've just learned contained two personal pronouns that you'll need in order to talk about yourself and to address the person you're talking to.

ich	ikh	*I*
Sie	zee	*you*

Did you notice the slight difference in the forms of the verbs that are used with them? With **ich**, the verbs end in **-e**, as in:

| ich heiße | ikh HĪ-seh | *my name is* |
| ich komme | ikh KOH-meh | *I come (from)* |

With **Sie**, they end in **-en**, as in:

| Sie heißen | zee HĪ-sen | *your name is* |
| Sie kommen | zee KOH-men | *you're from/you come (from)* |

Also, the pronoun **ich** contains another sound that makes German sound like German: **ch**. It's pronounced a bit like the sound *h* in English words like *hit*, but with more of a hissing quality: the back of the tongue is raised and moved forward, and the air escapes by its sides. Let's try it once more: **ich, ich**.

By the way, the pronoun **Sie** is only used when talking to a stranger or to a person that you don't know well. With family and friends, a different pronoun is used: **du** [doo]. You will learn more about other pronouns and the accompanying verb forms in Lesson 3.

�eqⅡ

✎ Work Out 1

Now let's review some of the expressions that you've learned in this lesson. Listen to the German on the audio, and fill in the missing words. Repeat the correct answers in the pauses provided for practice.

▶ 1G Work Out 1 (CD 1, Track 7)

Hello!	1. Guten _____!
My name is …	2. _____ heiße …
I'm from …	3. Ich _____ aus …
I speak a little German.	4. Ich _____ ein bisschen Deutsch.
It's nice here.	5. Es ist _____ hier.
What's your name?	6. Wie _____ Sie?
How are you?	7. _____ geht's?
And where are you from?	8. Und _____ kommen Sie her?
Do you speak English?	9. _____ Sie Englisch?
Good-bye.	10. _____ Wiedersehen.

ANSWER KEY
1. Tag; 2. Ich; 3.komme; 4. spreche; 5. schön; 6. heißen; 7. Wie; 8. wo; 9. Sprechen; 10. Auf

⏸

❝ Bring It All Together

▶ 1H Bring It All Together (CD 1, Track 8)

Now let's bring it all together, adding a little more vocabulary and structure. Imagine a dialogue between two people who have just met—Paula, from the United States, and Philipp, from Germany. As earlier, you'll hear each phrase in English first and then in German.

Hello!
Guten Tag!
GOO-ten tahk

How are you?
Wie geht's?
vee gayts

Very well, thanks.
Danke, sehr gut.
DAHN-keh, zayr goot

My name is Philipp.
Ich heiße Philipp.
ikh HĪ-seh FIH-lip

And what's your name?
Und wie heißen Sie?
uhnt vee HĪ-sen zee

My name is Paula.
Ich heiße Paula.
ikh HĪ-seh POW-lah

Where are you from?
Wo kommen Sie her?
voh KOH-men zee hehr

I'm from Philadelphia.
Ich komme aus Philadelphia.
ikh KOH-meh ows fih-lah-DEL-fee-yah

Welcome to Frankfurt.
Willkommen in Frankfurt.
vihl-KOH-men in FRAHNK-fort

It's nice here.
Es ist schön hier.
es ist shuh(r)n heer

I think so, too.

Das finde ich auch.

das FIN-deh ikh owkh

See you soon then.

Also, bis bald.

AHL-zoh bis bahlt

⏸

Take It Further 2

▶ 1I Take It Further (CD 1, Track 9)

Okay, you've learned quite a few words already in this lesson, and in this section we've added a few more. Let's go over them briefly.

und	uhnt	*and*
auch	owkh	*too, also, as well*
Das finde ich auch.	dass FIHN-deh ikh owkh	*I think so, too. (lit., "That find I, too.")*

You've also seen more verbs used with the pronoun **ich** (*I*), such as:

finde	FIHN-deh	*I find*
spreche	SHPREH-kheh	*I speak*

And did you notice that questions have a different word order than statements? Questions like the following have the verb before the pronoun.

Und wie heißen Sie?	uhnt vee HĪ-sen zee	*And what's your name?*
Wo kommen Sie her?	voh KOH-men zee hayr	*Where are you from?*

We will discuss the topic of word order in more detail in Lesson 6.

✎ Work Out 2

Let's practice what you've learned. Match the English in Column A to the correct German translation in Column B.

1. *Very well.*	a. **Danke.**
2. *Thank you.*	b. **Wie heißen Sie?**
3. *Good evening.*	c. **Wo kommen Sie her?**
4. *A little bit.*	d. **Bis bald.**
5. *What's your name?*	e. **Ein bisschen.**
6. *Where are you from?*	f. **Guten Abend.**
7. *My name is . . .*	g. **Sehr gut.**
8. *See you soon.*	h. **Ich heiße . . .**

ANSWER KEY
1. g; 2. a; 3. f; 4. e; 5. b; 6. c; 7. h; 8. d.

▶ 1J Work Out 2 (CD 1, Track 10)

Now listen to the audio for some more audio-only practice. This will help you master the material you've learned so far!

⏸

✎ Drive It Home

Throughout this course you'll see Drive It Home sections that include practices on key constructions that you've learned. At first glance, these exercises may seem simple and repetitive, so you may be tempted to skip them. But don't! They are designed to help make the structures that you learn more automatic, and to move them into your long-term memory. So take the time to do each exercise completely, writing out all the answers, and speaking them aloud to yourself. This will really help you retain the information.

First, let's start with something simple. Fill in the blanks of each greeting, according to the time of day given in parentheses. Then speak the whole sentence aloud for practice.

1. Guten _____, Monika. Wie geht's? (*morning*)

2. Guten _____, Hans. Wie geht's? (*afternoon*)

3. Guten _____, Heike. Wie geht's? (*morning*)

4. Guten _____, Karl. Wie geht's? (*evening*)

5. Guten _____, Sabine. Wie geht's? (*afternoon*)

ANSWER KEY
1. Morgen; 2. Tag; 3. Morgen; 4. Abend; 5. Tag

Now, complete each answer with **Ich komme aus ...** (*I'm from ...*), following the cues provided. Again, say each question and answer aloud for practice. Can you guess the translations of the countries?

1. **Wo kommen Sie her?** _____ Kanada.

2. **Wo kommen Sie her?** _____ Deutschland.

3. **Wo kommen Sie her?** _____ Österreich.

4. **Wo kommen Sie her?** _____ Frankreich.

5. **Wo kommen Sie her?** _____ Japan.

6. **Wo kommen Sie her?** _____ Südafrika.

ANSWER KEY
1. **Ich komme aus …** (*Canada*); 2. **Ich komme aus …** (*Germany*); 3. **Ich komme aus …** (*Austria*);
4. **Ich komme aus …** (*France*); 5. **Ich komme aus …** (*Japan*); 6. **Ich komme aus …** (*South Africa*)

Parting Words

Danke! *Thank you!* You've finished your first lesson of German. How did you do? You should now be able to:

☐ Greet someone and ask how they're doing (Still unsure? Go back to page 11.)

☐ Use basic courtesy expressions (Still unsure? Go back to page 13.)

☐ Ask simple questions when you meet someone (Still unsure? Go back to page 15.)

☐ Use both formal and informal forms of address (Still unsure? Go back to page 16.)

☐ Put it all together in a simple conversation between two people meeting for the first time (Still unsure? Go back to page 18.)

Don't forget to practice and reinforce what you've learned by visiting **www.livinglanguage.com/ languagelab** for flashcards, games, and quizzes for Lesson 1!

Take It Further 3

▶ 1K Take It Further (CD 1, Track 11)

Depending on whether you're in Germany, Austria, or Switzerland, you'll also hear people using expressions other than the ones you've just learned. For example, in southern Germany and Austria, you may hear people greet each other with:

| Grüß Gott! | grews got | *Hello!* |
| Servus! | SEHR-vus | *Hello!* |

Auf Wiedersehen bis zur Lektion 2! *Good-bye until Lesson 2!*

⏸

Word Recall

You'll see this section between each lesson. It gives you the chance to review key vocabulary from all of the previous lessons up to that point, not only the lesson you've just completed. This will reinforce the vocabulary, as well as some of the structures, that you've learned so far in the course, so that you can retain them in your long-term memory. For now, though, we'll only review the key vocabulary you learned in Lesson 1.

1. *What's the opposite of* ja?

   _____

2. *How do you greet someone in the morning?*

   _____

3. *How do you greet someone in the afternoon?*

   _____

4. *How do you greet someone in the evening?*

   _____

5. *What would you say to welcome a friend visiting your city?*

   _____

6. *How do you ask how someone is doing?*

   _____

7. *What are four things that you can say to someone when they're leaving?*

   _____

8. *Manners are important! How do you say "thank you"?*

_____

9. *If someone asks you,* **Sprechen Sie Deutsch?***, how do you say "a little"?*

_____

10. *How do you ask what someone's name is?*

_____

11. *If someone asks you,* **Wo kommen Sie her?***, and you're from* **Kanada***, what do you say?*

_____

12. *Finally, how do you tell your new friends that it's nice here, in their country?*

_____

ANSWER KEY

1. **nein**; 2. **Guten Morgen.** 3. **Guten Tag.** 4. **Guten Abend.** 5. **Willkommen.** 6. **Wie geht's?** 7. **Auf Wiedersehen, tschüss, bis bald,** or **mach's gut.** 8. **Danke.** 9. **Ein bisschen.** 10. **Wie heißen Sie?** 11. **Ich komme aus Kanada.** 12. **Es ist schön hier.**

Lesson 2: People and the Family

Lektion zwei: Leute und Familie

lek-tsee-OHN tsvī: LOY-teh uhnt fah-MEE-lyeh

Willkommen zurück! [VIL-koh-men tsoo-REWK] Welcome back! Are you ready for a new challenge? In this lesson, you'll learn how to:

☐ Talk about your immediate family

☐ Say *the* in German and use grammatical gender

☐ Talk about your extended family

☐ Say *a/an* in German

☐ Put it all together in a conversation about the family

Once again, we'll start with vocabulary building. You'll hear the English first, and then you'll hear the German. Repeat each new word or phrase every time you hear it. Let's begin!

Vocabulary Builder 1

▶ 2B Vocabulary Builder 1 (CD 1, Track 13)

the family	**die Familie**	dee fah-MEE-lyeh
the parents	**die Eltern**	dee EHL-tern
the mother	**die Mutter**	dee MUH-ter
the father	**der Vater**	dayr FAH-ter
the child	**das Kind**	das kihnt
the son	**der Sohn**	dayr zohn
the daughter	**die Tochter**	dee TOHKH-ter
the brother	**der Bruder**	dayr BROO-der
the sister	**die Schwester**	dee SHVES-ter
the grandmother	**die Großmutter**	dee GROHS-muh-ter
the grandfather	**der Großvater**	dayr GROHS-fah-ter

⏸

✎ Vocabulary Practice 1

Time to practice the vocabulary you just learned. Fill in the blanks with the word that best fits the description.

1. **Die Mutter** *and* **der Vater** *are* **die** _____.

2. *My* **Schwester** *is* **die** _____ *of my* **Eltern**.

3. **Der Sohn** *of my* **Eltern** *is my* _____.

4. *My* _____ *is* **die Mutter** *of my* **Mutter**.

5. *My* **Vater** *is der* _____ *of my* **Großvater**.

6. *A young* **Sohn** *or* **Tochter** *can also be called a* _____.

ANSWER KEY
1. **Eltern**; 2. **Tochter**; 3. **Bruder**; 4. **Großmutter**; 5. **Sohn**; 6. **Kind**

Grammar Builder 1

▶ 2C Grammar Builder 1 (CD 1, Track 14)

Have you noticed that many of these words are similar to English words? That's because English and German are related languages with a common origin—siblings in a language family, if you will.

Of course, there are also important differences between them. One such difference is gender. In German, all nouns have an inherent grammatical gender. They are either masculine, feminine, or neuter. That's also why German has three definite articles:

der [dayr]	
die [dee]	*the*
das [das]	

GENDER OF NOUN	DEFINITE ARTICLE	EXAMPLE	ENGLISH
masculine	**der**	**der Vater**	*the father*
feminine	**die**	**die Mutter**	*the mother*
neuter	**das**	**das Kind**	*the child*

You can sometimes guess the gender of a word based on what it refers to. For example, many words that describe men are masculine, while many that describe women are feminine. But this pattern is not absolute, and the noun **Kind** (*child*) is neuter, whether the word is used to refer to a boy or a girl. Basically, gender is often unpredictable and has to be memorized with the word.

The good news is that you don't have to worry about it for the plural: the plural definite article is always **die**, as in **die Eltern** (*the parents*). Now, let's continue with some more words and expressions.

Take It Further 1

▶ 2D Take It Further (CD 1, Track 15)

In the previous lesson, you learned that all German nouns are capitalized, regardless of whether they're a proper name (**Deutschland** [DOYCH-lahnt], *Germany*; **Anne** [AH-neh], *Anne*) or a common noun (**das Kind** [das KIHNT], *the child*; **der Sohn** [dayr ZOHN], *the son*). You also learned a few important points of German spelling and pronunciation. Let's review them:

ü	[ew]: *like ee in see, with lips rounded*	**Tschüss!** [chewss] *(bye)*
ch	[kh]: *similar to ch in Scottish Loch*	**mach's gut** [makhs goot] *(take care)*
w	[v]: *like v in very*	**auf Wiedersehen** [owf VEE-der-zay-en] *(good-bye)*
au	[ow]: *like ow in owl*	**auf** [owf] *(on, upon)*
ei	[ī]: *like i in hi or y in fly*	**eins** [īns] *(one)*
ie	[ee]: *like ee in see*	**wieder** [VEE-der] *(again)*

Before we go further with some other important points on German spelling and pronunciation, this is a good time to introduce you to a typical characteristic of German: compounds, or words (sometimes *long* words!) formed from smaller parts. You already know a perfect example: **Wiedersehen**. You can see in the last example above that **wieder** means *again*. **Sehen** [ZAY-en] is a verb that means *to see*. So, **Wiedersehen** means something like *seeing [each other] again*. **Auf** means *on* or *upon*, so the whole expression **auf Wiedersehen** can be translated roughly as *"until we see each other again."* Don't worry too much about this now, but as you learn more German, you'll come across a lot of long compound words. Eventually, you'll be able to break them down, and figure out what they mean part-by-part.

Now, though, let's take a look at some other important points of German spelling and pronunciation.

eu	[oy]: *like oy in toy*	**Leute** [LOY-teh] (*people*)
ä	[ay] *or* [eh]: *like ay in say or e in set*	**Mädchen** [MAYD-khen] (*girl*)
v	[f]: *similar to f in fox*	**Vater** [FAH-ter] (*father*)
s	[z] *at the beginning of a word, like z in zoo*	**Sohn** [zohn] (*son*)
s	[s] *at the end of a word, like s in see*	**es** [ess] (*it*)
ss	[s]: *like s in see*	**missen** [MIH-sehn] (*to miss*)
ß	[s]: *like s in see*	**Großmutter** [GROHS-muh-ter] (*grandmother*)
sch	[sh]: *like sh in show*	**Schwester** [SHVES-ter] (*sister*)
s	[sh]: *like sh in show (at beginning of a word before* p *or* t)	**Spaß** [shpass] (*fun*) **Stadt** [shtaht] (*city*)
tsch	[ch]: *like ch in church*	**Deutsch** [doych] (*German*)

Again, don't worry too much about committing all of this to memory right away. It will come naturally as you learn, but we'll point out some important tips as you progress.

Vocabulary Builder 2

2E Vocabulary Builder 2 (CD 1, Track 16)

This is …	**Das ist …**	dass ist …
a woman	**eine Frau**	ī-neh frow
This is a woman.	**Das ist eine Frau.**	dass ist ī-neh frow

Who is that?	Wer ist das?	vehr ist dahs
a man	ein Mann	īn mahn
a child	ein Kind	īn kihnt
the boy	der Junge	dayr YOONG-eh
the girl	das Mädchen	dahs MAYD-khen
the uncle	der Onkel	dayr OHN-kehl
the aunt	die Tante	dee TAHN-teh

✎ Vocabulary Practice 2

Ready for more practice? Give the correct German translation.

1. *Who is that?* _____

2. *This is …* _____

3. *the girl* _____

4. *the aunt* _____

5. *the father* _____

6. *a woman* _____

7. *a man* _____

8. *a child* _____

ANSWER KEY
1. Wer ist das? 2. Das ist … 3. das Mädchen; 4. die Tante; 5. der Vater; 6. eine Frau; 7. ein Mann;
8. ein Kind

Grammar Builder 2

▶ 2F Grammar Builder 2 (CD 1, Track 17)

So now you've learned more nouns that describe people. In most cases, the grammatical gender matches up with the natural gender of the person that is referred to, with one exception: **das Mädchen** (*the girl*) is neuter. That's because this noun ends in **-chen**, which marks the diminutive, a form that indicates that something is small or endearing. All words that have this ending are neuter, as are those that end in **-lein**, which has a similar meaning to **-chen**. You may know the word **Fräulein** [FROY-līn], which means *Miss*—literally, a little **Frau**. Because of its ending, this word is neuter as well: **das Fräulein**.

Notice that some of the words that you just learned were preceded by the indefinite article. There are only two different forms of this article:

GENDER OF NOUN	INDEFINITE ARTICLE	EXAMPLE	
masculine	**ein** [īn]	**ein Mann**	*a man*
neuter	**ein** [īn]	**ein Kind**	*a child*
feminine	**eine** [ī-neh]	**eine Frau**	*a woman*

As in English, there is no indefinite article in the plural.

⦿

✎ Work Out 1

▶ 2G Work Out 1 (CD 1, Track 18)

Let's review. As in the previous lesson, listen to the audio, and fill in the missing words. Repeat the correct answers in the pauses provided for practice. Note that **Frau** means *Mrs.* or *Ms.*, and **Herr** means *Mr.*

1. *This is the Klein family.*

   _____ die Familie Klein.

2. *This is Ms. Klein.*

   Das ist _____ Klein.

3. *This is Mr. Klein.*

   Das ist _____ Klein.

4. *Max is a boy.*

   Max ist _____ Junge.

5. *Sophie is a girl.*

   Sophie ist ein _____.

6. *Ms. Klein is the mother.*

   Frau Klein ist _____.

7. *Mr. Klein is the father.*

   Herr Klein ist _____.

8. *Max is the son.*

   Max ist _____.

9. *Sophie is the daughter.*

   Sophie ist _____.

   ANSWER KEY
   1. Das ist; 2. Frau; 3. Herr; 4. ein; 5. Mädchen; 6. die Mutter; 7. der Vater; 8. der Sohn; 9. die Tochter

🔊 Bring It All Together

▶ 2H Bring It All Together (CD 1, Track 19)

Now let's bring it all together, adding a little more vocabulary and structure. Remember Paula and Philipp, who met in the first lesson? Now Philipp is showing Paula pictures of his family. As usual, you'll hear each phrase in English first, and then in German, with pauses for repetition.

Look, Paula!
Guck mal, Paula!
gook mahl, POW-lah

Here is a photograph.
Hier ist ein Foto.
heer ist īn FOH-toh

This is my family.
Das ist meine Familie.
dass ist MĪ-neh fah-MEE-lyeh

Who is that?
Wer ist das?
vayr ist dass

This is my mother.
Das ist meine Mutter.
dass ist MĪ-neh MUH-ter

And this is my father.
Und das ist mein Vater.
uhnt dass ist mīn FAH-ter

And who is the boy?
Und wer ist der Junge?
uhnt vayr ist dayr YUHNG-eh

That is my brother.
Das ist mein Bruder.
dass ist mīn BROO-der

His name is Stephan.
Er heißt Stephan.
ayr hīst SHTAY-fahn

Here is another photograph.
Hier ist noch ein Foto.
heer ist nokh īn FOH-toh

This is my uncle Walter from Hamburg.
Das ist mein Onkel Walter aus Hamburg.
dass ist mīn OHN-kel VAHL-ter owss HAHM-boorg

Who is the woman?
Wer ist die Frau?
vayr ist dee frow

This is my aunt Lotte.
Das ist meine Tante Lotte.
dass ist MĪ-neh TAHN-teh LOH-teh

Take It Further 2

▶ 2I Take It Further 2 (CD 1, Track 20)

You have already learned most of the words in this conversation, but there were some new ones, too. I'm sure you've guessed that **Foto** means *photograph*. With the definite article, it's **das Foto**; the word is neuter. You use **Guck mal** to invite someone to take a look at something. Philipp also used the possessive pronoun **mein** (*my*) to talk about his family members. Just like the indefinite article, this pronoun has a different ending depending on the gender of the noun:

masculine	mein	mein Onkel	my uncle
neuter	mein	mein Foto	my photo
feminine	meine	meine Tante	my aunt

You will learn more possessive pronouns in Lesson 8.

⏸

✎ Work Out 2

A. Fill in the blank with the correct indefinite article, **ein** or **eine**, and then read the sentences out loud. The translations are provided to help you.

1. **Ursula ist** _____ **Frau.** (*Ursula is a woman.*)

2. **Klaus ist** _____ **Mann.** (*Klaus is a man.*)

3. **Hier ist noch** _____ **Foto.** (*Here is another photo.*)

4. **Frau Schneider ist** _____ **Tante.** (*Mrs. Schneider is an aunt.*)

5. **Sebastian ist** _____ **Kind.** (*Sebastian is a child.*)

B. Now let's do the same thing with the definite articles **der**, **die**, or **das**.

1. _____ **Sohn meiner Tante heißt Felix.** (*The son of my aunt is named Felix.*)

2. **Das ist** _____ **Mutter.** (*That's the mother.*)

3. _____ **Frau heißt Susanne Segebrecht.** (*The woman's name is Susanne Segebrecht.*)

4. **Wer ist** _____ **Junge?** (*Who is the boy?*)

5. **Herr Klein ist** _____ **Großvater.** (*Mr. Klein is the grandfather.*)

   ANSWER KEY
   A: 1. **eine**; 2. **ein**; 3. **ein**; 4. **eine**; 5. **ein** B: 1. **Der**; 2. **die**; 3. **Die**; 4. **der**; 5. **der**

▶ 2J Work Out 2 (CD 1, Track 21)

Now listen to the audio for some more audio-only practice. This will help you master the material you've learned so far!

⏸

✎ Drive It Home

It's time for another Drive It Home section, designed to help make the new structures you're learning become more automatic. Don't forget that these exercises will seem simple and repetitive, but they're supposed to! Spend a little time with them, write out each exercise completely, and speak the answers aloud.

First, let's round up some of the masculine nouns you've learned so far. Fill in the blank with **der**, and say the sentence aloud.

1. **Das ist** _____ **Mann.**

2. **Das ist** _____ **Vater.**

3. Das ist _____ Junge.

4. Das ist _____ Onkel.

5. Das ist _____ Bruder.

6. Das ist _____ Großvater.

Now let's try the same with feminine nouns, and **die**.

1. Das ist _____ Frau.

2. Das ist _____ Schwester.

3. Das ist _____ Familie.

4. Das ist _____ Tante.

5. Das ist _____ Mutter.

6. Das ist _____ Großmutter.

And finally, let's not forget about neuter nouns, and **das**.

1. Das ist _____ Kind.

2. Das ist _____ Mädchen.

3. Das ist _____ Foto.

Parting Words

Herzlichen Glückwunsch! *Congratulations!* You've finished Lesson 2. How did you do? You should now be able to:

☐ Talk about your immediate family (Still unsure? Go back to page 28.)

☐ Say *the* in German and use grammatical gender (Still unsure? Go back to page 29.)

☐ Talk about your extended family (Still unsure? Go back to page 31.)

☐ Say *a/an* in German (Still unsure? Go back to page 33.)

☐ Put it all together in a conversation about the family (Still unsure? Go back to page 35.)

Don't forget to practice and reinforce what you've learned by visiting **www.livinglanguage.com/languagelab** for flashcards, games, and quizzes for Lesson 2!

Take It Further 3

▶ 2K Take It Further 3 (CD 1, Track 22)

You've learned the basic vocabulary that you need in order to talk about your family. Of course, there will be times when you want to talk about other family members, like your:

female cousin	**eine Cousine**	ī-neh koo-ZEE-neh
male cousin	**ein Cousin**	īn koo-ZUH(N)
nephew	**ein Neffe**	īn NEH-feh
niece	**eine Nichte**	ī-neh NIKH-teh

And if you're a grandparent, you'll certainly want to talk about your:

grandchild	**Enkelkind**	EN-kel-kint
grandson	**der Enkel**	dayr EN-kel
granddaughter	**die Enkelin**	dee EN-keh-lin

Bis zum nächsten Mal! [biss tsuhm NEKH-sten mal] *Till next time!*

Word Recall

Let's review some of the key vocabulary you've learned in the two lessons you've completed so far. Remember that this is a great chance to be reminded of words and structures that you've learned earlier, so that you can retain them in your long-term memory.

A. Fill in the following family tree with the correct German word for each member of the family. Make sure to include **der**, **die**, or **das** before each German word.

1. _____ (Father)

2. _____ (Mother)

3. _____ (Sister)

you

4. _____ (Brother)

B. Now tell us something about them all. Fill in the blanks with the
missing German word.

1. _____ **Mutter kommt aus Berlin.**

   The mother comes from Berlin.

2. **Der Vater** _____ **Horst.**

   The father is named Horst.

3. **Der Bruder kommt** _____ **Stuttgart.**

   The brother comes from Stuttgart.

4. _____ **Schwester heißt Gisela.**

   The sister is named Gisela.

5. **Ich** _____ **aus Köln.**

   I come from Köln.

ANSWER KEY
A: 1. **die Mutter**; 2. **der Vater**; 3. **die Schwester**; 4. **der Bruder**
B: 1. **Die**; 2. **heißt**; 3. **aus**; 4. **Die**; 5. **komme**

Lesson 3: Numbers

Lektion drei: Zahlen

lek-tsee-OHN drī: TSAH-len

Willkommen! *Welcome!* In Lesson 3, you'll learn how to:

☐ Count from zero to ten in German

☐ Use plurals like *the men* and *the women* in German

☐ Count from eleven to one hundred

☐ Do some basic math

☐ Put it all together in a telephone call

So let's get started right away. By now, you know that you'll hear the English followed by the German. Repeat each new word or phrase every time you hear it.

Vocabulary Builder 1

▶ 3B Vocabulary Builder 1 (CD 1, Track 24)

zero	**null**	nuhl
one	**eins**	īns
two	**zwei**	tsvī
three	**drei**	drī
four	**vier**	feer
five	**fünf**	fewnf
six	**sechs**	zekhs
seven	**sieben**	ZEE-ben
eight	**acht**	akht
nine	**neun**	noyn
ten	**zehn**	tsayn

⏸

Take It Further 1

So now you can count **von eins bis zehn**, *from one to ten*. The word **eins** sounds familiar, doesn't it? It's almost like the indefinite article, **ein**. In fact, when the number is followed by a noun, you don't use **eins**; you use the article **ein**. So, **eine Schwester** means both *a sister* and *one sister*.

✎ Vocabulary Practice 1

A. Time to put what you've learned into practice. Translate, first from German to English and then from English to German.

1. **zwei** _____

2. **fünf** _____

3. **sieben** _____

4. **neun** _____

5. _three_ _____

6. _ten_ _____

7. _eight_ _____

8. _one_ _____

ANSWER KEY
A: 1. _two_; 2. _five_; 3. _seven_; 4. _nine_; 5. **drei**; 6. **zehn**; 7. **acht**; 8. **eins**

Grammar Builder 1
▶ 3C Grammar Builder 1 (CD 1, Track 25)

In German, there are several different ways of making a noun plural. Some nouns take the ending **-n**:

SINGULAR NOUN	PLURAL NOUN	
Schwester [SHVES-ter]	**Schwestern** [SHVES-tern]	_sister/sisters_
Tante [TAHN-teh]	**Tanten** [TAHN-tehn]	_aunt/aunts_

Some nouns don't have a separate plural form at all:

SINGULAR NOUN	PLURAL NOUN	
Mädchen [MAYD-khen]	**Mädchen** [MAYD-khen]	_girl/girls_

Some nouns indicate the plural by changing a vowel to an **Umlaut**: **a** becomes **ä**, **u** becomes **ü** and **o** becomes **ö**.

SINGULAR NOUN	PLURAL NOUN	
Vater [FAH-ter]	**Väter** [FAY-ter]	*father/fathers*
Mutter [MOO-ter]	**Mütter** [MEW-ter]	*mother/mothers*
Tochter [TOKH-ter]	**Töchter** [TU(R)KH-ter]	*daughter/daughters*

And some nouns form the plural just like English, by adding an **-s**.

SINGULAR NOUN	PLURAL NOUN	
Foto [FOH-toh]	**Fotos** [FOH-tohs]	*picture/pictures*

It's not always easy to know which word takes which plural ending, and so by far the best way to keep the plurals straight is to learn the plural form along with the singular word.

Take It Further 2
▷ 3D Take It Further 2 (CD 1, Track 26)

In the previous lesson we talked about the gender of nouns and definite articles. The good news, as you may remember, is that you don't have to worry about the gender of nouns in the plural, because the plural definite article is always **die**, no matter whether the noun is masculine, feminine, or neuter: **die Väter** (*the fathers*), **die Mütter** (*the mothers*), and **die Mädchen** (*the girls*).

We've also talked about the sounds of the German **Umlaut** in the previous lessons. As you've noticed, the **Umlaut** is really quite important with the plural. Let's go over **ä** and **ü** again:

ä	[ay] or [eh]: *like ay in say or e in set*	**Väter** [FAY-ter] (*fathers*)
ü	[ew]: *like a mixture of i in kiss and oo in food.*	**Mütter** [MEW-ter] (*mothers*)

The third in the bunch, **ö**, is has a long and a short version:

ö	[u(r)]: *like ur in fur but short*	**Töchter** [TU(R)KH-ter] (*daughters*)
ö	[uh(r)]: *like ur in fur but held longer*	**schön** [shuh(r)n] (*beautiful*)

We've also talked about the diminutive endings **-chen** and **-lein** used as terms of endearment:

die Tochter	das Töchterchen	*daughter*
der Vater	das Väterchen	*father*
das Kind	das Kindlein	*child*

Note that if a word with **a**, **o**, or **u** adds the diminutive ending, the vowels become **Umlaut ä, ö,** or **ü: Mutter/Mütterlein**. But there is good news here, too: all words with this diminutive ending are neuter and take the singular article **das**. And what's more, all words with a diminutive ending stay the same in the singular and plural:

das Töchterchen	die Töchterchen	*daughter/daughters*

Ⅱ

✎ Vocabulary Builder 2

▶ 3E Vocabulary Builder 2 (CD 1, Track 27)

eleven	**elf**	ehlf
twelve	**zwölf**	tsvu(r)lf
thirteen	**dreizehn**	DRĪ-tsayn
fourteen	**vierzehn**	FEER- tsayn
fifteen	**fünfzehn**	FEWNF- tsayn
sixteen	**sechzehn**	ZEKH- tsayn
seventeen	**siebzehn**	ZEEP- tsayn
eighteen	**achtzehn**	AKHT- tsayn
nineteen	**neunzehn**	NOYN- tsayn
twenty	**zwanzig**	TSVAHN-tsig
twenty-one	**einundzwanzig**	ĪN-uhnt-tsvahn-tsig

⏸

✎ Vocabulary Practice 2

Time to practice again. Write out the German equivalents of the numbers below.

1. *two grandmothers* _____ **Großmütter**

2. *twenty grandchildren* _____ **Enkel**

3. *eleven cousins* _____ **Kusinen**

4. *twelve nieces* _____ **Nichten**

5. *twenty-nine children* _____ **Kinder**

ANSWER KEY
1. zwei; 2. zwanzig; 3. elf; 4. zwölf; 5. neunundzwanzig

Grammar Builder 2

▶ 3F Grammar Builder 2 (CD 1, Track 28)

The German numbers are really quite similar to the English ones, aren't they? **Elf** and **zwölf** are easily recognizable, and so are the teens. Note that German differs from English in the word order of numbers over twenty. In German, the second digit is named first, so **zweiundzwanzig** (*twenty-two*) is literally *two and twenty*, and you continue on to **dreiundzwanzig** (*twenty-three*), **vierundzwanzig** (*twenty-four*), and so on.

thirty	dreißig	DRĪ-sig
forty	vierzig	FEER-tsig
fifty	fünfzig	FEWNF-tsig
sixty	sechzig	ZEKH-tsig
seventy	siebzig	ZEEP-tsig
eighty	achtzig	AKHT-tsig
ninety	neunzig	NOYN-tsig
hundred	hundert	HUHN-dert

⏸

✎ Work Out 1

▶ 3G Work Out 1 (CD 1, Track 29)

Let's do some math in German to practice the numbers. As in the previous lesson, listen to the audio, then give the answer. Repeat the correct answers in the pauses provided for practice. Note that **und** means *and* and **sind** means *are*.

1. **Zwei und zwei sind** _____.

2. **Vier und drei sind** _____.

3. **Sieben und fünf sind** _____.

4. **Zwölf und eins sind** _____ .

5. **Dreizehn und acht sind** _____ .

Ⅱ

ANSWER KEY
1. vier; 2. sieben; 3. zwölf; 4. dreizehn; 5. einundzwanzig

Bring It All Together
▶ 3H Bring It All Together (CD 1, Track 30)

Now let's listen to a dialogue that uses some of the words and structures you've learned. Our friend Paula would like to use Philipp's phone to call her mother in Philadelphia. Philipp dials the number for her and hands her the phone.

Philipp, I would like to call America, please.
Philipp, ich möchte bitte in Amerika anrufen.
FIH-lip, ikh MU(R)KH-teh BIH-teh in ah-MEH-ree-kah AHN-roo-fen

It's my mother's birthday.
Meine Mutter hat Geburtstag.
MĪ-neh MUH-tehr haht geh-BUHRTS-tahk

She is forty-eight.
Sie ist achtundvierzig.
zee ist AKHT-unht-feer-tsig

What's the number?
Was ist die Nummer?
vahs ist dee NUH-mehr

Zero-zero-one for America.
Null null eins für Amerika.
nuhl nuhl īns fewr ah-MEH-ree-kah

Two-one-five for Philadelphia.
Zwei eins fünf für Philadelphia.
tsvī īns fewnf fewr fih-lah-DEHL-fee-yah

And then it's four-five-six-two.
Und dann vier, fünf, sechs, zwei.
uhnt dahn feer, fewnf, zekhs, tsvī

And three ones.
Und dreimal die Eins.
uhnt drī mahl dee īns

Please go ahead, Paula; here is my phone.
Bitte Paula, hier ist mein Telefon.
BIH-teh POW-lah, heer ist mīn TEH-leh-fohn

Thank you, Philipp.
Danke schön, Philipp.
DAHN-keh shuh(r)n, FIH-lip

I'll call for ten minutes only.
Ich telefoniere nur zehn Minuten.
ikh teh-leh-foh-NEE-reh noor tsayn mih-NOO-tehn

Take It Further 3

▶ 31 Take It Further 3 (CD 1, Track 31)

Could you follow this conversation? There were some new words, but you probably recognized some of them right away, like **Telefon** (*telephone*), **Nummer** (*number*), and **Minuten** (*minutes*). An important and versatile word that was used twice in the dialogue is **bitte**.

bitte	*please*
bitte	*you're welcome*
Bitte Paula, hier ist mein Telefon.	*Here you go, Paula, my phone.*

You also heard two verbs:

anrufen	*to call on the telephone*
telefonieren	*to call on the telephone*

We'll learn more about verbs soon, in Lesson 5.

✎ Work Out 2

Fill in the blanks with the correct plural from the choices provided below, and then read the sentences out loud.

Brüder, Mütter, Kinder, Frauen, Schwestern, Fotos, Männer, Autos

1. **Klaus, Peter und Barbara sind** _____ (*children*).

2. **Die** _____ (*women*) **sind vierzig.**

3. **Zwei** _____ (*men*) **telefonieren.**

4. _____ (*mothers*) **haben Kinder.**

5. **Das sind neun** _____ (*cars*).

6. **Ich habe vier** _____ (*sisters*).

7. **Mein Vater hat zwei** _____ (*brothers*).

8. **Die** _____ (*pictures*) **sind schön.**

ANSWER KEY
1. **Kinder**; 2. **Frauen**; 3. **Männer**; 4. **Mütter**; 5. **Autos**; 6. **Schwestern**; 7. **Brüder**; 8. **Fotos**

▶ 3J Work Out 2 (CD 1, Track 32)

Now listen to the audio for some more audio-only practice. This will help you master the material you've learned so far!

⏸

✎ Drive It Home

Time to commit the new structures to your memory. These fairly easy exercises will help make German seem natural to you. Don't forget to write out and read aloud each exercise.

A. First, count how many men there are from one to five.

1. _____ **Mann**

2. _____ **Männer**

3. _____ **Männer**

4. _____ **Männer**

5. _____ **Männer**

B. Now, count how many women there are from six to ten.

1. _____ Frauen

2. _____ Frauen

3. _____ Frauen

4. _____ Frauen

5. _____ Frauen

C. Now let's count pictures in tens from ten to fifty.

1. _____ Fotos

2. _____ Fotos

3. _____ Fotos

4. _____ Fotos

5. _____ Fotos

D. And finally let's count a few cars in tens from sixty to one hundred.

1. _____ Autos

2. _____ Autos

3. _____ Autos

4. _____ Autos

5. _____ Autos

ANSWER KEY
A: 1. **ein**; 2. **zwei**; 3. **drei**; 4. **vier**; 5. **fünf**
B: 1. **sechs**; 2. **sieben**; 3. **acht**; 4. **neun**; 5. **zehn**
C: 1. **zehn**; 2. **zwanzig**; 3. **dreissig**; 4. **vierzig**; 5.**fünfzig**
D: 1. **sechzig**; 2. **siebzig**; 3. **achtzig**; 4. **neunzig**; 5. **hundert**

Parting Words

Herzlichen Glückwunsch! *Congratulations!* You've completed another lesson, and you're learning quickly. You've learned how to:

☐ Count from zero to ten in German (Still unsure? Go back to page 44.)

☐ Use plurals like *the men* and *the women* in German (Still unsure? Go back to page 45.)

☐ Count from eleven to one hundred (Still unsure? Go back to page 48.)

☐ Do some basic math (Still unsure? Go back to page 49.)

☐ Put it all together in a telephone call (Still unsure? Go back to page 50.)

Don't forget to practice and reinforce what you've learned by visiting **www.livinglanguage.com/languagelab** for flashcards, games, and quizzes for Lesson 3!

Take It Further 4

By the way, when answering the phone, it is customary in German-speaking countries to say your name and a greeting after picking up, rather than just "hello":

Hello, [this is] Philip.	**Hier Philipp.**	heer FIH-lip
Hello, [this is Mr./Mrs.] Meier.	**Hier Meier.**	heer MĪ-er
Bauer, hello.	**Bauer, guten Tag.**	BOW-er, goo-ten tahk

And when you're hanging up at the end of a conversation, you say:

| *Until next time* | **Auf Wiederhören** | owf VEE-der-hu(r)-ren |

You've probably noticed that **auf Wiederhören** looks a lot like **auf Wiedersehen**. That's no accident. **Wieder** means *again*, **sehen** means *to see*, and **hören** means *to hear*. **Auf** usually means *on,* but in this context it can be better translated as *until*. So, the expression **auf Wiedersehen** means something like "until we see each other again," and **auf Wiederhören** means "until we hear each other again." Perfect for the phone!

We'll review the numbers in later lessons. You will need them to tell time, to go shopping, and, of course, to remember telephone numbers. **Bis bald!** *See you soon!*

Word Recall

And now you'll have a chance to review the vocabulary and structures we've worked on in the three lessons you've already completed.

A. From the word bank below, choose the best word to complete each sentence.

Mutter, Sohn, Foto, vierundsiebzig, Kinder

1. **Mein** _____ **kommt aus Hannover.**

2. **Mein Sohn hat keine** _____ **.**

3. **Mein Onkel ist** _____ **Jahre alt.**

4. **Meine** _____ **ist auch so alt.**

5. **Das ist ein schönes** _____ **.**

B. Match the English word in column A with its appropriate translation in column B.

1. *the daughter*
2. *the grandfather*
3. *a photo*
4. *Take care.*
5. *the parents*

a. **der Großvater**
b. **die Eltern**
c. **Mach's gut.**
d. **ein Foto**
e. **die Tochter**

ANSWER KEY
A. 1. **Sohn**; 2. **Kinder**; 3. **vierundsiebzig**; 4. **Mutter**; 5. **Foto**
B. 1. e; 2. a; 3. d; 4. c; 5. b

Lesson 4: Around the Home

Lektion vier: Zuhause
lek-tsee-OHN feer: tsuh-HOW-seh

Hallo, da sind Sie ja wieder! *There you are again!* In Lesson 4 you'll learn how to:

☐ Name the rooms in your house or apartment

☐ Use prepositions and learn how to say where things are

☐ Name some furniture in your house or apartment

☐ Use the preposition **in**

☐ Put it all together in a conversation describing an apartment

So, let's get started with the new words and phrases. As usual, you'll hear the English words first, and then you'll hear the German words, which you should repeat every time you hear them.

Vocabulary Builder 1

▶ 4B Vocabulary Builder 1 (CD 1, Track 34)

the apartment	die Wohnung	dee VOH-nuhng
the living room	das Wohnzimmer	das VOHN-tsih-mehr
the bedroom	das Schlafzimmer	das SHLALHF-tsih-mehr
the office	das Arbeitszimmer	das AHR-bīts-tsih-mehr
the table	der Tisch	dayr tish
on the table	auf dem Tisch	owf daym tish
the bed	das Bett	das beht
on the bed	auf dem Bett	owf daym beht
the couch	die Couch	dee kowch
on the couch	auf der Couch	owf der kowch

⏸

✎ Vocabulary Practice 1

Ready for practice?

Match the English in column A with the German in column B.

1. *living room*

2. *couch*

3. *on the bed*

4. *on the couch*

5. *office*

6. *apartment*

a. **auf dem Bett**

b. **das Arbeitszimmer**

c. **die Wohnung**

d. **die Couch**

e. **auf der Couch**

f. **das Wohnzimmer**

ANSWER KEY

1. f; 2. d; 3. a; 4. e; 5. b; 6. c

Grammar Builder 1
"AUF" AND CASES

Now you've learned some words that you need in order to describe an apartment. You also learned the preposition **auf**, which means *on* or *on top of*. You also noticed, no doubt, that the articles change a bit after **auf**. **Der Tisch** (*the table*) becomes **auf dem Tisch** (*on the table*), **die Couch** (*the couch*) becomes **auf der Couch** (*on the couch*), and so on. You've just had your first introduction to German cases!

A case simply refers to the role that a noun or related word is playing in a sentence, for example subject, direct object, object of a preposition, and so on. In a lot of languages, nouns, articles, pronouns, and even adjectives change—typically by taking different endings—depending on which case they're in. So a noun that's playing the role of a subject (in the *nominative* case) will look slightly different than when it's playing the role of a direct object (in the *accusative* case).

English has cases, but they tend to show up mostly with pronouns. We say "**he** sees the dog," but "the dog sees **him**." The only time nouns change in English because of case is when they show possession; an apostrophe *s* is added: *John's dog, the woman's dog*, etc.

In German, not only do pronouns change (nominative **er**/*he* becomes accusative **ihn**/*him*), but so do articles like **der**, **die**, **das**, **ein**, and **eine**. Sometimes, the nouns themselves take endings, but we'll get to that later. For now, let's just start simply by looking at what's going on in the examples you just learned with **auf** (*on*).

Auf, like a lot of German prepositions that express location, takes the dative case. The noun forms you've been seeing so far have been in the nominative case, which is the case of subjects. But compare:

Der Tisch ist gross.
The table is big.
(*The table/***der Tisch** is the subject of the sentence, so it's in the nominative.)

Das Buch liegt auf dem Tisch.
The book is lying on the table.
(*The table/***dem Tisch** follows **auf**, expressing location, so it's in the dative.)

Notice that masculine singular **der** becomes **dem** in the dative. Here's a summary of how the other definite articles change.

NOMINATIVE	DATIVE	NOM. EXAMPLE	DAT. EXAMPLE
der (*m. sing.*)	**dem**	**der Tisch** (*the table*)	**auf dem Tisch** (*on the table*)
die (*f. sing.*)	**der**	**die Couch** (*the couch*)	**auf der Couch** (*on the couch*)
das (*n. sing.*)	**dem**	**das Bett** (*the bed*)	**auf dem Bett** (*on the bed*)

The masculine singular **der Tisch** (*the table*) becomes **auf dem Tisch** (*on the table*), the feminine singular **die Couch** becomes **auf der Couch**, and the neuter singular **das Bett** (*the bed*) becomes **auf dem Bett** (*on the bed*). Note that the feminine dative is the same as the masculine nominative **der**.

Again, we'll cover cases gradually, but if you're curious, German has four of them. The nominative is the case of subjects. The accusative is the case of direct objects and certain prepositions, especially ones that express motion. The dative is the case of indirect objects and of certain prepositions, especially ones that express location, such as **auf**. And the genitive is the case of possession, as well as of a few prepositions. But don't worry about committing this to memory now! We'll cover it slowly and gradually.

▶ 4C Grammar Builder 1 (CD 1, Track 35)

Now listen to an audio-only version of this grammar builder. The additional practice will help you retain the material, and of course you'll hear all of the new essential vocabulary pronounced.

⏸

Take It Further 1

▶ 4D Take It Further 1 (CD 1, Track 36)

Auf is one of many prepositions. Some other common ones are:

under	**unter**	UHN-tehr
next to	**neben**	NAY-behn
in front of	**vor**	fohr
behind	**hinter**	HIHN-tehr

All these prepositions take the dative when they express location. Therefore, like with **auf** (*on*), the masculine and neuter definite articles become **dem**, and the feminine definite article becomes **der**.

	MASCULINE	**FEMININE**	**NEUTER**
	der Tisch (*the table*)	**die Couch** (*the couch*)	**das Bett** (*the bed*)
under ...	**unter dem Tisch**	**unter der Couch**	**unter dem Bett**
next to ...	**neben dem Tisch**	**neben der Couch**	**neben dem Bett**
in front of ...	**vor dem Tisch**	**vor der Couch**	**vor dem Bett**
behind ...	**hinter dem Tisch**	**hinter der Couch**	**hinter dem Bett**

⏸

Vocabulary Builder 2

▶ 4E Vocabulary Builder 2 (CD 1, Track 37)

there is/there are	es gibt	ehs gihpt
you are (informal)	du bist	doo bihst
you are (formal)	Sie sind	zee zihnt
we are	wir sind	veer zihnt
the closet	der Schrank	dayr shrahnk
in the closet	im Schrank	ihm shrahnk
the kitchen	die Küche	dee KEW-kheh
in the kitchen	in der Küche	ihn dayr KEW-kheh
the bathroom	das Bad	dahs baht
in the bathroom	im Bad	ihm baht
next to the bathroom	neben dem Bad	NAY-behn daym baht
the door	die Tür	dee tewr
the window	das Fenster	dahs FEHNS-tehr

⏸

✎ Vocabulary Practice 2

Let's practice identifying the rooms of a house. Fill in the floor plan below with the correct German word for each room.

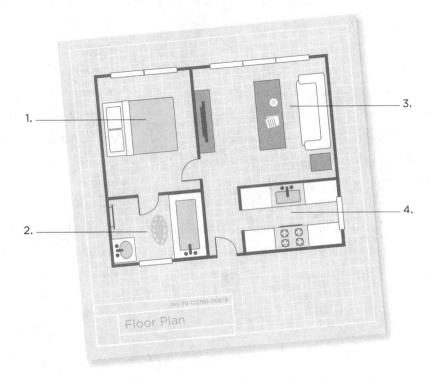

1. _____

2. _____

3. _____

4. _____

ANSWER KEY
1. **das Schlafzimmer**; 2. **das Bad**; 3. **das Wohnzimmer**; 4. **die Küche**

Grammar Builder 2

▶ 4F Grammar Builder 2 (CD 1, Track 38)

Did you notice that the preposition **in** merges with the masculine and neuter dative article **dem** to form **im**?

das Bad (*bathroom*)	im Bad (*in the bathroom*)	ihm bahd
der Schrank (*closet*)	im Schrank (*in the closet*)	ihm shrahnk

Note that **in** doesn't merge with **der**, so with feminine nouns, the preposition and the article stay separate.

| die Küche (*kitchen*) | in der Küche (*in the kitchen*) | ihn dayr KEW-khe |

We'll encounter other such contracted prepositions later, in Lesson 6.

Ⅱ

✎ Work Out 1

Let's review. As usual, listen to the audio first, then fill in the missing German words. Finally, repeat the correct answers in the pauses provided for practice. Remember that **ist** means *is* and **sind** means *are*.

▶ 4G Work Out 1 (CD 1, Track 39)

1. *There are three rooms, a kitchen, and a bathroom in the apartment.*

   In der _____ **sind drei Zimmer, eine Küche und ein Bad.**

2. *There are two windows in the living room.*

   Im Wohnzimmer sind zwei _____.

3. *There's a window in the kitchen.*

   In der _____ **ist ein Fenster.**

4. *The bathroom is next to the kitchen.*

   Das _____ **ist neben der Küche.**

5. *The bedroom is next to the living room.*

   Das Schlafzimmer ist _____ **Wohnzimmer.**

6. *There is a closet in the bedroom.*

   Im Schlafzimmer ist ein _____.

7. *There is also an office.*

   _____ **auch ein Arbeitszimmer.**

8. *Next to the door, there is a window.*

   Neben der _____ **ist ein Fenster.**

   ANSWER KEY
   1. Wohnung; 2. Fenster; 3. Küche; 4. Bad; 5. neben dem; 6. Schrank; 7. Es gibt; 8. Tür

Bring It All Together

4H Bring It All Together (CD 1, Track 40)

Now let's bring it all together, and add a little more vocabulary and structure. Listen to our friend Philipp as he shows Paula his apartment. As usual, you'll hear each phrase in English first and then in German. Repeat the German phrases in the pauses provided.

Welcome to my apartment!
Willkommen in meiner Wohnung!
vil-KOH-mehn ihn MĪ-nehr VOH-nuhng

I have three rooms.
Ich habe drei Zimmer.
ikh HAH-beh drī TSIH-mehr

Here we are in my living room.
Hier sind wir in meinem Wohnzimmer.
heer zihnt veer in MĪ-nehm VOHN-tsih-mehr

Next to the couch is a lamp.
Neben der Couch ist eine Lampe.
NAY-behn dayr kowch ist ī-neh LAHM-peh

Next to the window is a photograph.
Neben dem Fenster ist ein Foto.
NAY-behn daym FEHNS-tehr ist īn FOH-toh

The phone is on the table.
Das Telefon ist auf dem Tisch.
dahs TEH-leh-fohn ist owf daym tish

The TV is in the living room.
Der Fernseher ist im Wohnzimmer.
dayr FEHRN-zay-ehr ist im VOHN-tsih-mehr

There is also a radio in the kitchen.
In der Küche ist auch ein Radio.
in dayr KEW-kheh ist owkh īn RAH-dee-oh

This is the bedroom.
Das ist das Schlafzimmer.
dass ist dass SHLAHF-tsih-mehr

You really have a nice apartment!
Du hast aber eine schöne Wohnung!
doo hahst AH-behr ī-neh SHU(R)-neh VOH-noong

Take It Further 2

▶ 41 Take It Further 2 (CD 1, Track 41)

Could you follow the conversation? There were a few new words, like **der Fernseher** (*the television*). But I'm sure you didn't have a problem understanding that **eine Lampe** is, of course, *a lamp*, and **ein Radio**, *a radio*. Philipp also used the possessive pronoun **mein** a few times. I'm sure you noticed that the possessive adjective had different endings after the prepositions. In fact, the possessive adjective endings are the same as those for the definite article: **-em** for masculine and neuter nouns and **-er** for feminine ones:

MASCULINE			
der Schrank	**im Schrank**	**in meinem Schrank**	*in my closet*

FEMININE			
die Küche	**in der Küche**	**in meiner Küche**	*in my kitchen*

NEUTER			
das Wohnzimmer	**im Wohnzimmer**	**in meinem Wohnzimmer**	*in my living room*

Finally, you also heard two forms of the verb **haben** (*to have*):

I have	**ich habe**	ikh HAH-beh
you have	**du hast**	doo hahst

We will return to the topic of verbs soon, in Lesson 5.

Ⅱ

✎ Work Out 2

A. Match the English in column A with the German in column B.

1. *in the kitchen*	a. **im Schrank**
2. *on the couch*	b. **neben dem Wohnzimmer**
3. *behind the closet*	c. **in der Küche**
4. *in the closet*	d. **hinter dem Schrank**
5. *next to the living room*	e. **auf der Couch**

B. Fill in the blanks with the German words from the word bank that provide the best translation of the English words in parentheses. Choose from: **neben dem, im, hinter der, in der, auf dem.**

1. **Das Telefon ist** _____ **Tisch.** (*on the*)

2. **Du bist** _____ **Tür.** (*behind the*)

3. **Der Tisch ist** _____ **Bett.** (*next to the*)

4. **Der Schrank ist** _____ **Schlafzimmer.** (*in the*)

5. **Das Fenster ist** _____ **Küche.** (*in the*)

ANSWER KEY
A: 1. c; 2. e; 3. d; 4. a; 5. b
B: 1. **auf dem**; 2. **hinter der**; 3. **neben dem**; 4. **im**; 5. **in der**

▶ 4J Work Out 2 (CD 1, Track 42)

Now listen to the audio for some audio-only practice. This will help you master the material you've learned so far!

⏸

✎ Drive It Home

It's time for another Drive It Home section, which will make sure that the new material becomes second nature. As always, write out each exercise completely and speak the answers out loud for extra practice.

First, let's go over the use of the dative form of the masculine and neuter article with the prepositions. Fill in the blanks with **dem**.

1. auf _____ Bett

2. neben _____ Fenster

3. hinter _____ Bad

4. neben _____ Schrank

5. auf _____ Tisch

Now let's do the same with the dative version of the feminine article, **der**.

1. auf _____ Couch

2. neben _____ Küche

3. hinter _____ Tür

4. neben _____ Tür

5. hinter _____ Couch

Let's practice the contraction of the preposition **in** with the dative version of the masculine and neuter article **dem**. Fill in the blanks with **im**.

1. **Der Schrank ist** _____ **Bad.**

2. **Die Couch ist** _____ **Wohnzimmer.**

3. **Das Telefon ist** _____ **Schlafzimmer.**

4. **Der Fernseher ist** _____ **Wohnzimmer.**

5. **Der Tisch ist** _____ **Arbeitszimmer.**

And now let's fill in the blanks with **in der**—the preposition **in** and the dative version of the feminine definite article **der**.

1. **Das Fenster ist** _____ **Küche.**

2. **Der Schrank ist** _____ **Küche.**

3. **Das Telefon ist** _____ **Küche.**

4. **Der Tisch ist** _____ **Küche.**

5. **Der Fernseher ist** _____ **Küche.**

Parting Words

Herzlichen Glückwunsch! *Congratulations!* You've finished another lesson, and you've learned a lot. Now you know how to:

☐ Name the rooms in your house or apartment (Still unsure? Go back to page 59.)

☐ Use prepositions and how to say where things are
(Still unsure? Go back to page 60.)

☐ Name some furniture in your house or apartment
(Still unsure? Go back to page 59.)

☐ Use the preposition **in** (Still unsure? Go back to page 63.)

☐ Put it all together in a conversation describing an apartment
(Still unsure? Go back to page 66.)

Don't forget to practice and reinforce what you've learned by visiting **www.livinglanguage.com/ languagelab** for flashcards, games, and quizzes for Lesson 4!

Take It Further 3

 4K Take It Further 3 (CD 1, Track 43)

You've learned many of the words you need to describe your apartment. Here are a few more that will help you navigate a classified ad for rentals.

classified ad	**die Annonce**	dee ah-NOHN-seh

Many young people in Germany share apartments with roommates.

roommate	**der Mitbewohner**	dayr MIHT-beh-voh-nehr
roommates	**die Mitbewohner**	dee MIHT-beh-voh-nehr

When they do, the apartment is called a:

shared flat	**die Wohngemeinschaft**	dee VOHN-geh-mīn-shaft
shared flat	**die WG**	dee veh-GEH

Both words come from the verb:

to reside	**wohnen**	VOH-nehn

You'll start learning much more about verbs in the next lesson. **Auf Wiedersehen bis dann!** [owf VEE-dehr-zay-ehn bihs dahn] *Good-bye until then!*

Word Recall

Ready to practice some of the key vocabulary you've learned in the four lessons you've completed so far? This is a great chance to work on words and structures you've learned earlier. If you're having trouble with these exercises, go back to the previous lessons and review.

A. Fill in the blanks with the appropriate word from the word bank:

zwei, Wohnung, Schrank, kommt, Zimmer

1. **Meine Schwester _____ aus Hamburg.**

2. **Sie wohnt in einer _____.**

3. **Die Wohnung hat drei _____.**

4. **Das Bad hat _____ Fenster.**

5. **Die Fenster sind neben dem _____.**

B. Fill in the blanks in the conversation below.

1. **Guten Tag, _____?**

   Good day, how are you (informal)?

2. **Gut, _____.**

   Good, thanks.

3. **Ich möchte meine _____ anrufen.**

   I want to call my daughter.

4. **Sie hat heute** _____.

   It's her birthday.

5. **Sie ist** _____ **Jahre alt.**

   She is twenty years old.

6. **Das Telefon ist** _____.

   The phone is in the living room.

7. **Tisch** _____ **Couch.**

   on the table next to the couch

8. **Danke.**

   Thanks.

ANSWER KEY

A. 1. kommt; 2. Wohnung; 3. Zimmer; 4. zwei; 5. Schrank

B. 1. wie geht's; 2. danke; 3. Tochter; 4. Geburtstag; 5. zwanzig; 6. Wohnzimmer, 7. auf dem, neben der

Lesson 5: Everyday Life

Lektion fünf: Tägliches Leben

lek-tsee-OHN fewnf: TEHG-likh-ehs LAY-behn

Da sind Sie ja wieder! *Here you are again!* In Lesson 5, you will learn how to:

☐ Talk about things you do

☐ Use personal pronouns and verb forms together

☐ Talk about everyday activities

☐ Use the accusative case

☐ Put it all together in a conversation about making plans for the evening

Let's begin by looking at one verb and its different forms in the present tense. You know that you'll hear the English first, and then you'll hear the German. Repeat each new word or phrase every time you hear it.

Vocabulary Builder 1

▶ 5B Vocabulary Builder 1 (CD 2, Track 2)

I go	**ich gehe**	ikh GAY-eh
you go (singular, informal)	**du gehst**	doo gayst
you go (singular, formal)	**Sie gehen**	zee GAY-ehn
he goes	**er geht**	ayr gayt
she goes	**sie geht**	zee gayt
it goes	**es geht**	ehs gayt
we go	**wir gehen**	veer GAY-ehn
you go (plural, informal)	**ihr geht**	eer gayt
they go	**sie gehen**	zee GAY-ehn

⏸

✎ Vocabulary Practice 1

Let's practice what you've just learned.

A. First fill in the blanks with the appropriate verb form. Please note that **nach Hause** means *(to) home*.

1. **Er** _____ **nach Hause.**

2. **Wir** _____ **nach Hause.**

3. **Sie** (*formal*) _____ **nach Hause.**

4. **Ich** _____ **nach Hause.**

5. **Ihr** _____ **nach Hause.**

B. Now choose the appropriate personal pronoun to match the translation in parentheses. Note that **ins Büro** means to the office.

1. *(We)* _____ **gehen ins Büro.**

2. *(I)* _____ **gehe ins Büro.**

3. *(He)* _____ **geht ins Büro.**

4. *(You, plural informal)* _____ **geht ins Büro.**

5. *(They)* _____ **gehen ins Büro.**

ANSWER KEY
A. 1. **geht**; 2. **gehen**; 3. **gehen**; 4. **gehe**; 5. **geht**
B. 1. **Wir**; 2. **Ich**; 3. **Er**; 4. **Ihr**; 5. **Sie**

Grammar Builder 1
▶ 5C Grammar Builder 1 (CD 2, Track 3)

You've already encountered some pronouns in previous lessons, but now you have seen them all together.

I	**ich**	ikh
you (singular, informal)	**du**	doo
you (singular, formal)	**Sie**	zee
he	**er**	ayr
she	**sie**	zee
it	**es**	ehs
we	**wir**	veer
you (plural, informal)	**ihr**	eer
you (plural, formal)	**Sie**	zee
they	**sie**	zee

German has a few more pronouns than English, because the English *you* corresponds to three different forms in German: **du**, **Sie**, and **ihr**.

you have (singular, informal)	**du hast**	doo hahst
you have (plural, informal)	**ihr habt**	eer hahbt
you have (singular/plural, formal)	**Sie haben**	zee HAH-behn

Like **du**, **ihr** is used to address family or friends, except that it's plural. So use **ihr** when you address several people at once, just as some speakers of English might say *y'all* or *you guys*.

Did you also notice that the word **sie** can have three different meanings? It's either formal *you*, or *she*, or *they*. Don't worry; you can distinguish these meanings easily from the context of the pronoun, and by the ending of the verb that goes with it.

you have (singular/plural, formal)	**Sie haben**	zee HAH-behn
she has (singular)	**sie hat**	zee haht
they have (plural)	**sie haben**	zee HAH-behn

When **sie** means *she*, the verb ends in a **-t**, as, for example, in **sie heißt** (*her name is*). When **Sie/sie** is used to mean *you* or *they*, the verb ends in **-en**, so for example, we get **Sie/sie heißen** (*your name is* or *their name is*).

Finally, there are also two verb endings that you have encountered before:

| *I have* | **ich habe** | ikh HAH-beh |
| *you have (singular, informal)* | **du hast** | doo hahst |

With **ich**, verbs end in **-e**, as in **ich habe**, **ich heiße**, or **ich gehe**. After **du**, the ending is **-st**, as in **du hast**, **du bist**, or **du gehst**.

Now let's continue your vocabulary building with a few more words and phrases.

Vocabulary Builder 2

▶ 5D Vocabulary Builder 2 (CD 2, Track 4)

He sits.	**Er sitzt.**	ehr zitst
I see.	**Ich sehe.**	ikh ZAY-eh
You see a movie.	**Du siehst einen Film.**	doo zeest ī-nehn film
I listen to music.	**Ich höre Musik.**	ikh HUH(R)-eh moo-ZEEK
We read the paper.	**Wir lesen die Zeitung.**	veer LAY-zehn dee TSī-toong
You write a letter.	**Du schreibst einen Brief.**	doo SHRīPST ī-nehn breef
They go for a walk.	**Sie gehen spazieren.**	zee GAY-ehn shpah-TSEE-rehn
She visits a friend.	**Sie besucht einen Freund.**	zee beh-ZOOKHT ī-nehn froynt
I eat ice cream.	**Ich esse ein Eis.**	ikh EH-seh īn īs
in the morning	**am Morgen**	ahm MOHR-gen
in the afternoon	**am Nachmittag**	ahm NAKH-mih-tahk
in the evening	**am Abend**	ahm AH-bent

⏸

✎ Vocabulary Practice 2

Time to put the vocabulary you've just learned to work. Choose the word from the word bank that best completes the sentence:

sehe, eine Freundin, ein Eis, Am Abend, Musik

1. **Am Nachmittag esse ich** _____.

2. **Ich** _____ **einen Film.**

3. **Du hörst** _____.

4. _____ schreiben wir einen Brief.

5. Sie besucht _____.

ANSWER KEY
1. ein Eis; 2. sehe; 3. Musik; 4. Am Abend; 5. eine Freundin

Grammar Builder 2

While German verb endings are for the most part regular, there are some very common verbs whose vowels shift in the present tense. This is limited to the **du** and **er/sie/es** forms. One common example is **sehen** (*to see*), where the vowel **e** becomes **ie**:

I see	**ich sehe**	ikh ZAY-eh
you (informal) see	**du siehst**	doo zeest
he/she/it sees	**er/sie/es sieht**	ayr/zee/ehs zeet
we see	**wir sehen**	veer ZAY-ehn
you (informal, plural) see	**ihr seht**	eer zayt
they see	**sie sehen**	zee ZAY-ehn
Sie (formal, singular and plural)	**Sie sehen**	zee ZAY-ehn

Earlier, you learned the expression **es gibt** (*there is/there are*), which literally means *it gives* and comes from the verb **geben** (*to give*). Here you can see the same sort of shift: **ich gebe** [ikh GAY-beh], but **du gibst** [doo gipst] and **es gibt** [ess gipt].

Now is a good time to take a look at another German case. In Lesson 4 you were introduced to cases, and focused on the dative case. Now let's talk about the accusative case, which is the case of direct objects, and which also follows certain prepositions, especially those that express motion or direction. Remember that a direct object is the noun (or pronoun) in a sentence that receives the action of the verb. Here are some English examples, underlined.

I see the film. (The film is the thing being seen.)

She is writing a book. (The book is the thing being written.)

We ate a wonderful meal. (The meal is the thing being eaten.)

The boy kissed his grandmother. (The grandmother is the person being kissed.)

Each of those nouns is in the accusative case. In German, the only articles that change from the nominative to the accusative are masculine: **der** becomes **den**, and **ein** becomes **einen**.

Der Film ist gut.
The film is good.
(**Der Film** is the subject, so it's nominative.)

Du siehst den Film.
You see the film.
(**Den Film** is the direct object, so it's accusative.)

Ein Film läuft im Kino.
A film is playing (lit., "is running") at the movies.
(**Ein Film** is the subject, so it's nominative.)

Wir sehen einen Film.
We're seeing a film.
(**Einen Film** is the direct object, so it's accusative.)

▶ 5E Grammar Builder 2 (CD 2, Track 5)

Now, listen to your audio for an audio-only version of the grammar note that you just read. This will help you with your pronunciation, and it will also help reinforce everything that you've learned here.

�𝍣

Take It Further 1

In the previous lesson we learned that the preposition **in** contracts with the dative version of the masculine and neuter article **dem** to **im**. The same is true for the preposition **an**: **an** + **dem** becomes **am**:

der Morgen (*morning*)	am Morgen (*in the morning*)	ahm MOHR-gehn
der Abend (*evening*)	am Abend (*in the evening*)	ahm AH-behnt
der Nachmittag (*afternoon*)	am Nachmittag (*in the afternoon*)	ahm NAKH-mih-tahk

�𝍣

✎ Work Out 1

Now that you've learned some words and expressions that you need to describe what you do in the course of a day, let's see how they go together. Listen to the audio first, then fill in the missing German words, and finally, repeat the correct answers in the pauses provided. Note that when a time expression like *in the morning* is at the beginning of the sentence, the verb precedes the subject instead of following it.

▶ 5F Work Out 1 (CD 2, Track 6)

1. *In the morning I read the newspaper.*

   Am Morgen lese _____ **die Zeitung.**

2. *Then I listen to music on the radio.*

   Dann höre ich _____ **im Radio.**

3. *And I write a letter.*

   Und ich schreibe _____ **.**

4. *In the afternoon, I visit my brother.*

   Am Nachmittag besuche ich _____ **.**

5. *We go for a walk.*

   _____ **gehen spazieren.**

6. *And we eat ice cream.*

   _____ **wir essen ein Eis.**

7. *In the evening we sit on the couch in the living room.*

   Am Abend sitzen wir _____ **im Wohnzimmer.**

8. *We watch a movie on TV.*

   Wir _____ **einen Film im Fernsehen.**

   ANSWER KEY
   1. ich; 2. Musik; 3. einen Brief; 4. meinen Bruder; 5. Wir; 6. Und; 7. auf der Couch; 8. sehen

Ⅱ

❝ Bring It All Together

▶ 5G Bring It All Together (CD 2, Track 7)

Now let's listen to a dialogue that brings together everything you've learned in this lesson so far. Paula and Philipp are sitting in Philipp's living room. Philipp is reading a book. Remember to repeat the German phrases in the pauses provided.

What are you reading, Philipp?
Was liest du da, Philipp?
vahs leest doo dah, FEE-lihp

I'm reading a novel.
Ich lese einen Roman.
ikh LAY-zeh ī-nehn roh-MAHN

And what are you doing, Paula?
Und was machst du, Paula?
uhnt vahs mahkhst doo POW-lah

I'm looking out the window.
Ich sehe aus dem Fenster.
ikh ZAY-eh ows dehm FEHNS-tehr

What do you see there?
Was siehst du da?
vahs zeest doo dah

I see a child in the park.
Ich sehe ein Kind im Park.
ikh ZAY-eh īn kihnt ihm pahrk

What are we doing tonight?
Was machen wir heute Abend?
vahs MAH-khehn veer HOY-teh AH-behnt

There's a new movie in the movie theater.
Im Kino läuft ein neuer Film.
ihm KEE-noh loyft īn NOY-ehr fihlm

Oh yes, I'd like to see a new movie.
Au ja, ich sehe gerne einen neuen Film.
ow yah, ikh ZAY-eh gayrn ī-nehn NOY-ehn fihlm

Do you know my friend Tim?
Kennst Du meinen Freund Tim?
kehnst doo Mī-nehn froynt tīm

No, not yet.
Nein, noch nicht.
nīn, nokh nihkht

I want to call him.
Ich will ihn anrufen.
ikh vil een AHN-roo-fehn

Maybe he'll come, too.
Vielleicht kommt er auch.
feel-īkht kohmt ayr owkh

Ⅱ

Take It Further 2

▶ 5H Take It Further 2 (CD 2, Track 8)

There were a few new words in this dialogue. Could you understand them? An important one is the verb **es läuft,** which literally means *it runs,* but applies here to a showing of a movie. You already knew the verb **lesen** (*to read*), but note that it also changes its vowel:

I read	**ich lese**	ikh LAY-zeh
you (informal) read	**du liest**	doo leest
he reads	**er liest**	ehr leest

And did you notice that there were some unfamiliar grammatical examples as well?

NOMINATIVE		ACCUSATIVE	
a new film	**ein neuer Film** īn NOY-ehr fihlm	*a new film*	**einen neuen Film** īn-ehn NOY-ehn fihlm
the new film	**der neue Film** dehr NOY-eh fihlm	*the new film*	**den neuen Film** dayn NOY-ehn fihlm

As you can see, adjectives like **neu** change their form depending on the case, just like the articles. You'll learn more about adjectives in Lesson 8.

Ⓘ

Work Out 2

Let's put to practice what you've learned.

A. Complete the sentences with the accusative form of the appropriate noun and the definite or indefinite article that goes with it.

1. **Das ist ein Brief. Ich schreibe** _____.

2. **Das ist der Mann. Kennst du** _____ **?**

3. **Das ist ein neuer Film. Wir sehen** _____.

   (Don't forget the -en on neu!)

4. **Das ist mein Bruder. Er besucht** _____.

   (Don't forget the -en on mein!)

5. **Das ist ein Kind. Haben Sie** _____ **?**

B. Complete the sentences using the appropriate form of the verb in parentheses.

1. **Hans-Peter** _____ **einen neuen Film.** *(to see)*

2. **Du** _____ **ein Buch.** *(to write)*

3. **Ich** _____ **ein Eis.** *(to eat)*

4. **Wir** _____ **einen Freund.** *(to visit)*

5. **Claudia** _____ **die Zeitung.** *(to read)*

ANSWER KEY
A. 1. einen Brief; 2. den Mann; 3. einen neuen Film; 4. meinen Bruder; 5. ein Kind
B. 1. sieht; 2. schreibst; 3. esse; 4. besuchen; 5. liest

▶ 5I Work Out 2 (CD 2, Track 9)

Now listen to the audio for some more audio-only practice. This will help you
master the material you've learned so far!

Ⅱ

✎ Drive It Home

As usual, the following drills will help you master the grammar points we studied in this lesson. Write out all the answers, and read aloud each exercise.

A. Complete the sentences with the masculine definite article in the accusative.

1. **Ich kenne** _____ **Mann.**

2. **Ich sehe** _____ **Film.**

3. **Ich schreibe** _____ **Brief.**

B. Complete the sentences with the masculine indefinite article in the accusative.

1. **Er sieht** _____ **Film.**

2. **Er besucht** _____ **Freund.**

3. **Er hat** _____ **Bruder.**

C. Complete the sentences with the correct form of the adjective **neu.**

1. **Wir schreiben einen** _____ **Brief.**

2. **Wir sehen einen** _____ **Film.**

3. **Wir haben einen** _____ **Freund.**

D. Complete the sentences with the correct form of the verb in parentheses.

1. **Horst** _____ **ein Buch. (lesen)**

2. **Klaus** _____ **den Brief. (schreiben)**

3. **Susanne** _____ **den Film. (sehen)**

E. Complete the sentences with the correct form of the verb in parentheses.

1. **Wir** _____ **den Mann. (kennen)**

2. **Was** _____ **wir heute Abend? (machen)**

3. **Thomas und ich** _____ **einen Film. (sehen)**

ANSWER KEY
A. 1. den; 2. den; 3. den
B. 1. einen; 2. einen; 3. einen
C. 1. neuen; 2. neuen; 3. neuen
D. 1. liest; 2. schreibt; 3. sieht
E. 1. kennen; 2. machen; 3. sehen

Parting Words

Herzlichen Glückwunsch! *Congratulations!* You've finished another lesson, and you're learning so much. You can now:

☐ Talk about things you do (Still unsure? Go back to page 76 and page 79.)

☐ Use personal pronouns and verb forms together (Still unsure? Go back to page 77.)

☐ Talk about everyday activities (Still unsure? Go back to page 79.)

☐ Use the accusative case (Still unsure? Go back to page 80.)

☐ Put it all together in a conversation about making plans for the evening (Still unsure? Go back to page 84.)

Don't forget to practice and reinforce what you've learned by visiting **www.livinglanguage.com/languagelab** for flashcards, games, and quizzes for Lesson 5!

Take It Further 3

 5J Take It Futher (CD 2, Track 10)

When you're discussing plans for the evening or the weekend, the following expressions might come in handy:

Do you feel like it? (*informal, singular*)	**Hast du Lust?**	hahst doo loost
Yes, I feel like it.	**Ja, ich habe Lust.**	yah, ikh HAH-beh loost
Do you feel like it? (*formal, singular*)	**Haben Sie Lust?**	HAH-behn zee loost
Do you feel like it? (*informal, plural*)	**Habt ihr Lust?**	habt eer loost

Haben Sie Lust to learn more German? Then let's move on to the next lesson. **Auf Wiedersehen!** *Good-bye!*

Word Recall

Let's review and use some of the vocabulary you've learned so far. Match the English in column A to the correct German translation in column B.

1. *next to*   a. **der Brief**

2. *closet*   b. **die Schwester**

3. *apartment*   c. **kennen**

4. *in the evening*   d. **der Geburtstag**

5. *letter*   e. **ein bisschen**

6. *to call*   f. **neben**

7. *a little*   g. **am Abend**

8. *birthday*   h. **die Wohnung**

9. *to know*   i. **anrufen**

10. *sister*   j. **der Schrank**

ANSWER KEY
1. f; 2. j; 3. h; 4. g; 5. a; 6. i; 7. e; 8. d; 9. c; 10. b

Quiz 1

Eine kleine Nachprüfung 1
Ī-neh KLĪ-neh NAKH-prew-foong īns

Now let's see how you've done so far. In this section you'll find a short quiz testing what you learned in Lessons 1–5. After you've answered all of the questions, score your quiz and see how you did! If you find that you need to go back and review, please do so before continuing on to Lesson 6.

You'll get a second quiz after Lesson 10, followed by a final review with five dialogues and comprehension questions.

Let's get started!

A. Match the following English words to the correct German translations:

1. **die Wohnung**   a. *the kitchen*

2. **das Schlafzimmer**   b. *the apartment*

3. **das Bad**   c. *the closet*

4. **die Küche**   d. *the bedroom*

5. **der Schrank**   e. *the bathroom*

B. Translate the following English expressions into German:

1. *What's your name? (formal)* _____

2. *See you soon.* _____

3. *How are you? (informal)* _____

4. *Where are you from? (formal)* _____

5. *Take care. (informal)* _____

C. Fill in the blanks with **der**, **die**, or **das**:

1. _____ Mädchen

2. _____ Freund

3. _____ Eltern

4. _____ Familie

5. _____ Großvater

D. Fill in the table with the correct forms of **gehen** (*to go*):

I go	1.
you go (informal)	2.
she goes	3.
you go (formal/plural)	4.
we go	5.

E. Complete the sentences with the correct form of **der**, **die**, or **das** (*the*) and **ein**, **eine**, or **ein** (*a/an*):

1. **Mein Vater liest** _____ **Roman.** (*a*)

2. **Siehst du** _____ **Mann am Fenster?** (*the*)

3. **Ich sehe** _____ **Kind am Fenster.** (*the*)

4. **Wir besuchen** _____ **Freundin.** (*a*)

5. **Wir essen** _____ **Eis.** (*a*)

ANSWER KEY
A. 1. b; 2. d; 3. e; 4. a; 5. c
B. 1. Wie heißen Sie? 2. Bis bald. 3. Wie geht's? 4. Wo kommen Sie her? 5. Mach's gut.
C. 1. das; 2. der; 3. die; 4. die; 5. der
D. 1. ich gehe; 2. du gehst; 3. sie geht; 4. Sie gehen; 5. wir gehen
E. 1. einen; 2. den; 3. das; 4. eine; 5. ein

How Did You Do?

Give yourself a point for every correct answer, then use the following key to determine whether or not you're ready to move on:

0–10 points: It's probably best to go back and study the lessons again to make sure you understood everything completely. Take your time; it's not a race! Make sure you spend time reviewing the vocabulary and reading through each Grammar Builder section carefully.

11–18 points: If the questions you missed were in sections A or B, you may want to review the vocabulary from previous lessons again; if you missed answers mostly in sections C, D, or E, check the Grammar Builder sections to make sure you have your grammar basics down.

19–25 points: Feel free to move on to Lesson 6! You're doing a great job.

points

Lesson 6: Around Town

Lektion sechs: In der Stadt

Herzlich Willkommen! *Welcome again!* You are already on Lesson 6. In this lesson, you will learn how to:

- ☐ Ask for directions
- ☐ Use question words
- ☐ Talk about visiting a town
- ☐ Use the dative case with new prepositions
- ☐ Put it all together in a conversation about going into town to shop

Note that we'll stop using phonetic transliterations in Lesson 6. But that's **kein Problem!** (*No problem!*) You've got enough German under your belt by now, and you've also got the audio to help you continue to improve your pronunciation. Let's start with a few new words and expressions.

Vocabulary Builder 1

▶ 6B Vocabulary Builder 1 (CD 2, Track 12)

When?	**Wann?**
Where?	**Wo?**
How?	**Wie?**
Why?	**Warum?**
the city center	**die Innenstadt**
the bus stop	**die Bushaltestelle**
the street car	**die Straßenbahn**
the bus goes …	**der Bus fährt …**
the ticket	**die Fahrkarte**
it costs	**es kostet**
to buy	**kaufen**
to shop	**einkaufen**

Ⅱ

✎ Vocabulary Practice 1

Let's practice the vocabulary you just learned. Complete the sentences with the most appropriate word from the word bank:

kostet, einkaufen, fährt, Wo, Innenstadt

1. **Ich gehe** _____.

2. **Thomas fährt in die** _____.

3. **Die Fahrkarte** _____ **20 Euro.**

4. _____ **ist die Bushaltestelle?**

5. **Die Straßenbahn** _____ **in die Innenstadt.**

ANSWER KEY
1. **einkaufen**; 2. **Innenstadt**; 3. **kostet**; 4. **Wo**; 5. **fährt**

Grammar Builder 1

▶ 6C Grammar Builder 1 (CD 2, Track 13)

You have already encountered some question words before, in questions like:

What's your name?	**Wie heißen Sie?**
Who is that?	**Wer ist das?**

All German question words start with a **w,** pronounced _v_. They are placed at the beginning of the sentence and are followed by the verb and then the subject (pro)noun. This is just like the structure of the English _Where are you?_

WORD ORDER IN QUESTIONS		
QUESTION WORD	**VERB**	**SUBJECT**
Where	_are_	_you?_
Wo	**bist**	**du?**

In German, this same order is found with all verbs, not just with _to be_, so you get:

	QUESTION WORD	VERB	SUBJECT
What do you see?	**Was**	**siehst**	**du?**
How much is it?	**Was**	**kostet**	**das?**

(Note that you don't use the "helping verb" _do_ or _does_ in German questions!)

This reversed order of subject and verb also indicates a question when there is no question word at all:

	QUESTION WORD	VERB	SUBJECT
Are you coming?	-	**Kommst**	**du?**
Would you like?	-	**Möchtest**	**du?**

These are questions that are usually answered with ja or nein. Now let's look at some more words and phrases.

Vocabulary Builder 2

6D Vocabulary Builder 2 (CD 2, Track 14)

I'm looking for ...	Ich suche ...
from me	von mir
with you (informal)	mit dir
with you (formal)	mit Ihnen
the post office	die Post
to the post office	zur Post
from the train station	vom Bahnhof
the store	das Geschäft
the department store	das Kaufhaus
to the right	rechts
to the left	links

Vocabulary Practice 2

Let's use the vocabulary you've just learned.

Which German words in column A and column B most logically go together?

1. die Post

2. suchen

3. das Geschäft

a. links

b. einkaufen

c. der Brief

4. rechts   d. **die Bushaltestelle**

5. **der Bus**   e. **Wo?**

ANSWER KEY
1. c; 2. e; 3. b; 4. a; 5. d

Grammar Builder 2

▶ 6E Grammar Builder 2 (CD 2, Track 15)

The word list that you just heard contained some new prepositions:

with	**mit**
to, towards	**zu**
from	**von**

The last two prepositions have contracted forms:

from + (m/n) article	**von + dem = vom**	*BUT: from + (f) article*	**von + der = von der**
	vom Bahnhof		**von der Post**

By contrast, **zu** also contracts with the feminine article, so *to the post office* is **zur Post**, not **zu der Post**.

to + (m/n) article	**zu + dem = zum**	*AND: to + (f) article*	**zu + der = zur**
	zum Bahnhof		**zur Post**

All four of these new prepositions require the noun or pronoun following to take the dative case. You already know how to form the dative of a noun by changing the form of the article or merging it with a preposition.

	NOMINATIVE	**DATIVE**
the (m.)	**der**	**dem**
the (f.)	**die**	**der**

	NOMINATIVE	DATIVE
the (n.)	das	dem
a/an (m.)	ein	einem
a/an (f.)	eine	einer
a/an (m.)	ein	einem

However, the personal pronouns have special case forms:

	NOMINATIVE	DATIVE
I	ich	mir
you (informal)	du	dir
you (formal)	Sie	Ihnen
he	er	ihm
she	sie	ihr
it	es	ihm

(Note: We'll discuss the dative plural forms of the personal pronouns in a later lesson.)

Work Out 1

6F Work Out 1 (CD 2, Track 16)

You can use the words and expressions that you just learned to ask for directions in a new city. Let's practice together. As usual you'll hear the English first, then fill in the missing German words, and finally, repeat the correct answers in the pauses provided.

1. *How do I get to the city center?*

   Wie komme ich in _____ **?**

2. *Take the street car.*

   Fahren Sie doch mit _____ **.**

3. *How much is a ticket? (How much does a ticket cost?)*

   Was _____ **eine Fahrkarte?**

4. *Two euros twenty.*

   _____ **Euro** _____ **.**

5. *When does the street car go?*

   _____ **fährt die Straßenbahn?**

6. *In five minutes.*

   In _____ **Minuten.**

7. *Where is the stop?*

   _____ **ist die Haltestelle?**

8. *Next to the post office.*

   Neben _____ **.**

   ANSWER KEY
   1. die Innenstadt; 2. der Straßenbahn; 3. kostet; 4. zwei/zwanzig; 5. Wann; 6. fünf; 7. Wo; 8. der Post

🔊 Bring It All Together

▶ 6G Bring It All Together (CD 2, Track 17)

Now let's listen to a dialogue that highlights more of the structures and words from this lesson. Philipp wants to go shopping, and he asks Paula to come along. Listen to the English sentence first, and then you'll hear the German sentence, which you should repeat for practice in the pause provided.

Would you like to go shopping with me?
Möchtest du mit mir einkaufen gehen?

Yes, I would like to come with you.
Ja, ich komme gerne mit dir.

Are we taking the bus?
Fahren wir mit dem Bus?

No, I prefer to ride the street car.
Nein, ich fahre lieber mit der Straßenbahn.

Why?
Warum?

It goes straight to the city center.
Sie fährt direkt zur Innenstadt.

So, what would you like to buy?
Was möchtest du denn kaufen?

I'm looking for a book about music.
Ich suche nach einem Buch über Musik.

And I would like to buy shoes.
Und ich möchte gerne Schuhe kaufen.

Great, I know a good shoe store, next to the post office.
Super, ich kenne ein gutes Schuhgeschäft neben der Post.

Ⓘ

Take It Further 2

▶ 6H Take It Further 2 (CD 2, Track 18)

That wasn't hard to understand, was it? Most of the words you knew already. Did you remember the verb **mögen** (*to like*) from Lesson 3? You'll hear and use these forms a lot:

I would like	**ich möchte**
you (informal) would like	**du möchtest**
you (formal) would like	**Sie möchten**

But there were also some new words in the dialogue. Did you notice the word **denn**:

| *So, what would you like to buy?* | **Was möchtest du denn kaufen?** |

It can often be translated as *then*, but here it's kind of a filler word best translated as *so*, which indicates that Paula is asking for additional information—she already knows that Philipp wants to buy something.

German speakers use a lot of filler words like that. It's best to learn them as part of expressions.

Ⓘ

Lesson 6: Around Town   103

✎ Work Out 2

Time to practice. First, complete the sentences with the correct preposition.
Sometimes you'll need to add an article or the contracted form of an article
with that preposition. Then, starting with number five, answer the questions by
replacing the underlined words with the correct dative pronoun.

1. **Kommst du _____ in die Stadt?** (*with*)

2. **Fährst du _____ Bus?** (*with*)

3. **Der Bus fährt _____ Bahnhof _____ Innenstadt.** (*from/to*)

4. **Fährt die Straßenbahn _____ Post?** (*to*)

5. **Die Haltestelle ist _____ Post.** (*next to*)

6. **Fährst du mit <u>Thomas</u> in die Stadt? Ja, ich fahre mit _____ in**

   die Stadt.

7. **Kommen Sie mit <u>mir</u> zur Bushaltestelle? Ja, ich komme mit _____**

   zur Bushaltestelle.

8. **Kommen Sie mit <u>Susanne</u> zur Party? Ja, ich komme mit _____**

   zur Party.

9. **Geht Sabine mit <u>Horst</u> zur Post? Ja, Sabine geht mit _____**

   zur Post.

10. **Fahre ich mit dir oder mit <u>Andrea</u>? Du fährst mit _____ , nicht**

    mit Andrea.

    ANSWER KEY
    1. mit; 2. mit dem; 3. vom/in die; 4. zur; 5. neben der; 6. ihm; 7. Ihnen; 8. ihr; 9. ihm; 10. mir

▶ 6I Work Out 2 (CD 2, Track 19)

As usual, listen to the audio for some more audio-only practice. These audio practices will help tune your ear to German and develop both your listening comprehension and spoken proficiency.

✎ Drive It Home

Time to drive home the grammar points of the lesson.

A. Ask questions with the German for *where?*

1. _____ ist die Bushaltestelle?

2. _____ ist das Kaufhaus?

3. _____ ist der Bahnhof?

B. Ask questions with the German for *when?*

1. _____ fährt der Bus?

2. _____ kommst du?

3. _____ gehen wir einkaufen?

C. Ask questions with the German for what?

1. _____ kostet das denn?

2. _____ kaufts du denn?

3. _____ möchtest du denn essen?

D. Decide whether to use **zum** or **zur**.

1. **Der Bus fährt** _____ **Post.**

2. **Die Straßenbahn fährt** _____ **Bahnhof.**

3. **Kommst du** _____ **Kaufhaus?**

4. **Kommst du** _____ **Bushaltestelle?**

E. Decide whether to use **vom** or **von der**.

1. **Der Bus fährt** _____ **Post in die Innenstadt.**

2. **Kommst du** _____ **Kaufhaus?**

3. **Kommst du** _____ **Bushaltestelle?**

4. **Die Straßenbahn fährt** _____ **Bahnhof in die Innenstadt.**

ANSWER KEY
A. 1. Wo; 2. Wo; 3. Wo
B. 1. Wann; 2. Wann; 3. Wann
C. 1. Was; 2. Was; 3. Was
D. 1. zur; 2. zum; 3. zum; 4. zur
E. 1. von der; 2. vom; 3. von der; 4. vom

Parting Words

Herzlichen Glückwunsch! _Congratulations!_ You've finished another lesson, and you've learned how to:

☐ Ask for directions (Still unsure? Go back to page 100.)

☐ Use question words (Still unsure? Go back to page 97.)

☐ Talk about visiting a town (Still unsure? Go back to page 96 and page 98.)

☐ Use the dative case with new prepositions (Still unsure? Go back to page 99.)

☐ Put it all together in a conversation about going into town to shop (Still unsure? Go back to page 102.)

Don't forget to practice and reinforce what you've learned by visiting **www.livinglanguage.com/ languagelab** for flashcards, games, and quizzes for Lesson 6!

Take It Further 3

▶ 6J Take It Further 3 (CD 2, Track 20)

You know how to ask questions now, so if you go shopping for clothes and shoes, you will be fine, even if you need to ask additional questions. Here are some words that will help.

size	**die Größe**
to try on	**anprobieren**
on sale	**im Angebot**
on sale	**im Sonderangebot**
pedestrian zones	**die Fußgängerzonen**

Shopping in most German cities will lead you to the city centers, which have been largely closed off to traffic to create **Fußgängerzonen** (*pedestrian zones*) with many shops, outdoor cafés and restaurants, and sometimes outdoor markets. **Auf Wiedersehen!** *Good-bye!*

⏸

Word Recall

Time to review the vocabulary from the previous six lessons. Choose which word fits best in the blanks.

links, Wohnzimmer, suche, Wohnung, am Morgen, mit, Sohn, Post, Wo, möchtest

1. Ich _____ nach einem Buch über Musik.

2. Was _____ du denn essen?

3. Die Bushaltestelle ist _____ von dir.

4. Am Nachmittag geht Frau Schneider zur _____.

5. Meine _____ hat vier Zimmer.

6. Das Telefon ist im _____.

7. Mein _____ ist vierzehn Jahre alt.

8. Mein Vater liest _____ die Zeitung.

9. Ich komme _____.

10. _____ wohnen Sie?

ANSWER KEY

1. suche; 2. möchtest; 3. links; 4. Post; 5. Wohnung; 6. Wohnzimmer; 7. Sohn; 8. am Morgen; 9. mit; 10. Wo

Lesson 7: At a Restaurant

Lektion sieben: Im Restaurant

Willkommen! Welcome to Lesson 7. In this lesson, you will learn how to:

☐ Order at a restaurant

☐ Use the accusative case

☐ Talk about food

☐ Use the imperative to make requests

☐ Put it all together in a conversation about dinner

So let's get started with some new words and phrases.

Vocabulary Builder 1

▶ 7B Vocabulary Builder 1 (CD 2, Track 22)

the menu	die Speisekarte
the appetizer	die Vorspeise
the main course	das Hauptgericht
the dessert	der Nachtisch
I would like to have …	Ich hätte gerne …
you wish (formal)	Sie wünschen
I recommend the salad.	Ich empfehle den Salat.
the soup	die Suppe
with rice	mit Reis
without potatoes	ohne Kartoffeln
for me	für mich

⏸

✎ Vocabulary Practice 1

Let's practice the vocabulary.

Can you find the German translations of the following English words in the puzzle below?

1. *salad*

2. *dessert*

3. *rice*

4. *soup*

5. *without*

6. *appetizer*

S	A	L	A	T	Ü	H	R	S
A	O	H	N	R	A	U	B	U
ß	Ö	C	H	S	E	W	A	P
O	H	N	E	N	A	I	H	P
V	O	R	S	P	E	I	S	E
N	A	C	H	T	I	S	C	H

Grammar Builder 1

▶ 7C Grammar Builder 1 (CD 2, Track 23)

Did you notice the word **gerne** (often shortened to **gern**)? This is an adverb that you have already encountered in previous lessons. Together with a verb, it indicates that an activity is liked.

GERN(E) + VERB	
I'd like to have	**ich hätte gerne**
I like to eat	**ich esse gerne**
I like to drink	**ich trinke gerne**

If you want to add a noun to such an expression with **gerne**, it has to be in the accusative case. You already know how to form the accusative of nouns.

GERN(E) + VERB + ACCUSATIVE OBJECT	
I'd like to have the salad.	**Ich hätte gern den Salat.**
I'd like to have the rice.	**Ich hätte gern den Reis.**

Personal pronouns have an accusative, too, but there are some special forms that you need to know.

PERSONAL PRONOUNS	
NOMINATIVE	ACCUSATIVE
ich	mich
du	dich
er	ihn
sie/Sie	sie
es	es

For instance, ich and du have the accusative forms mich and dich, and er becomes ihn in the accusative. Not all pronouns change their form, though. The accusative of Sie is also Sie, and that's true for all three meanings of sie/Sie.

Take It Further 1

▶ 7D Take It Further 1 (CD 2, Track 24)

The accusative pronoun forms are used not only when the pronoun is the direct object of the sentence, but also after certain prepositions that take the accusative.

PREPOSITIONS THAT TAKE THE ACCUSATIVE	
about	über
for	für
without	ohne

Now let's listen to some more words and expressions.

Vocabulary Builder 2

▷ 7E Vocabulary Builder 2 (CD 2, Track 25)

He drinks coffee.	**Er trinkt Kaffee.**
Have the cutlet. (informal)	**Nimm das Schnitzel.**
Bring a beer. (formal)	**Bringen Sie ein Bier.**
a glass of white wine	**ein Glas Weißwein**
the chicken	**das Hühnchen**
the meat	**das Fleisch**
fresh fish	**frischer Fisch**
the vegetables	**das Gemüse**
the cake	**der Kuchen**
the mineral water	**das Mineralwasser**

✎ Vocabulary Practice 2

Time to practice. Translate the following English sentences into German.

1. *She drinks mineral water.*

   _____

2. *Bring a glass of white wine. (informal)*

   _____

3. *Take the vegetables. (informal)*

   _____

4. *I'd like to have the Schnitzel.*

   _____

5. *I recommend the cake.*

ANSWER KEY

1. Sie trinkt Mineralwasser. 2. Bring ein Glass Weißwein. 3. Nimm das Gemüse. 4. Ich hätte gern das Schnitzel. 5. Ich empfehle den Kuchen.

Grammar Builder 2

▶ 7F Grammar Builder 2 (CD 2, Track 26)

When you ask another person to do something for you, such as when you order at a restaurant, you often need to use an imperative form of the verb. This is another aspect of grammar where you have to make a distinction between the formal **Sie** and the informal **du**, depending on whom you're talking to. With the **Sie** form, the imperative form is the same as the form of the verb in the present tense, except that the verb comes first.

IMPERATIVE (FORMAL) SIE GEBEN. → GEBEN SIE!	
Give me.	**Geben Sie mir!**
Take the vegetables.	**Nehmen Sie das Gemüse!**
Bring the coffee.	**Bringen Sie den Kaffee!**

By contrast, there is a special imperative form for the informal **du**. The informal imperative is the **du** form of the verb in the present tense, but without the **-st** or **-t** ending.

IMPERATIVE (INFORMAL) DU GIBST. → GIB!	
Give me.	**Gib mir!**
Take the vegetables.	**Nimm das Gemüse!**
Bring the coffee.	**Bring den Kaffee!**

⏸

✎ Work Out 1
▶ 7G Work Out 1 (CD 2, Track 27)

Now let's practice what you just learned by listening to a dialogue. Listen to the audio, and fill in the missing words.

1. *Hello, what would you like?*

   Guten Tag, was hätten Sie _____?

2. *As an appetizer, I'd like a salad.*

   Zur Vorspeise hätte ich gerne einen _____.

3. *And what would you like for your main course?*

   Und was wünschen Sie zum _____?

4. *Can you recommend something to me?*

   Können Sie mir etwas _____?

5. *Today we have fresh fish with rice.*

   Heute haben wir frischen Fisch _____.

6. *Thanks, but I would like to eat meat.*

   Danke, aber ich _____ gerne Fleisch essen.

7. *Then why don't you have a cutlet?*

   Dann nehmen Sie doch _____.

8. *Yes, I would like to have that.*

   Ja, das _____ ich gerne.

⏸

ANSWER KEY
1. gerne; 2. Salat; 3. Hauptgericht; 4. empfehlen; 5. mit Reis; 6. möchte; 7. ein Schnitzel; 8. hätte

🎧 Bring It All Together
▶ 7H Bring It All Together (CD 2, Track 28)

Now listen to a conversation that highlights the structures you have learned in this lesson and introduces a bit more vocabulary. Philipp and Paula are going out for dinner, and they are discussing what they will have. You'll hear the English sentence first; then, listen to and repeat the German sentence.

What will you have, Philipp?
Was nimmst du, Philipp?

As an appetizer, I'll have a pea soup.
Zur Vorspeise nehme ich eine Erbsensuppe.

And then I'd like chicken with rice.
Und dann möchte ich ein Hühnchen mit Reis.

And for you, Paula?
Und für dich, Paula?

I don't know yet.
Ich weiß noch nicht.

Please, give me the menu once more.
Gib mir bitte noch einmal die Speisekarte.

Here you go.
Bitte sehr.

Have the fish, why don't you?
Nimm doch den Fisch.

Yes, I like to eat fish.
Ja, Fisch esse ich gerne.

Would you like to drink a glass of white wine?
Möchtest Du ein Glas Weißwein trinken?

Oh yes, and a bottle of mineral water.
Au ja, und eine Flasche Mineralwasser.

Ⅱ

Take It Further 2

▶ 7I Take It Further 2 (CD 2, Track 29)

Okay, you're learning more and more vocabulary with each lesson. Did you notice that some phrases included an extra word to indicate a quantity of food or drink?

cake	der Kuchen	a piece of cake	ein Stück Kuchen
mineral water	das Mineralwasser	a bottle of mineral water	eine Flasche Mineralwasser

Another point you may have noticed is that imperatives very often come with an extra little word: When you make a request, you often use the word **bitte** (*please*).

Please give me the menu.	**Gib mir bitte die Speisekarte.**

If you use the imperative to make a suggestion, it is common to add the word **doch**.

Why don't you give me the menu.	**Gib mir doch bitte die Speisekarte.**

In both cases, the extra word serves to make the request or suggestion sound less direct and more polite.

Ⅱ

✎ Work Out 2

A. Rewrite the following sentences as a request. Add the word in parentheses.

1. **Du nimmst den Kuchen. (doch)**

   _____

2. **Sie geben mir ein Glas Wein. (bitte)**

   _____

3. **Sie nehmen den Salat. (doch)**

   _____

4. **Du nimmst das Schnitzel. (doch)**

   _____

5. **Du bringst mir ein Bier. (bitte)**

   _____

B. Answer the questions using the words in parentheses.

1. **Was nehmen Sie als Vorspeise? (der Salat)**

   _____

2. **Was empfehlen Sie? (das Schnitzel)**

   _____

3. **Was hätten Sie gern? (ein Glas Wein)**

   _____

4. **Was möchtest du? (das Gemüse)**

   _____

5. Was suchen Sie? (die Speisekarte)

_____

ANSWER KEY
A. 1. Nimm doch den Kuchen. 2. Geben Sie mir bitte ein Glas Wein. 3. Nehmen Sie doch den Salat.
4. Nimm doch das Schnitzel. 5. Bring bitte ein Bier.
B. 1. Ich nehme den Salat. 2. Ich empfehle das Schnitzel. 3. Ich hätte gern ein Glas Wein. 4. Ich
möchte das Gemüse. 5. Ich suche die Speisekarte.

▶ 7J Work Out 2 (CD 2, Track 30)

Now listen to the audio for some audio-only practice.

⏸

✎ Drive It Home

Let's practice the grammar points of the lesson and try to make some of the
structures you've learned a bit more automatic. Remember to write down the
exercises, and read them out loud as well.

A. Complete the sentences with the accusative form of the noun in parentheses.

1. Ich nehme _____. (der Reis)

2. Ich nehme _____. (das Gemüse)

3. Ich nehme _____. (der Salat)

4. Ich nehme _____. (die Kartoffeln)

5. Ich nehme _____. (der Wein)

B. Complete the sentences with the informal imperative form of the verb in parentheses.

1. _____ mir die Speisekarte, bitte. (geben)

2. _____ doch das Hühnchen. (nehmen)

3. _____ doch etwas. (empfehlen)

4. _____ doch ein Glas Wein. (bringen)

5. _____ doch mit mir zum Bahnhof. (kommen)

C. Now complete the sentences with the formal imperative form of the verb in parentheses.

1. _____ mir die Speisekarte, bitte. (geben)

2. _____ doch das Hühnchen. (nehmen)

3. _____ doch etwas. (empfehlen)

4. _____ doch ein Glas Wein. (bringen)

5. _____ doch mit mir zum Bahnhof. (kommen)

ANSWER KEY
A. 1. den Reis; 2. das Gemüse; 3. den Salat; 4. die Kartoffeln; 5. den Wein
B. 1. Gib; 2. Nimm; 3. Empfiehl; 4. Bring; 5. Komm
C. 1. Geben Sie; 2. Nehmen Sie; 3. Empfehlen Sie; 4. Bringen Sie; 5. Kommen Sie

Parting Words

Danke! *Thank you!* You're making great progress as you're learning to use German in some real-life situations that you might encounter when visiting Germany. You now know how to:

☐ Order at a restaurant (Still unsure? Go back to page 110.)

☐ Use the accusative case (Still unsure? Go back to page 111.)

☐ Talk about food (Still unsure? Go back to page 113.)

☐ Use the imperative to make requests (Still unsure? Go back to page 114.)

☐ Put it all together in a conversation about dinner (Still unsure? Go back to page 116.)

Don't forget to practice and reinforce what you've learned by visiting **www.livinglanguage.com/languagelab** for flashcards, games, and quizzes for Lesson 7!

Take It Further 3
▶ 7K Take It Further 3 (CD 2, Track 31)

There are a lot more food terms that you may want to learn, such as:

beef	**das Rindfleisch**
noodles, pasta	**die Nudeln**
fruit	**das Obst**
Enjoy your meal!	**Guten Appetit!**

Auf Wiedersehen in Lektion Acht! *See you in Lesson 8!*

⏸

Word Recall

Let's go over some of the important vocabulary from all previous lessons. Fill in the blanks with the German words from the word bank that best fit the storyline.

Kinder, Gemüse, Wohnung, Wein, kommt, heißt, gern, ein Glas, Innenstadt, Sohn

Mein Bruder _____ (1) aus Berlin. Er hat eine große _____ (2) in der _____ (3). Er hat zwei _____ (4). Seine Tochter _____ (5) Sabine, und sein _____ (6) heißt Sebastian. Sebastian isst _____ (7) Nachtisch. Sabine isst gern _____ (8). Im Restaurant bestellen beide gern _____ (9) Mineralwasser. Mein Bruder trinkt lieber ein Glas _____ (10).

ANSWER KEY
1. kommt; 2. Wohnung; 3. Innenstadt; 4. Kinder; 5. heißt; 6. Sohn; 7. gern; 8. Gemüse; 9. ein Glas; 10. Wein

Lesson 8: Describing Things

Lektion acht: Gegenstände beschreiben

Hallo! *Hi!* Welcome to Lesson 8, where you'll learn how to:

☐ Use the words for colors and other adjectives

☐ Describe objects such as items of clothing

☐ Use possessive pronouns such as my

☐ Use demonstrative pronouns such as that one

☐ Put it all together in a conversation about dressing up for a party

Let's begin with a few new words and phrases.

Vocabulary Builder 1

▶ 8B Vocabulary Builder 1 (CD 2, Track 33)

the color	die Farbe
red	rot
blue	blau
green	grün
brown	braun
black	schwarz
yellow	gelb
the yellow shirt	das gelbe Hemd
a large shirt	ein großes Hemd
a small bag	eine kleine Tasche

Ⅱ

✎ Vocabulary Practice 1

Let's see if you know your colors. Match the word in column A with the color that best describes it.

1. *sun*   a. **grün**

2. *grass*   b. **blau**

3. *sky*   c. **braun**

4. *dirt*   d. **rot**

5. *rose*   e. **gelb**

ANSWER KEY
1. e; 2. a; 3. b; 4. c; 5. d

Grammar Builder 1

Now you've learned some words for colors, and you've seen how to use them with a noun. Like other adjectives, their form depends on where in the sentence they are used. When they're not right next to the noun they describe, for example after a verb like **sein**, adjectives don't take any agreement endings.

The chair is red.	Der Stuhl ist rot.
Grass is green.	Das Gras ist grün.
The city is beautiful.	Die Stadt ist schön.

But when a German adjective is used right before the noun it describes, it has to agree with that noun by taking endings that match the noun's gender, number, and even case. There are two different types of endings for adjectives, often called "strong" and "weak." You don't have to worry about these labels, but they're actually helpful. Think of it this way: A German adjective wants you to know whether the noun it's describing is masculine, feminine, or neuter. In some instances, there's something else in the sentence that already does that, so the adjective doesn't need to do the work. In these instances, it takes the "weak" endings.

If you think of the definite articles, **der**, **die**, and **das**, you know that each one gives you all the the information you need about the noun's gender. So, after definite articles, adjective can stay "weak," and just take the lazy ending: **-e**.

der kleine Mann
the small man

die kleine Frau
the small woman

das kleine Kind
the small child

But now think about the indefinite articles. **Eine** is only used with feminine nouns, but **ein** is used with both masculine and neuter nouns. In other words, the adjective has to pick up the slack and use the "strong" endings. These endings even look a lot like the endings of the definite article: **-er** for masculine (like **der**), **-e** for feminine (like **die**), and **-es** for neuter (like **das**).

ein kleiner Mann
a small man

eine kleine Frau
a small woman

ein kleines Kind
a small child

Keep in mind that these endings only cover the nominative case. Adjective endings also differ according to the case of the noun, but we'll cover that later.

▶ 8C Grammar Builder 1 (CD 2, Track 34)

Now, listen to your audio for an audio-only version of this grammar note. This will be a great review, and it will also give you the chance to hear the pronunciation of key words and phrases.

⏸

Vocabulary Builder 2
▶ 8D Vocabulary Builder 2 (CD 2, Track 35)

the skirt	**der Rock**
the pants	**die Hose**
the shoe	**der Schuh**

the sweater	der Pullover
your jacket	deine Jacke
an old dress	ein altes Kleid
the new dress	das neue Kleid
this dress	dieses Kleid
her dress	ihr Kleid
his pants	seine Hose

✎ Vocabulary Practice 2

Time to practice the vocabulary. Find the German translations for the following words:

1. *pants*

2. *shoe*

3. *skirt*

4. *jacket*

5. *dress*

6. *old*

7. *new*

A	L	J	N	H	O	H	O	S
L	J	A	L	T	N	E	W	N
ß	S	C	H	U	H	M	S	E
R	O	K	U	R	O	C	K	U
K	L	E	I	D	S	W	K	U
Ä	L	T	E	R	E	S	C	H

Grammar Builder 2

▶ 8E Grammar Builder 2 (CD 2, Track 36)

You've just learned some more words for items of clothing along with more adjectives to describe them. Instead of using articles, you can also combine nouns with possessives like **mein** (*my*) and demonstratives like **dieser** (*this*).

my	mein
your	dein
your (formal)	Ihr
his	sein
her	ihr
its	sein

When it comes to endings, **mein**, **dein**, and the other possessives behave a lot like the indefinite article **ein**. They have the same gender and case endings, and they also have the same effect on accompanying adjectives.

my blue sweater	mein blauer Pullover
your new bag	deine neue Tasche
my black shirt	mein schwarzes Hemd

By contrast, the demonstrative **dieser** (*this*) behaves more like the definite article **der**. It has a different form for each gender—**dieser**, **diese**, **dieses**—while a following adjective always ends in -e.

this blue sweater	dieser blaue Pullover
this new bag	diese neue Tasche
this black dress	dieses schwarze Hemd

Ⅱ

✎ Work Out 1

▶ 8F Work Out 1 (CD 2, Track 37)

Now let's review what you have just learned about adjectives. The following advertisement for a yard sale describes the items that are for sale. You'll hear adjectives and nouns together, in the accusative case. Note that those adjectives that precede masculine nouns have an accusative case ending in **-n**, while the feminine and neuter forms are unchanged. You'll hear the English first, then the German. You'll have to fill in the adjectives in their correct form, then listen to the German again, which you should repeat for practice.

1. *We sell a large table,*

   Wir verkaufen einen _____ **Tisch,**

2. *two black chairs,*

   zwei _____ **Stühle,**

3. *a blue chair,*

   einen _____ **Stuhl,**

4. *a red lamp,*

   eine _____ **Lampe,**

5. *a small radio,*

   ein _____ **Radio,**

6. *a green couch,*

   eine _____ **Couch,**

7. *a new TV,*

   einen _____ **Fernseher,**

8. *and an old wardrobe.*

   und einen _____ Schrank.

   ⏸

   ANSWER KEY
   1. großen; 2. schwarze; 3. blauen; 4. rote; 5. kleines; 6. grüne; 7. neuen; 8. alten

Bring It All Together
▶ 8G Bring It All Together (CD 2, Track 38)

Now let's listen to a dialogue that highlights more of the structures and words from this lesson. Paula and Philipp are going to a party. They are talking about what to wear.

Listen to the English sentence first, and then you'll hear the German sentence repeated.

Would you like to borrow a dress from my sister?
Möchtest du ein Kleid von meiner Schwester leihen?

Yes, I'd like to; what color is it?
Ja gerne, welche Farbe hat es?

It's brown, with a yellow pattern.
Es ist braun, mit einem gelben Muster.

That's a beautiful dress.
Das ist ein schönes Kleid.

But maybe it's too small for me.
Aber vielleicht ist es mir zu klein.

I believe it's the right size.
Ich glaube es hat die richtige Größe.

Yes, you're right.
Ja, du hast recht.

It goes well with your new shoes.
Es passt gut zu deinen neuen Schuhen.

And what are you going to wear?
Und was ziehst du an?

I'll wear white pants and a shirt.
Ich werde eine weiße Hose anziehen und dazu ein Hemd.

⏸

Take It Further 1

▶ 8H Take It Further 1 (CD 3, Track 1)

Did you notice the question word **welche** in **welche Farbe** (*which color*)? It works just like the demonstrative **dies-**, in that it has three different gender forms:

WHICH?		
MASCULINE	**FEMININE**	**NEUTER**
welcher	welche	welches

There were also a few new words in this dialogue:

to dress, to wear	**anziehen**
to borrow	**leihen**
to lend	**verleihen**

⏸

✎ Work Out 2

Fill in the blanks with the correct form of the possessive pronoun that suits the pronoun in parentheses.

Example: **Das ist _____ blaues Kleid. (ich) → Das ist mein blaues Kleid.**

1. **Das ist _____ grüne Jacke. (er)**

2. **Das ist _____ weißes Hemd. (ich)**

3. **Das sind _____ grünen Schuhe. (ich)**

4. **Das ist _____ schwarzer Rock. (sie)**

5. **Das ist _____ roter Pullover. (du)**

Now complete the sentences with the correct form of the adjective in parentheses. Note that **gehören** means *to belong to*, and **wem** means *to whom?*

1. **Das _____ Kleid steht dir sehr gut.** (*red*)

2. **Wem gehört dieser _____ Pullover?** (*white*)

3. **Die Tasche ist _____.** (*old*)

4. Meine _____ Schuhe passen nicht. (*new*)

5. Aber sie sind die _____ Größe. (*right*)

6. Dieses _____ Hemd passt zu deiner _____ Hose. (*green/black*)

ANSWER KEY
1. seine; 2. mein; 3. meine; 4. ihr; 5. dein
1. rote; 2. weiße; 3. alt; 4. neuen; 5. richtige; 6. grüne/schwarzen

▶ 8I Work Out 2 (CD 3, Track 2)

Okay, now let's practice some of what you've learned in an audio-only exercise.

⏸

✎ Drive It Home

Let's practice some grammar so that we can help make the patterns more automatic for you. We'll focus on adjective endings.

A. Fill in the blanks following the example. (Clue: These are the "weak" endings! The articles **der, die, das** do all the work in telling you the gender of the noun, so the adjective can be lazy.)
Example: **das** _____ Gemüse (gut) → **das gute Gemüse**

1. das _____ Hemd (schön)

2. die _____ Tasche (neu)

3. der _____ Rock (lang)

4. die _____ Jacke (braun)

5. der _____ Pullover (warm)

B. Now fill in the blanks with the "strong" endings, following the example. Remember that after **ein** or **eine** (or similar words like **mein**), the adjective has to do a bit more work and show the gender of the noun. Note that **voll** means *full*.
Example: **ein** _____ Geschäft (gut) → **ein gutes Geschäft**

1. ein _____ Kind (klein)

2. eine _____ Speisekarte (neu)

3. ein _____ Freund (alt)

4. eine _____ Freundin (gut)

5. ein _____ Glas (voll)

C. Now, rewrite the sentences following the example. Change the definite article to an indefinite article, but look out for changes in the adjective ending as well!
Example: **Das neue Geschäft ist teuer.** → **Ein neues Geschäft ist teuer.**

1. **Der grüne Salat ist gut.** _____

2. **Die rote Bluse steht mir.** _____

3. **Das große Foto ist schön.** _____

4. **Der neue Pullover ist gelb.** _____

5. **Die grüne Tasche gehört mir.** _____

D. Now, rewrite the sentences using **dieser**, **diese**, or **dieses** instead of the underlined possessives. Again, look out for changes you'll need to make to the adjective endings.

1. <u>**Ihr**</u> **rotes Kleid ist schön.** _____

2. <u>**Seine**</u> **neue Hose ist zu teuer.** _____

3. **Dein** grünes Hemd steht mir. _____

4. **Dein** roter Pullover hat ein schönes Muster. _____

5. **Mein** alter Fernseher ist kaputt. _____

ANSWER KEY
A. 1. schöne; 2. neue; 3. lange; 4. braune; 5. warme
B. 1. kleines; 2. neue; 3. alter; 4. gute; 5. volles
C. 1. Ein grüner; 2. Eine rote; 3. Ein großes; 4. Ein neuer; 5. Eine grüne
D. 1. Dieses rote; 2. Diese neue; 3. Dieses grüne; 4. Dieser rote; 5. Dieser alte

Parting Words

Herzlichen Glückwunsch! *Congratulations!* This was a difficult lesson, but you've done remarkably well. Make sure you can now:

☐ Use the words for colors and other adjectives (Still unsure? Go back to page 124.)

☐ Describe objects such as items of clothing (Still unsure? Go back to page 124 and page 125.)

☐ Use possessive pronouns such as 'my' (Still unsure? Go back to page 128.)

☐ Use demonstrative pronouns such as 'that one' (Still unsure? Go back to page 128.)

☐ Put it all together in a conversation about dressing up for a party (Still unsure? Go back to page 130.)

Don't forget to practice and reinforce what you've learned by visiting **www.livinglanguage.com/languagelab** for flashcards, games, and quizzes for Lesson 8!

Take It Further 2

8J Take It Further (CD 3, Track 3)

The adjective endings are a complicated topic; maybe you'll want to practice some more with other adjectives.

MORE ADJECTIVES	
violet	lila
pink	rosa
cold	kalt
hot	heiß

MORE NOUNS	
hat	der Hut
scarf	der Schal
tie	die Kravatte
boots	die Stiefel

Auf Wiedersehen! See you in Lesson 9.

Word Recall

Ready? Let's review the vocabulary from the eight lessons we've gone through so far. Translate the following sentences, using the clues provided to help you with vocabulary and grammar that might be challenging.

1. *I have a new apartment.*

   _____

2. *My old bed is next to the new couch. (Remember: Dative after* neben*!)*

   _____

3. *I'd like to have a glass of wine. (Would like is one word,* möchte*.)*

   _____

4. *Do you recommend the meat? (formal)*

   _____

5. *Bring me a cold beer, please (informal). (Me in this sentence is* mir*.)*

   _____

6. *She buys a new hat. ("Hat" is masculine in German, so there are some changes to watch out for in the accusative!)*

   _____

7. *The new hat is expensive.*

   _____

8. *Why don't you give me your old jacket? (The flavoring word* **doch** *can be translated as "why don't you … ?" Start the answer with:* **Gib mir doch bitte …**)

_____

9. *This yellow sweater costs fifty Euros. (Use the singular* **Euro** *for the price here.)*

_____

10. *My black sweater costs only forty nine Euro. (Only is* **nur.**)

_____

ANSWER KEY

1. **Ich habe eine neue Wohnung.**
2. **Mein altes Bett ist neben der neuen Couch.**
3. **Ich möchte ein Glas Wein.**
4. **Empfehlen Sie das Fleisch?**
5. **Bring mir bitte ein kaltes Bier.**
6. **Sie kauft einen neuen Hut.**
7. **Der neue Hut ist teuer.**
8. **Gib mir doch bitte deine alte Jacke.**
9. **Dieser gelbe Pullover kostet fünfzig Euro.**
10. **Mein schwarzer Pullover kostet nur neunundvierzig Euro.**

Lesson 9: At Work

Lektion neun: Bei der Arbeit

Willkommen zur Lektion 9! Welcome to Lesson 9! In this lesson, you'll learn how to:

- ☐ Tell time
- ☐ Talk about events in the past tense
- ☐ Use new vocabulary related to work and professions
- ☐ Talk about the days of the week
- ☐ Put it all together in a conversation about a regular day at work

Vocabulary Builder 1

▶ 9B Vocabulary Builder 1 (CD 3, Track 5)

I worked.	**Ich habe gearbeitet.**
I phoned.	**Ich habe telefoniert.**
He drove.	**Er ist gefahren.**
I studied law.	**Ich habe Jura studiert.**
to run a business	**ein Geschäft leiten**
He ran the company.	**Er hat die Firma geleitet.**
at one o'clock	**um ein Uhr**
half past three	**halb vier**
quarter to nine	**Viertel vor neun**
quarter past eight	**Viertel nach acht**

Take It Further 1

So now you know how to tell time in German.

at	**um**
… o'clock	**… Uhr**
at five o' clock	**um fünf Uhr**
quarter	**Viertel**
to	**vor**
past	**nach**
quarter to three	**Viertel vor drei**
quarter past three	**Viertel nach drei**
half	**halb**
half past seven	**halb acht**

Just be careful not to confuse the meaning of forms like **halb acht**: it means *half past seven*, not *half past eight*. It's like saying you're halfway to eight o'clock.

✎ Vocabulary Practice 1

Let's practice the new vocabulary.

A. Match the English in column A with the German translation in column B.

1. *I studied German.*	a. **Er ist zum Bahnhof gefahren.**
2. *at three o'clock*	b. **Mein Vater hat gearbeitet.**
3. *He drove to the train station.*	c. **um drei Uhr**
4. *quarter past six*	d. **Ich habe Deutsch studiert.**
5. *My father worked.*	e. **viertel nach sechs**

B. Complete the sentences with the appropriate word from the word bank.
   bin, um, neun Uhr, geleitet, studiert

1. **Mein Vater kommt um _____.**

2. **Mein Bruder hat Jura _____.**

3. **Ich _____ mit dem Bus gefahren.**

4. **Mein Mann hat ein Kaufhaus _____.**

5. **_____ halb drei gibt es Abendessen.**

ANSWER KEY
A. 1. d; 2. c; 3. a; 4. e; 5. b
B. 1. neun Uhr; 2. studiert; 3. bin; 4. geleitet; 5. Um

Grammar Builder 1

Back in Lesson 5 you learned how to use verbs in the present tense. Here's a quick reminder, with **arbeiten** (*to work*). Notice that since the stem ends in -**t**, an extra -**e**- is used before the endings in the **du**, **er/sie/es**, and **ihr** forms.

ich arbeite	wir arbeiten
du arbeitest	ihr arbeitet
er, sie, es arbeitet	sie arbeiten

In the past tense, spoken German looks a lot like one of the constructions that English uses to express the past:

ich habe gearbeitet
I worked/I have worked

wir haben gesprochen
we spoke/we have spoken

Notice that there's a form of **haben** (*to have*), and then a special verb form, called the past participle, just like in English. There's one difference to keep in mind, though. German also uses **sein** (*to be*) for the past tense, especially with verbs that indicate a change of state or location, such as **kommen** (*to come*), **gehen** (*to go*), **fahren** (*to drive*), **fallen** (*to fall*), and **laufen** (*to run*).

ich bin gefahren
I drove/I have driven

The regular way to form a past participle in German is to add the prefix **ge-** and then the ending -**(e)t** to the verb stem.

haben (*to have*) → **gehabt** (*had*)
danken (*to thank*) → **gedankt** (*thanked*)

arbeiten (*to work*) → **gearbeitet** (*worked*)
leiten (*to run, lead*) → **geleitet** (*run, led*)

Many verbs add the ending **-en** instead.
fahren (*to drive*) → **gefahren** (*driven*)
kommen (*to come*) → **gekommen** (*come*)

Many verbs that take **-en** in the past participle also have vowel changes, just like English *speak/spoken, get/gotten, sleep/slept,* and so on.
gehen (*to go*) → **gegangen** (*gone*)
sprechen (*to speak*) → **gesprochen** (*spoken*)

There are a few verbs, usually ending in **-ieren** or beginning with a prefix like **be-** or **ver-**, that don't take **ge-** in the past participle.
studieren (*to study*) → **studiert** (*studied*)
verstehen (*to understand*) → **verstanden** (*understood*)

One important difference between German and English is the word order in the past tense. The past participle usually goes to the end of the sentence. So, in a simple sentence, the word order may seem the same in German as it is in English.

Sie hat gearbeitet.
She worked.

But, if you add anything to that sentence, such as a location or time reference, you see the difference:
Sie hat gestern gearbeitet.
She worked yesterday.

Sie hat im Büro gearbeitet.
She worked in the office.

Here are some other examples:

Ich bin ins Büro gekommen.

I came into the office.

Du bist mit dem Bus gefahren.

You went by bus.

Seine Töchter haben Jura studiert.

His daughters studied law.

▶ 9C Grammar Builder 1 (CD 3, Track 6)

Now listen to your audio for an audio-only version of this grammar note.

⏸

Vocabulary Builder 2

▶ 9D Vocabulary Builder 2 (CD 3, Track 7)

the lawyer (male)	**der Anwalt**
the lawyer (female)	**die Anwältin**
the teacher (male)	**der Lehrer**
the architect (female)	**die Architektin**
the baker (male)	**der Bäcker**
He was a doctor.	**Er war Arzt.**
Monday	**Montag**
Tuesday	**Dienstag**
Wednesday	**Mittwoch**
Thursday	**Donnerstag**
Friday	**Freitag**

Saturday	**Samstag**
Sunday	**Sonntag**

Take It Further 2

▶ 9E Take It Further (CD 3, Track 8)

So now you've also learned the names for the days of the week. Many are similar to their English counterparts, except for Wednesday: **Mittwoch** comes from the two words **Mitte** (*middle*) and **Woche** (*week*), so literally, it's the day in the middle of the week.

✎ Vocabulary Practice 2

Let's put the vocabulary we've just learned to use. Take a look at Susanne's calendar, and then answer the questions below based on her schedule. Don't worry if you can't understand every single word. Try to make out the meaning by looking for key words that you do understand. One handy word to know, though, is **war** (*was*).

Example: **Wann war Susanne einkaufen? → Am Montag um halb neun.**

MONTAG	8:30 einkaufen	10:30 Büro		
DIENSTAG		10:30 Büro		
MITTWOCH		10:30 Büro	4:00 Kaffee mit Andreas	
DONNERSTAG		10:30 Büro		7:30 Kino
FREITAG		10:30 Büro		8:15 Abendessen mit Thomas

SAMSTAG			
SONNTAG	11:45 Brunch		

1. **Wann hat Susanne mit Andreas Kaffee getrunken?**

   _____

2. **Wann ist Susanne ins Kino gegangen?**

   _____

3. **Wann hat Susanne mit Thomas gegessen?**

   _____

4. **Wann war Susanne zum Brunch verabredet?**

   _____

5. **Wann ist Susanne ins Büro gegangen?**

   _____

ANSWER KEY
1. **Am Mittwoch um vier Uhr.** 2. **Am Donnerstag um halb acht.** 3. **Am Freitag um Viertel nach acht.**
4. **Am Sonntag um Viertel vor zwölf.** 5. **Am Montag, Dienstag, Mittwoch, Donnerstag und Freitag um halb elf.**

Grammar Builder 2
▶ 9F Grammar Builder 2 (CD 3, Track 9)

You learned some names of professions, which are different for men and women.
First, you'll use either a masculine or a feminine article, depending on the gender
of the person. And if you are talking about a woman, you also have to add the
ending -**in** to the masculine form.

	MALE	FEMALE
architect	der Architekt	die Architektin
teacher	der Lehrer	die Lehrerin

Some names of professions add an **Umlaut**:

lawyer	der Anwalt	die Anwältin
doctor	der Arzt	die Ärztin

When talking about both men and women, the two forms are usually used together. So job ads often ask for **Lehrer oder Lehrerin** (*male teacher or female teacher*).

⏸

✎ Work Out 1

▶ 9G Work Out 1 (CD 3, Track 10)

Now let's review some of the new grammar and vocabulary. Philipp is telling us about the professions of his family members. As usual you'll hear the English first, then fill in the missing German words, and finally, repeat the correct answers in the pauses provided.

1. *My sister studied law.*

   Meine Schwester hat _____ **studiert.**

2. *Now she's a lawyer.*

   Jetzt ist sie _____ **.**

3. *My brother is an architect.*

   Mein Bruder ist _____ **.**

4. *My parents are retired.*

   Meine _____ **sind pensioniert.**

5. *My mother was a teacher.*

   Meine Mutter war _____ **.**

6. *My father worked for the postal service.*

   Mein Vater _____ **bei der Post** _____.

7. *My grandfather was a baker.*

   Mein Großvater war _____.

8. *My grandmother ran the store.*

   Meine Großmutter _____ **den Laden** _____.

   ANSWER KEY
   1. **Jura**; 2. **Anwältin**; 3. **Architekt**; 4. **Eltern**; 5. **Lehrerin**; 6. **hat/gearbeitet**; 7. **Bäcker**; 8. **hat/geleitet**

Bring It All Together

▶ 9H Bring It All Together (CD 3, Track 11)

Now let's listen to a dialogue that highlights more of the structures and phrases from this lesson. Listen to Paula asking Philipp about his day at work. Listen to the English sentence first, and then you'll hear the German sentence, which you should repeat for practice.

What did you do today?
Was hast du heute gemacht?

I worked in the office.
Ich habe im Büro gearbeitet.

I drove to work at nine.
Um neun bin ich zur Arbeit gefahren.

At half past ten I talked on the phone with a client.
Um halb elf habe ich mit einem Kunden telefoniert.

At quarter to one I had lunch with a colleague.
Um Viertel vor eins habe ich mit einer Kollegin zu Mittag gegessen.

Then we had a meeting, as we do every Thursday.
Dann haben wir eine Besprechung gehabt, wie jeden Donnerstag.

And at five o'clock, I went home.
Und um fünf Uhr bin ich nach Hause gefahren.

Do you work in the office every day?
Arbeitest Du jeden Tag im Büro?

No, on Monday I went to Cologne on a business trip.
Nein, am Montag war ich auf Geschäftsreise in Köln.

Ⓘ

Take It Further 3
▶ 9I Take It Further 3 (CD 3, Track 12)

You're learning more and more vocabulary with each lesson. Let's sum up the new words used in the comprehension piece above.

in the office	im Büro
colleagues	Kollegen
clients	Kunden
a meeting	eine Besprechung
a business trip	eine Geschäftsreise

Ⓘ

✎ Work Out 2

Time for some written practice. Rewrite the sentence in the past tense with **haben** and **sein**, or use **war**.

1. **Ich arbeite am Montag.**

   _____

2. **Meine Schwester leitet das Büro.**

   _____

3. **Am Sonntag fahren wir nach München.**

   _____

4. **Sie studiert Jura.**

   _____

5. **Heute essen wir um Viertel vor acht.**

   _____

6. **Herr Schneider kommt auch.**

   _____

7. **Du hast um halb sieben eine Besprechung.**

   _____

8. **Mein Großvater ist Bäcker.**

   _____

9. **Was machen Sie heute?**

   _____

10. **Ich gehe in die Stadt.**

ANSWER KEY

1. Ich habe am Montag gearbeitet. 2. Meine Schwester hat das Büro geleitet. 3. Am Sonntag sind wir nach München gefahren. 4. Sie hat Jura studiert. 5. Heute haben wir um viertel vor acht gegessen. 6. Herr Schneider ist auch gekommen. 7. Du hast um halb sieben eine Besprechung gehabt. 8. Mein Großvater war Bäcker. 9. Was haben Sie heute gemacht? 10. Ich bin in die Stadt gegangen.

▶ 9K Work Out 2 (CD 3, Track 13)

And now listen to your audio for some more practice.

⏸

✎ Drive It Home

Time to drive home the grammar points of the lesson.

A. Fill in the appropriate form of haben.

1. **Wir** _____ **heute im Büro gearbeitet.**

2. **Du** _____ **Jura studiert.**

3. **Dieter** _____ **gestern nichts gemacht.**

4. **Ich** _____ **das Geschäft geleitet.**

5. _____ **Sie schon gegessen?**

B. Fill in the appropriate form of sein.

1. **Ihr** _____ **in die Stadt gefahren.**

2. **Ich** _____ **mit dem Bus gefahren.**

3. **Wann** _____ **du gekommen?**

4. **Frau Heinemann** _____ **am Dienstag nach München gefahren.**

5. **Wir** _____ **mitgekommen.**

C. Fill in the appropriate past participle.

1. **Ursula hat Medizin** _____ . (studieren)

2. **Meine Mutter hat das Geschäft** _____ . (leiten)

3. **Wann bist du denn** _____ ? (kommen)

4. **Ich habe ein neues Kleid** _____ . (kaufen)

5. **Sie haben den ganzen Tag** _____ . (arbeiten)

ANSWER KEY
A. 1. haben; 2. hast; 3. hat; 4. habe; 5. Haben
B. 1. seid; 2. bin; 3. bist; 4. ist; 5. sind
C. 1. studiert; 2. geleitet; 3. gekommen; 4. gekauft; 5. gearbeitet

Parting Words

Herzlichen Glückwunsch! *Congratulations!* You have completed another lesson. You should be able to:

☐ Tell time (Still unsure? Go back to page 140.)

☐ Talk about events in the past tense (Still unsure? Go back to page 142.)

☐ Use new vocabulary related to work and professions (Still unsure? Go back to page 144.)

☐ Talk about the days of the week (Still unsure? Go back to page 144.)

☐ Put it all together in a conversation about a regular day at work (Still unsure? Go back to page 148.)

Don't forget to practice and reinforce what you've learned by visiting **www.livinglanguage.com/languagelab** for flashcards, games, and quizzes for Lesson 9!

Take It Further 4

▶ 9J Take It Further 4 (CD 3, Track 14)

There are many names of professions other than the ones we've learned.

trade	**das Handwerk**
a butcher	**ein Metzger**
an electrician	**ein Elektriker**
a carpenter	**ein Tischler**
dentist	**der Zahnarzt**
scientist	**der Wissenschaftler**
accountant	**der Buchhalter**
journalist	**der Journalist**

Auf Wiedersehen! See you in Lesson 10.

⏸

Word Recall

Let's go back and look at the vocabulary we learned in the past nine lessons. Find the German translations of the English words in the puzzle below.

1. *lawyer*

2. *bed*

3. *study*

4. *afternoon*

5. *telephone*

6. *letter*

7. *buy*

8. *work*

9. *see*

10. *no*

B	A	N	W	A	L	T	Ä	H	T	E
E	R	S	T	U	D	I	E	R	E	N
S	B	B	K	A	U	F	E	N	L	E
G	E	H	R	H	O	H	D	B	E	U
Ö	I	H	C	I	R	F	B	E	F	S
M	T	H	E	R	E	V	E	T	O	S
N	E	I	N	N	W	F	U	T	N	H
S	N	A	C	H	M	I	T	T	A	G

Lesson 10: Socializing and Entertainment

Lektion zehn: Beschäftigungen und Unterhaltung

Willkommen! Welcome to the tenth and final lesson. You've done a great job and learned a lot of basic German. In this lesson, you'll learn how to:

☐ Express likes and dislikes

☐ Use the German words **nicht** and **kein**

☐ Use the comparative and superlative forms of adjectives

☐ Use words that relate to sports and entertainment

☐ Put it all together in a conversation about making plans

Let's get started right away.

Vocabulary Builder 1

▶ 10B Vocabulary Builder 1 (CD 3, Track 16)

entertainment	die Unterhaltung
people	die Leute
viewers	die Zuschauer
We play cards.	Wir spielen Karten.
the sport	die Sportart
soccer	Fußball
the bike	das Rad
to swim	schwimmen
not	nicht
I like it.	Das gefällt mir.
I don't like it.	Das gefällt mir nicht.
no work	keine Arbeit

⏸

✎ Vocabulary Practice 1

Let's practice the new vocabulary. First, translate from German to English, and then do the reverse.

1. keine Arbeit _____

2. die Sportart _____

3. die Leute _____

4. Wir spielen Karten. _____

5. das Rad _____

6. *soccer* _____

7. *the bike* _____

8. *to swim* _____

9. *I like it.* _____

10. *not* _____

ANSWER KEY

1. *no work*; 2. *the sport*; 3. *people*; 4. *We play cards.* 5. *the bike* 6. **Fußball**; 7. **das Rad**; 8. **schwimmen**; 9. **Das gefällt mir.** 10. **nicht**

Grammar Builder 1

There are two important negative words to know in German: **nicht** and **kein**. **Nicht** is used with verbs, so it's the equivalent of *not*. **Kein** is used with nouns, so it's the equivalent of *no* or *not any*. **Nicht** never changes form, but **kein** agrees with the noun it negates.

Ich arbeite nicht.
I'm not working.

Ich habe keine Arbeit.
I don't have any work./I have no work.

Kein takes the same endings as **ein, mein, dein** and so on:

a man	ein Mann	no man	kein Mann
a woman	eine Frau	no woman	keine Frau
a child	ein Kind	no child	kein Kind

Nicht doesn't change form. It usually comes at the end of the sentence, or right before the past participle in past tense sentences.

Ich spiele.
I play./I'm playing.

Ich spiele nicht.
I don't play./I'm not playing.

Ich habe gespielt.
I played.

Ich habe nicht gespielt.
I didn't play.

Notice that German doesn't use an auxiliary verb like *do* or *does* in negative sentences. To negate a verb, just use **nicht**, never a translation of the English helping verb.

▶ 10C Grammar Builder 1 (CD 3, Track 17)

Now, listen to your audio for an audio-only version of this grammar note.

⏸

Take It Further 1
▶ 10D Take It Further (CD 3, Track 18)

Did you also notice the expression **Es gefällt mir** (*I like it*)? Literally, it means *it pleases me*, so the person who likes something is in the dative case, while the thing being liked is the subject. We'll practice later, but first, we'll look at some other ways of expressing likes and dislikes.

⓫

Vocabulary Builder 2

▶ 10E Vocabulary Builder 2 (CD 3, Track 19)

popular	beliebt
rather	lieber
few	wenige
fewer than	weniger als
I like it better.	Es gefällt mir besser.
He swims best.	Er schwimmt am besten.
many	viele
more	mehr
the most	am meisten
other people	andere Leute

⓫

✎ Vocabulary Practice 2

Let's practice the new words. Complete the sentences using the most appropriate word from the word bank below.

beliebt, gefällt, viele, mehr, schwimme

1. Tennis hat _____ Zuschauer.

2. **Fußball ist** _____.

3. **Fußball hat** _____ **Zuschauer als Tennis.**

4. **Ich** _____ **gern.**

5. **Es** _____ **mir besser.**

ANSWER KEY
1. viele; 2. beliebt; 3. mehr; 4. schwimme; 5. gefällt

Grammar Builder 2

Just as in English, German adjectives have comparative (*bigger than*) and superlative (*biggest*) forms. The endings are even similar to English: **-er** is added to form comparatives, and **-ste** or **-sten** produces the superlative.

ADJECTIVE	COMPARATIVE	SUPERLATIVE
klein	kleiner	am kleinsten
small	*smaller*	*smallest*

Like other adjective forms, the comparative and superlative adjectives can stand before a noun or at the end of a sentence. If they come before a noun, they'll take agreement endings.

Peter ist das kleinere Kind.
Peter is the smaller child.

Das Mädchen ist am kleinsten.
The girl is the smallest.

The equivalent of *than* in comparative sentences is **als**.

Ich bin kleiner als du.
I'm smaller than you.

Sie hat mehr Geld als du.

She has more money than you.

There are a few common irregular forms to keep in mind.

good	**gut**	**besser**	**am besten**
a lot	**viel**	**mehr**	**am meisten**
gladly	**gern**	**lieber**	**am liebsten**

▶ 10F Grammar Builder 2 (CD 3, Track 20)

Now listen to your audio for an audio-only version of the grammar note you just read.

⏸

✎ Work Out 1

▶ 10G Work Out 1 (CD 3, Track 21)

Let's practice these forms and listen to a short text about home entertainment in Germany. You'll hear the English first, and then the German, which you should repeat for practice.

1. *What do people in Germany do for entertainment in the evening?*

   Was _____ die Leute in Deutschland am Abend zur Unterhaltung?

2. *Many people like to play cards.*

   Viele _____ spielen gerne Karten.

3. *The most popular card game is called Skat.*

   Das _____ Kartenspiel heißt Skat.

4. *Many people also like to watch sports on TV.*

   Viele Leute sehen auch _____ Sport im Fernsehen.

5. *Soccer is the most popular.*

   Fußball ist _____ .

6. *It always has the most viewers.*

   Er hat immer _____ **Zuschauer.**

7. *Tennis has fewer viewers than soccer.*

   Tennis hat weniger Zuschauer _____ **Fußball.**

8. *But it has more viewers than many other sports.*

   Aber es hat mehr Zuschauer als _____ **andere Sportarten.**

ANSWER KEY
1. **machen**; 2. **Leute**; 3. **beliebteste**; 4. **gerne**; 5. **am beliebtesten**; 6. **die meisten**; 7. **als**; 8. **viele**

Bring It All Together
10H Bring It All Together (CD 3, Track 22)

Now let's bring it all together and listen to a dialogue that highlights more of the structures and phrases from this lesson. Paula and Philipp are making plans for the day. Listen to the English sentence first, and then listen to and repeat the German sentence.

Do you feel like going swimming today?
Hast du Lust, heute Schwimmen zu gehen?

No, I don't feel like it.
Nein, dazu habe ich keine Lust.

Don't you like to swim?
Schwimmst Du nicht gerne?

No, I'd rather play tennis.
Nein, ich spiele lieber Tennis.

And I like bike riding best.
Und am liebsten fahre ich Rad.

I like that, too.
Das gefällt mir auch.

Let's do a bike tour then.
Dann lass uns doch eine Radtour machen.

Oh yes, and we can have a picnic along the way.
Au ja, und unterwegs können wir ein Picknick machen.

Do you think Tim wants to come, too?
Meinst du Tim will auch mitkommen?

No, he plays soccer today.
Nein, er spielt heute Fußball.

He likes that better.
Das gefällt ihm besser.

Ⅱ

Take It Further 2

▶ 10I Take It Further 2 (CD 3, Track 23)

Could you follow the conversation? It included several ways of expressing likes and dislikes, including a very common idiom:

to feel like doing something	**zu etwas Lust haben**
I feel like it	**Ich habe Lust**
I don't feel like it	**Ich habe keine Lust**

There were only a few new words in the dialogue, and most of them are very similar to their English counterparts:

tennis	**Tennis**
picnic	**Picknick**
to mean	**meinen**
Do you think?	**Meinst du?**

Remember that in German, you can often just stick two nouns together to form a new one.

a bike tour	**eine Radtour**

ⅠⅠ

✎ Work Out 2

Time for some written practice.

A. Complete the sentences with the comparative form of the adjective in parentheses.

1. **Thomas ist** _____ **als Horst. (klein)**

2. **Das rote Kleid ist** _____. **(schön)**

3. **Fußball ist** _____ **als Tennis. (beliebt)**

4. **Der Film gefällt mir** _____ **. (gut)**

5. **Wir haben** _____ **Zeit. (wenig)**

B. Now use the superlative form of the adjective in parentheses.

1. **Frau Heinrichs ist die** _____ **Lehrerin. (nett)**

2. **Am** _____ **esse ich Reis. (gern)**

3. **Das ist das** _____ **Restaurant in der Innenstadt. (gut)**

4. **Kinder singen am** _____ **. (schön)**

5. **Ich habe am** _____ **Geld. (wenig)**

ANSWER KEY
A. 1. kleiner; 2. schöner; 3. beliebter; 4. besser; 5. weniger
B. 1. netteste; 2. liebsten; 3. beste; 4. schönsten; 5. wenigsten

▶ 10J Work Out 22 (CD 3, Track 24)

Now turn on your audio for additional audio-only practice.

Ⅱ

✎ Drive It Home

Let's review some more of the grammar points. Remember to write and read the exercises.

A. Complete the sentences with **als**.

1. **Fußball ist beliebter** _____ **Tennis.**

2. **Tennis hat weniger Zuschauer** _____ **Fußball.**

3. Mein Sohn ist kleiner _____ dein Sohn.

4. Ihr Kleid ist kürzer _____ mein Kleid.

5. Mein Mann ist älter _____ Ihr Mann.

B. Rewrite the sentences in the negative using **nicht**.

1. Ich schwimme gern.

   _____

2. Mein Chef ist im Büro.

   _____

3. Sie hat heute gearbeitet.

   _____

4. Der Film gefällt mir.

   _____

5. Ich studiere.

   _____

C. Rewrite the sentences in the negative using **kein**.

1. Ich habe einen Bruder.

   _____

2. Hat er denn Zeit?

   _____

3. Heute sind Zuschauer im Stadion.

   _____

4. **Das ist ein gutes Spiel.**

_____

5. **Ich kenne einen Zahnarzt.**

_____

ANSWER KEY

A. 1. als; 2. als; 3. als; 4. als; 5. als

B. 1. Ich schwimme nicht gern. 2. Mein Chef ist nicht im Büro. 3. Sie hat heute nicht gearbeitet. 4. Der Film gefällt mir nicht. 5. Ich studiere nicht.

C. 1. Ich habe keinen Bruder. 2. Hat er denn keine Zeit? 3. Heute sind keine Zuschauer im Stadion. 4. Das ist kein gutes Spiel. 5. Ich kenne keinen Zahnarzt.

Parting Words

Herzlichen Glückwunsch! _Congratulations!_ You've done a great job in this course and have just completed its tenth and final lesson. You've learned a lot of practical vocabulary and useful basic grammar, which now you are all ready to put to use. You should now be able to:

☐ Express likes and dislikes (Still unsure? Go back to page 156.)

☐ Use the German words **nicht** and **kein** (Still unsure? Go back to page 157.)

☐ Use the comparative and superlative forms of adjectives (Still unsure? Go back to page 159.)

☐ Use words that relate to sports and entertainment (Still unsure? Go back to page 161.)

☐ Put it all together in a conversation about making plans (Still unsure? Go back to page 162.)

Don't forget to practice and reinforce what you've learned by visiting **www.livinglanguage.com/languagelab** for flashcards, games, and quizzes for Lesson 10!

And that brings us to the end of our last lesson. You can test yourself and practice what you've learned with the final Word Recall and quiz, followed by five conversational dialogues that will bring together the German you've seen so far. Until then, **auf Wiedersehen! Alles Gute!** *Good-bye! All the best!*

Word Recall

Let's go back and look at the vocabulary you've learned in this program. Match the English term in column A with the correct German translation in column B.

1. *doctor*
2. *When?*
3. *to be called*
4. *people*
5. *soon*
6. *the newspaper*
7. *to drive*
8. *Friday*
9. *left*
10. *to call*

a. **Leute**
b. **fahren**
c. **Freitag**
d. **die Zeitung**
e. **telefonieren**
f. **Wann?**
g. **links**
h. **heißen**
i. **bald**
j. **Arzt**

ANSWER KEY
1. j; 2. f; 3. h; 4. a; 5. i; 6. d; 7. b; 8. c; 9. g; 10. e

Quiz 2

Eine kleine Nachprüfung 2

Now let's review. In this section you'll find a final quiz testing what you've learned in Lessons 1–10. Once you've completed it, score yourself to see how well you've done. If you find that you need to go back and review, please do so before continuing on to the final section with review dialogues and comprehension questions.

A. Match the German expressions on the left to the correct English translations on the right.

1. Was kostet das?   a. *Good-bye.*

2. Was hätten Sie gerne?   b. *I like it.*

3. Guten Abend.   c. *What would you like?*

4. Das gefällt mir.   d. *Good evening.*

5. Auf Wiedersehen.   e. *How much is it?*

B. Rewrite the following times using numbers instead of words. For example, instead of halb zwei you might write 1 Uhr 30; instead of zweiundzwanzig Uhr fünfzehn you might write 22 Uhr 15, etc.

1. Es ist halb fünf. _____

2. Es ist zwanzig Uhr fünfzehn. _____

3. Es ist viertel nach drei. _____

4. Es ist dreiundzwanzig Uhr siebenundvierzig. _____

5. Es ist zehn Minuten nach Mitternacht. _____

C. Fill in the blanks with the appropriate German adjective in the correct form.

1. Der rote Pullover gefällt mir nicht, aber der _____ Pullover passt gut zu meiner Hose. (*I don't like the red sweater, but the white sweater goes well with my pants.*)

2. Meine alte Wohnung war sehr groß, aber meine _____ Wohnung hat nur vier Zimmer. (*My old apartment was big, but my new apartment only has four rooms.*)

3. Mein Grossvater ist ein _____ Mann. Er ist neunundachtzig Jahre alt. (*My grandfather is an old man. He is 89 years old.*)

4. Frau Bauer ist eine _____ Anwältin. Sie hat sehr viele Kunden. (*Mrs. Bauer is a good lawyer. She has many clients.*)

5. Das Mittagessen hat fünfzig Euro gekostet, und das Abendessen hat hundert Euro gekostet. Das war ein _____ Tag. (*Lunch cost fifty euros, and dinner cost one hundred euros. That was an expensive day!*)

D. Conjugate the verbs in parentheses in the correct form and then translate each sentence into English.

1. Wir _____ (kommen) gerne mit ins Kino.

2. Welches Buch _____ (lesen) du?

3. Welchen Fisch _____ (empfehlen) Sie?

4. Er _____ (fahren) mit dem Bus.

5. Ich _____ (suchen) ein Kaufhaus in der Stadt.

E. Change the following sentences from the present to the past tense using the participle in parentheses. Make sure you are using the correct form of haben or sein.

1. Der Bäcker arbeitet am Sonntag. (gearbeitet)

   _____

2. Liest du schon die Zeitung? (gelesen)

   _____

3. Wir spielen den ganzen Abend Karten. (gespielt)

   _____

4. Wann fährst du nach Hause? (gefahren)

   _____

5. Ich arbeite im Büro. (gearbeitet)

   _____

F. Rewrite the following sentences in the comparative or superlative, following the English translations provided.

1. Das sind gute Tomaten. *(These are good tomatoes.)*

   _____. *(These are the best tomatoes.)*

2. Ist das ein neuer Film? *(Is that a new film?)*

   _____? *(Is that a newer film?)*

3. Meine Nichte ist noch klein. *(My niece is small.)*

   _____. *(My niece is smaller.)*

4. Fußball ist beliebt. *(Soccer is popular.)*

   _____. *(Soccer is most popular.)*

5. Der Salat schmeckt nicht gut. *(The salad doesn't taste good.)*

   _____. *(The salad doesn't taste better.)*

How Did You Do?

Give yourself a point for every correct answer, then use the following key to determine whether or not you're ready to move on:

0–11 points: It's probably best to go back and study the lessons again. Take as much time as you need to. Review the vocabulary lists and carefully read through each Grammar Builder section.

12–24 points: If the questions you missed were in sections A, B, or C, you may want to review the vocabulary again; if you missed answers mostly in sections D, E, or F, check the Grammar Builder sections to make sure you have your conjugations and other grammar basics down.

25–30 points: Feel free to move on to the Review Dialogues! Great job!

[ ] [ ] **points**

ANSWER KEY

A. 1. e; 2. c; 3. d; 4. b; 5. a

B. 1. **4 Uhr 30**; 2. **20 Uhr 15**; 3. **3 Uhr 15**; 4. **23 Uhr 47**; 5. **0 Uhr 10**

C. 1. **weiße**; 2. **neue**; 3. **alter**; 4. **gute**; 5. **teurer**

D. 1. **kommen** (*We gladly come to the movies.*) 2. **liest** (*Which book are you [familiar] reading?*) 3. **empfehlen** (*Which fish do you [polite] recommend?*) 4. **fährt** (*He takes the bus.*) 5. **suche** (*I'm looking for a department store in the city.*)

E. 1. **Der Bäcker hat am Sonntag gearbeitet.** 2. **Hast du die Zeitung schon gelesen?** 3. **Wir haben den ganzen Abend Karten gespielt.** 4. **Wann bist du nach Hause gefahren?** 5. **Ich habe im Büro gearbeitet.**

F. 1. **Das sind die besten Tomaten.** 2. **Ist das ein neuerer Film?** 3. **Meine Nichte ist noch kleiner.** 4. **Fußball ist am beliebtesten.** 5. **Der Salat schmeckt nicht besser.**

Review Dialogues
Willkommen! *Welcome!*

Here's your chance to practice all the vocabulary and grammar you've mastered in ten lessons of *Living Language Essential German* with these five everyday dialogues. Each dialogue is followed by comprehension questions.

To practice your pronunciation, don't forget to listen to the audio. As always, look for ⊳ and ⅠⅠ. You'll hear the dialogue in German first, then in German and English. Next, for practice, you'll do some role play by taking part in the conversation yourself!

Dialogue 1
TREFFEN MIT DER FAMILIE
MEETING THE FAMILY

First, try to read (and listen to) the whole dialogue in German. Then read and listen to the German and English together. How much did you understand? Next, take part in the role play exercise in the audio and answer the comprehension questions here in the book.

Note that there will be words and phrases in these dialogues that you haven't seen yet. This is because we want to give you the feel of a real German conversation. As a result, feel free to use your dictionary or the glossary if you're unclear about anything you see. And of course, you'll see the English translations for each line, as well.

⊳ German Only – CD 3, Track 26 English and German – CD 3, Track 27
Role Play Exercise – CD 3, Track 28

Paula:	Ich bin Paula. Wie heißt du?
	I'm Paula. What's your name?
Stephan:	Hallo Paula, ich bin Stephan. Philipp ist mein Bruder.
	Hi, Paula! I'm Stephan. Philipp is my brother.
Paula:	Hallo, Stephan. Wie geht es dir?
	Hi, Stephan. How are you?
Stephan:	Sehr gut, danke. Und wie geht es dir?
	Very well, thank you. And how are you?
Paula:	Auch sehr gut, danke.
	Very well, also. Thank you.
Stephan:	Du sprichst aber gut Deutsch.
	But you speak German well.
Paula:	Danke, aber ich spreche nur ein bisschen.
	Thanks, but I speak only a little.
Stephan:	Willkommen in Frankfurt, Paula.
	Welcome to Frankfurt, Paula.
Paula:	Danke sehr. Es ist schön hier.
	Thank you. It's nice here.
Stephan:	Und wo kommst du her?
	And where are you from?
Paula:	Ich komme aus Philadelphia. Ich bin zu Besuch in Deutschland.
	I'm from Philadelphia. I'm in Germany for a visit.
Stephan:	Philadelphia ist sehr schön, finde ich.
	Philadelphia is very nice, I find.
Paula:	Das finde ich auch.
	I think so, too.

Ⅱ

✎ Dialogue 1 Practice

Now let's check your comprehension of the dialogue and review what you learned in Lessons 1–10. Ready?

1. **Ist Paula Amerikanerin?**

   _____

2. **Woher kommt Paula?**

   _____

3. **Ist Stephan Amerikaner?**

   _____

4. **Ist Philipp Paulas Bruder?**

   _____

5. **Wer ist Stephan?**

   _____

6. **Spricht Paula Deutsch?**

   _____

7. **Ist Paula zu Besuch in Deutschland?**

   _____

8. **Sind Stephan und Paula in Stuttgart oder in Frankfurt?**

   _____

9. **Findet Paula Frankfurt schön?**

   _____

10. **Findet Stephan Philadelphia schön?**

ANSWER KEY

1. Ja, Paula ist Amerikanerin. 2. Paula Kommt aus Philadelphia. 3. Nein, Stephan ist Deutscher. 4. Nein, Philipp ist Stephans Bruder. 5. Stephan ist Philipps Bruder. 6. Ja, Paula spricht ein bisschen Deutsch. 7. Ja, Paula ist zu Besuch in Deutschland. 8. Sie sind in Frankfurt. 9. Ja, Paula findet Frankfurt schön. 10. Ja, Stephan findet Philadelphia schön.

◉ Dialogue 2
ZUHAUSE BEI PHILIPPS ELTERN
PHILIPP'S PARENTS' HOUSE

As with Dialogue 1, first read and listen to the whole dialogue in German. Then read and listen to the German and English together. How much did you understand? Next, do the role play in the audio as well as the comprehension exercises here in the book.

▶ German Only – CD 3, Track 29 English and German – CD 3, Track 30
Role Play Exercise – CD 3, Track 31

Philipp:	**Hier wohnen meine Eltern.**
	Here is where my parents live.
Paula:	**Das ist aber ein schönes Haus, Philipp.**
	That's really a nice house, Philipp.
Philipp:	**Hier ist das Wohnzimmer.**
	Here is the living room.
Paula:	**Da sind aber viele Familienfotos.**
	There are many family photographs there.
Philipp:	**Ja, es sind vielleicht dreißig Fotos.**
	Yes, there are maybe thirty photographs.
Paula:	**Wer ist das?**
	Who is that?
Philipp:	**Das sind meine drei Tanten. Sie wohnen in Berlin.**

Those are my three aunts. They live in Berlin.

Paula:	**Und wer ist das?**
	And who is that?
Philipp:	**Das ist mein Cousin. Er wohnt in London.**
	That's my (male) cousin. He lives in London.
Paula:	**Wirklich? Meine Cousine wohnt auch in London.**
	Really? My (female) cousin lives in London, too.
Philipp:	**Hier ist auch ein Balkon. Auf dem Balkon ist ein Tisch.**
	There's also a balcony here. There's a table on the balcony.
Paula:	**Das ist schön.**
	That's nice.
Philipp:	**Im Garten ist auch ein Tisch. Und da sind vier Stühle.**
	There's also a table in the garden. And there are four chairs there.
Paula:	**Entschuldige, aber wo finde ich das Bad?**
	Excuse me, but where do I find the bathroom?
Philipp:	**Es ist neben der Küche.**
	It's next to the kitchen.
Paula:	**Danke.**
	Thanks.

✎ Dialogue 2 Practice

Let's practice what you've learned in this dialogue.

1. **Wer wohnt in dem Haus?**

   _____

2. **Wie viele Fotos sieht Paula?**

   _____

3. Wo sind die Fotos?

_____

4. Wie viele Tanten hat Philipp?

_____

5. Wo wohnen Philipps Tanten?

_____

6. Wo wohnt Paulas Cousine?

_____

7. Was steht auf dem Balkon?

_____

8. Hat das Haus einen Garten?

_____

9. Was steht im Garten?

_____

10. Wo ist das Bad?

_____

ANSWER KEY
1. Philipps Eltern wohnen in dem Haus. 2. Paula sieht etwa dreißig Fotos. 3. Die Fotos sind im Wohnzimmer. 4. Philipp hat drei Tanten. 5. Philipps Tanten wohnen in Berlin. 6. Paulas Cousine wohnt in London. 7. Ein Tisch steht auf dem Balkon. 8. Ja, das Haus hat einen Garten. 9. Ein Tisch und vier Stühle stehen im Garten. 10. Das Bad ist neben der Küche.

« Dialogue 3
IM SCHUHGESCHÄFT
AT THE SHOE STORE

Let's listen to a dialogue between **der Verkäufer** (*the salesperson*) and **die Kundin** (*the female customer*). Remember, feel free to use your dictionary or the glossary to look up any words you don't know.

▶ German Only – CD 3, Track 32 English and German – CD 3, Track 33
Role Play Exercise – CD 3, Track 34

Verkäufer:	**Guten Tag. Kann ich Ihnen helfen?**
	Hello. Can I help you?
Kundin:	**Ja, ich würde gerne ein Paar Schuhe kaufen.**
	Yes, I would like to buy a pair of shoes.
Verkäufer:	**Da ist ein schönes Paar im Fenster.**
	There is a nice pair in the window.
Kundin:	**Ja, die möchte ich gerne anprobieren.**
	Yes, I'd like to try those.
Verkäufer:	**Welche Größe haben Sie?**
	Which size are you?
Kundin:	**Ich habe Größe vierzig.**
	I'm size forty.
Verkäufer:	**Einen Moment bitte, ich gehe sie suchen. (…) Bitte sehr, hier sind die Schuhe in Größe vierzig.**
	One moment please; I'll go and look for them. (…) Here you go; here are the shoes in size forty.
Kundin:	**Danke sehr, ich werde sie anprobieren.**
	Thank you; I will try them on.
Verkäufer:	**Passen sie Ihnen?**
	Do they fit?
Kundin:	**Ja, sie passen gut.**

	Yes, they fit well.
Verkäufer:	**Das sehe ich.**
	I can see.
Kundin:	**Ich möchte sie gerne kaufen. Was kosten sie?**
	I would like to buy them. How much are they?
Verkäufer:	**Sie kosten hundertzwanzig Euro.**
	They cost one hundred twenty euros.
Kundin:	**Bitte sehr.**
	Here you go.
Verkäufer:	**Danke sehr.**
	Thank you very much.
Kundin:	**Auf Wiedersehen.**
	Good-bye.

Ⅱ

✎ Dialogue 3 Practice

Let's see if you've understood everything. Listen to the dialogue as often as you'd like to check your answers.

1. **Wo arbeitet der Verkäufer?**

_____

2. **Was möchte die Kundin kaufen?**

_____

3. **Welche Größe hat sie?**

_____

4. **Wo ist das schöne Paar Schuhe?**

_____

5. **Was möchte die Kundin machen?**

_____

6. **Was sucht der Verkäufer?**

_____

7. **Passen die Schuhe?**

_____

8. **Wer möchte die Schuhe kaufen?**

_____

9. **Wie viel kosten die Schuhe?**

_____

10. **Bezahlt die Kundin?**

_____

ANSWER KEY

1. Der Verkäufer arbeitet im Schuhgeschäft. 2. Die Kundin möchte Schuhe kaufen. 3. Sie hat Größe vierzig. 4. Das schöne Paar Schuhe ist im Fenster. 5. Die Kundin möchte die Schuhe anprobieren. 6. Der Verkäufer sucht die Schuhe in Größe vierzig. 7. Ja, die Schuhe passen (gut). 8. Die Kundin möchte die Schuhe kaufen. 9. Die Schuhe kosten hundertzwanzig Euro. 10. Ja, die Kundin bezahlt.

Dialogue 4
IM GEMÜSELADEN
AT THE GROCERY STORE

A good dinner needs good ingredients. Let's go shopping for groceries. **Der Kunde** is the male counterpart of **die Kundin** (*customer*) and **die Verkäuferin** is the female counterpart of **der Verkäufer** (*the salesperson*).

▷ German Only – CD 3, Track 35 English and German – CD 3, Track 36
Role Play Exercise – CD 3, Track 37

Verkäuferin:	**Möchten Sie Bananen kaufen?**
	Would you like to buy bananas?
Kunde:	**Nein, diese Bananen sind noch etwas grün.**
	No, these bananas are still a bit green.
Verkäuferin:	**Hier sind rote Äpfel.**
	Here are red apples.
Kunde:	**Ja, die möchte ich kaufen.**
	Yes, I want to buy those.
Verkäuferin:	**Was brauchen Sie sonst noch?**
	What else do you need?
Kunde:	**Vielleicht etwas frischen Salat.**
	Maybe some fresh salad (lettuce).
Verkäuferin:	**Hier ist Salat, und da sind auch Tomaten.**
	Here is salad, and there are tomatoes, too.
Kunde:	**Au ja, ich nehme ein Pfund Tomaten. Und dann möchte ich noch Kartoffeln kaufen.**
	Oh yes, I'll take a pound of tomatoes. And then I want to buy some potatoes, too.
Verkäuferin:	**Nehmen Sie doch diese kleinen Kartoffeln. Ein Pfund kostet nur ein Euro.**
	Take these small potatoes. One pound costs only one euro.
Kunde:	**Danke, die nehme ich gerne.**
	Thanks, I'll take those gladly.
Verkäuferin:	**Möchten Sie sonst noch etwas?**
	Would you like anything else?
Kunde:	**Nein, das ist alles.**
	No, that's everything.
Verkäuferin:	**Das macht acht Euro fünfzig.**
	That's eight Euros and fifty cents.

Ⓘ

✎ Dialogue 4 Practice

Beantworten Sie die folgenden Fragen. *Answer the following questions.*

1. **Wer arbeitet in dem Gemüseladen, ein Mann oder eine Frau?**

   _____

2. **Warum möchte der Kunde die Bananen nicht kaufen?**

   _____

3. **Welche Farbe haben die Äpfel?**

   _____

4. **Kauft der Kunde grüne Äpfel?**

   _____

5. **Möchte der Kunde Salat?**

   _____

6. **Ist der Salat frisch?**

   _____

7. **Wie viele Tomaten kauft der Kunde?**

   _____

8. **Hat die Verkäuferin große Kartoffeln?**

   _____

9. **Wie viel kosten die Kartoffeln?**

   _____

10. **Wie viel macht alles zusammen?**

   _____

ANSWER KEY

1. Eine Frau arbeitet in dem Gemüseladen. 2. Die Bananen sind noch etwas grün. 3. Die Äpfel sind rot. 4. Nein, der Kunde kauft rote Äpfel. 5. Ja, der Kunde möchte Salat. 6. Ja, der Salat ist frisch. 7. Der Kunde kauft ein Pfund Tomaten. 8. Nein, die Verkäuferin hat kleine Kartoffeln. 9. Die Kartoffeln kosten ein Euro pro Pfund. 10. Alles zusammen macht acht Euro fünfzig.

Dialogue 5

AUSGEHEN

GOING OUT

The last dialogue talks about a fun night in town. Viel Spass! *Enjoy!*

▶ German Only – CD 3, Track 38 English and German – CD 3, Track 39
Role Play Exercise – CD 3, Track 40

Philipp:	Was hast du gestern Abend gemacht?
	What did you do last night?
Paula:	Ich war mit meinem Freund im Kino. Und danach haben wir Eis gegessen.
	I went to the movies with my boyfriend. And afterwards, we ate ice cream.
Philipp:	Was für einen Film habt ihr gesehen?
	Which movie did you see?
Paula:	Wir haben einen alten Film von Hitchcock gesehen. Das Kino macht eine Retrospektive mit den besten Filmen aus den Fünfzigern.
	We saw an old movie by Hitchcock. The theater has a retrospective with the best movies from the fifties.
Philipp:	Das gefällt mir auch. Vielleicht können wir Morgen zusammen einen anderen Film sehen.
	I like that, too. Maybe tomorrow we can see another movie together.
Paula:	Au ja, das mache ich gerne. Und was hast Du gestern gemacht?
	Oh yes, I'd like to do that. And what did you do yesterday?
Philipp:	Ich habe Karten mit Freunden gespielt.

I played cards with friends.

Paula: **Dazu hätte ich auch Lust gehabt.**
I would have enjoyed that, too.

Philipp: **Ja, es hat Spaß gemacht. Wir waren in einer Kneipe und haben viel Wein getrunken.**
Yes, it was fun. We were in a pub and drank a lot of wine.

Paula: **Wer hat gewonnen?**
Who won?

Philipp: **Ich habe gewonnen, dabei haben die anderen besser gespielt als ich.**
I won, even though the others played better than I did.

Paula: **Und wer hat am meisten Wein getrunken?**
And who drank the most wine?

Philipp: **Das weiß ich nicht mehr!**
That I don't know anymore!

✎ Dialogue 5 Practice

Wie lautet die richtige Antwort? *What's the right answer?*

1. **Mit wem war Paula im Kino?**

   _____

2. **Was haben sie dann gegessen?**

   _____

3. **Hat Paula einen alten oder einen neuen Film gesehen?**

   _____

4. **Was zeigt die Retrospektive?**

   _____

5. **Was hat Philipp gespielt?**

_____

6. **Wer hat gewonnen?**

_____

7. **Wie haben die anderen gespielt?**

_____

8. **Hat Paula auch Lust zum Karten spielen?**

_____

9. **Wo war Philipp?**

_____

10. **Was hat er getrunken?**

_____

ANSWER KEY

1. Paula war mit ihrem Freund im Kino. 2. Sie haben dann ein Eis gegessen. 3. Paula hat einen alten Film gesehen. 4. Die Retrospektive zeigt die besten Filme aus den Fünfzigern. 5. Philipp hat Karten gespielt. 6. Philipp hat gewonnen. 7. Die anderen haben besser gespielt. 8. Ja, Paula hat auch Lust zum Karten spielen. 9. Philipp war in einer Kneipe. 10. Er hat Wein getrunken.

Pronunciation Guide

Vowels

LETTER	PRONUNCIATION	EXAMPLES
a	*(long) ah in father*	sagen, Datum, Laden, Tafel
	(short) o in hot	kann, Mann, Pfanne, was?
ä	*(long) ai in fair*	spät, Erklärung, Währung, Ernährung
	(short) e in bet	Männer
e	*(long) ay in may*	geben, stehen
	(short) e in bent	Adresse, Moment, wetten, rennen
	at the end of a word, e in pocket	beide, heute, Karte, seine
	followed by another e *or* h, *a in care*	Heer, mehr
i	*(long) ee in see*	Miete, dienen, Liebe, Dieb
	(short) i in ship	mit, Sitte, Witz, mittags
o	*(long) o in lone*	oben, Obst, Boden, holen
	(short) o in off	oft, kommen, Stoff, Loch
ö	*(long) like the German* e in geben, *but with rounded lips*	König, Löwe, hören, böse
	(short) like a short u with rounded lips, as in pup	können, Töchter, möchte, Röcke
u	*(long) oo in noon*	Blume, Huhn, Hut, gut

LETTER	PRONUNCIATION	EXAMPLES
	(short) u in bush	**muss, dumm, bummeln, Russland**
ü	*(long) ee in see but with rounded lips*	**über, drüben, früher, Frühstück**
	(short) like short i but with rounded lips	**Stück, Brücke, dünn, müssen**
y	*same as short ü*	**typisch, Lyrik**
ai	*y in by*	**Mai**
ei	*y in by*	**Ei, Heimat**
ie	*ee in see*	**sieht, mieten, vier**
au	*ou in house*	**Haus, Maus, Baum, Pflaume**
äu	*oy in boy*	**Häuser, träumen**
eu	*oy in boy*	**Leute, heute**

Consonants

LETTER	PRONUNCIATION	EXAMPLES
b	*b in before*	Bett, Gabe
	at the end of a word, p in trap	Grab, Trab
c	*before a, o, and u, k in kilt*	Cato
	before e, i, ä, ö, and y, ts in cats	Cäsar
d	*d in date*	Datum, Norden
	at the end of a word, t in but	Bad, Hund
f	*f in fuss*	Fliege, Fluss
g	*g in garden*	Garten

Essential German

LETTER	PRONUNCIATION	EXAMPLES
	in foreign words, s in pleasure	Genie
h	*h in help*	hundert, Heimat, Geheimnis, behalten
	silent	Schuh, fröhlich
j	*y in your*	Jahr, jemand
k	*k in keep*	Katze, Kind, Keller, Kunde
l	*l in land*	Land, Wolf, Leben
m	*m in mother*	Meile, Maler
n	*n in never*	nur, Neffe
p	*p in park*	Preis, Papier
q	*q in quiet*	Quelle, Qualität
r	*r in risk, but rolled and more strongly pronounced*	Rede, reine
s	*before a vowel, z in zoo*	süß, Sahne
	at the end of a word or syllable, s in son	Maus, Eis
ß	*ss in less*	süß, Straße
t	*t in tea, even when followed by* h	Tanz, Tasse, Theater, Thron
v	*f in fair*	Vogel, Vater
	when used in a word with Latin roots, v in victory	Vase, Vulkan
w	*v in vain*	Wein, Waffe
x	*x in next*	Axt, Hexe
z	*ts in cats*	Zahn, Zauber

Special Sounds and Spelling Combinations

LETTER	PRONUNCIATION	EXAMPLES
ch	*hard ch similar to Scottish ch in loch, after a, o, u, and au*	machen, auch, Loch, Buch
	soft ch like the initial h in Hughes, after e, i, eu, äu, ä, ö, and ü	China, Kirche, mich, sicher
	ch in character	Christ, Chor, Charakter
	when followed by s, x in next	Fuchs, Wachs
ig	*at the end of a word, like ch in ich*	ewig, König
	when followed by lich or e, like a hard g or k	wenigstens, richtige, königlich
sch	*sh in shoe*	Kirsche, Schuh, amerikanisch
tsch	*ch in choose*	Rutsch, tschüss
sp	*sh + p*	Spanien, Spiegel
st	*sh + t*	stehen, Stahl
ng	*ng in sing*	bringen, anfangen
tz	*ts in cats*	Mütze, Blitz
er	*at the end of a word, a in father*	kleiner, schöner, Vater, Wetter

Grammar Summary

1. CASES

CASE: PRINCIPAL USE	EXAMPLE
Nominative: Subject	Der Lehrer ist hier.
	The teacher is here.
Accusative: Direct object	Sie sieht den Lehrer.
	She sees the teacher.
Dative: Indirect object	Er gibt dem Lehrer einen Apfel.
	He gives an apple to the teacher.
Genitive: Possession	Ich weiss den Namen des Lehrers nicht.
	I don't know the teacher's name.

2. DEFINITE ARTICLES (*THE*)

	NOM.	ACC.	DAT.	GEN.
m.	der	den	dem	des
f.	die	die	der	der
n.	das	das	dem	des
pl.	die	die	den	der

3. INDEFINITE ARTICLES (*A, AN*)

	NOM.	ACC.	DAT.	GEN.
m.	ein	einen	einem	eines
f.	eine	eine	einer	einer
n.	ein	ein	einem	eines

4. THE NEGATIVE KEIN (*NOT A, NOT ANY, NO*)

	NOM.	ACC.	DAT.	GEN.
m.	kein	keinen	keinem	keines
f.	keine	keine	keiner	keiner
n.	kein	kein	keinem	keines
pl.	keine	keine	keinen	keiner

5. PERSONAL PRONOUNS

NOM.	ACC.	DAT.	GEN.
ich	mich	mir	meiner
du	dich	dir	deiner
er	ihn	ihm	seiner
sie	sie	ihr	ihrer
es	es	ihm	seiner
wir	uns	uns	unser
ihr	euch	euch	eurer
Sie	Sie	Ihnen	Ihrer
sie	sie	ihnen	ihrer

6. DEMONSTRATIVES (*THIS*)

	NOM.	ACC.	DAT.	GEN.
m.	dieser	diesen	diesem	dieses
f.	diese	diese	dieser	dieser
n.	dieses	dieses	diesem	dieses
pl.	diese	diese	diesen	dieser

7. POSSESSIVE ADJECTIVES

M./N. SG. NOM.	F. SG. NOM.	PL. NOM.	
mein	meine	meine	*my*
dein	deine	deine	*your (infml.)*
sein	seine	seine	*his, its*
ihr	ihre	ihre	*her*
unser	unsere	unsere	*our*
euer	eure	eure	*your (infml. pl.)*
Ihr	Ihre	Ihre	*your (fml.)*
ihr	ihre	ihre	*their*

Essential German

8. POSSESSIVE PRONOUNS

M. NOM.	F. NOM.	N. NOM.	
meiner	meine	meines	*mine*
deiner	deine	deines	*yours (infml.)*
seiner	seine	seines	*his*
ihrer	ihre	ihres	*hers*
unser	unsere	unseres	*ours*
euer	eure	eures	*yours (infml.)*
Ihrer	Ihre	Ihres	*yours (fml.)*
ihrer	ihre	ihres	*theirs*

9. RELATIVE PRONOUNS

	NOM. *(WHO)*	ACC. *(WHOM)*	DAT. *(TO WHOM)*	GEN. *(WHOSE)*
m.	der	den	dem	dessen
f.	die	die	der	deren
n.	das	das	dem	dessen
pl.	die	die	denen	deren

10. STRONG ADJECTIVE ENDINGS (WITHOUT ARTICLE OR PRONOUN)

	NOM.	ACC.	DAT.	GEN.
m.	roter Wein	roten Wein	rotem Wein	roten Weines
f.	rote Tinte	rote Tinte	roter Tinte	roter Tinte
n.	rotes Licht	rotes Licht	rotem Licht	roten Lichtes
pl.	rote Weine	rote Weine	roten Weinen	roter Weine

11. WEAK ADJECTIVE ENDINGS (WITH THE DEFINITE ARTICLE)

	NOM.	ACC.	DAT.	GEN.
m.	der rote Wein	den roten Wein	dem roten Wein	des roten Weines
f.	die rote Tinte	die rote Tinte	der roten Tinte	der roten Tinte
n.	das rote Licht	das rote Licht	dem roten Licht	des roten Lichtes
pl.	die roten Weine	die roten Weine	den roten Weinen	der roten Weine

12. MIXED ADJECTIVE ENDINGS (WITH EIN WORDS, KEIN WORDS, OR POSSESSIVES)

	NOM.	ACC.	DAT.	GEN.
m.	ein roter Wein	einen roten Wein	einem roten Wein	eines roten Weines
f.	seine rote Tinte	seine rote Tinte	seiner roten Tinte	seiner roten Tinte
n.	kein rotes Licht	kein rotes Licht	keinem roten Licht	keines roten Lichtes
pl.	meine roten Weine	meine roten Weine	meinen roten Weinen	meiner roten Weine

13. DEGREES OF ADJECTIVES

POSITIVE	COMPARATIVE	SUPERLATIVE
schlecht (*bad*)	schlechter (*worse*)	schlechtest (*worst*)
alt (*old*)	älter (*older*)	ältest (*oldest*)

14. IRREGULAR ADJECTIVES

POSITIVE	COMPARATIVE	SUPERLATIVE
gut	besser	der (die, das) beste, am besten
groß	größer	der (die, das) größte, am größten
hoch	höher	der (die, das) höchste, am höchsten
nahe	näher	der (die, das) nächste, am nächsten
viel	mehr	der (die, das) meiste, am meisten
gern	lieber	der (die, das) liebste, am liebsten

15. IRREGULAR ADVERBS

Common adverbs with irregular comparatives and superlatives

POSITIVE	COMPARATIVE	SUPERLATIVE
viel	mehr	am meisten
gern	lieber	am liebsten
bald	eher	am ehesten

16. ACCUSATIVE PREPOSITIONS

durch	*through, by*
für	*for*
gegen	*against, toward*
ohne	*without*
um	*round, about, at (time)*

17. DATIVE PREPOSITIONS

aus	*from, out of*
außer	*besides, except*
bei	*at, by, near, with*
mit	*with*
nach	*after, to (a place)*
seit	*since*
von	*of, from, by*
zu	*to, at*

18. "TWO-WAY" PREPOSITIONS

an	*at, to*
auf	*on, upon, in*
hinter	*behind*
in	*in, into, at*
neben	*beside, near*
über	*over, across*
unter	*under, among*
vor	*before, ago*
zwischen	*between*

19. GENITIVE PREPOSITIONS

statt, anstatt	*instead of*
trotz	*in spite of*
während	*during*
wegen	*because of*

sein
to be

ich	wir
du	ihr
er/sie/es	sie/Sie

Present		Imperative	
bin	sind		seien wir!
bist	seid	sei!	seid!
ist	sind		seien Sie!

Present Perfect		Simple Past	
bin gewesen	sind gewesen	war	waren
bist gewesen	seid gewesen	warst	wart
ist gewesen	sind gewesen	war	waren

Future		Past Perfect	
werde sein	werden sein	war gewesen	waren gewesen
wirst sein	werdet sein	warst gewesen	wart gewesen
wird sein	werden sein	war gewesen	waren gewesen

Subjunctive (II)		Past Subjunctive	
wäre	wären	wäre gewesen	wären gewesen
wärest	wäret	wärest gewesen	wäret gewesen
wäre	wären	wäre gewesen	wären gewesen

Conditional		Special Subjunctive (I)	
würde sein	würden sein	sei	seien
würdest sein	würdet sein	seist	seiet
würde sein	würden sein	sei	seien

haben
to have

ich	wir
du	ihr
er/sie/es	sie/Sie

Present		Imperative	
habe	haben		haben wir!
hast	habt	hab!	habt!
hat	haben		haben Sie!

Present Perfect		Simple Past	
habe gehabt	haben gehabt	hatte	hatten
hast gehabt	haben gehabt	hattest	hattet
hat gehabt	haben gehabt	hatte	hatten

Future		Past Perfect	
werde haben	werden haben	hatte gehabt	hatten gehabt
wirst haben	werdet haben	hattest gehabt	hattet gehabt
wird haben	werden haben	hatte gehabt	hatten gehabt

Subjunctive (II)		Past Subjunctive	
hätte	hätten	hätte gehabt	hätten gehabt
hättest	hättet	hättest gehabt	hättet gehabt
hätte	hätten	hätte gehabt	hätten gehabt

Conditional		Special Subjunctive (I)	
würde haben	würden haben	habe	haben
würdest haben	würdet haben	habest	habet
würde haben	würden haben	habe	haben

fragen
to ask

ich	wir
du	ihr
er/sie/es	sie/Sie

Present		Imperative	
frage	fragen		fragen wir!
fragst	fragt	frag(e)!	fragt!
fragt	fragen		fragen Sie!

Present Perfect		Simple Past	
habe gefragt	haben gefragt	fragte	fragten
hast gefragt	habt gefragt	fragtest	fragtet
hat gefragt	haben gefragt	fragte	fragten

Future		Past Perfect	
werde fragen	werden fragen	hatte gefragt	hatten gefragt
wirst fragen	werdet fragen	hattest gefragt	hattet gefragt
wird fragen	werden fragen	hatte gefragt	hatten gefragt

Subjunctive (II)		Past Subjunctive	
fragte	fragten	hätte gefragt	hätten gefragt
fragtest	fragtet	hättest gefragt	hättet gefragt
fragte	fragten	hätte gefragt	hätten gefragt

Conditional		Special Subjunctive (I)	
würde fragen	würden fragen	frage	fragen
würdest fragen	würdet fragen	fragest	fraget
würde fragen	würden fragen	frage	fragen

kommen
to come

ich	wir
du	ihr
er/sie/es	sie/Sie

Present		Imperative	
komme	kommen		kommen wir!
kommst	kommt	komm(e)!	kommt!
kommt	kommen		kommen Sie!

Present Perfect		Simple Past	
bin gekomnen	sind gekomnen	kam	kamen
bist gekomnen	seid gekomnen	kamst	kamt
ist gekomnen	sind gekomnen	kam	kamen

Future		Past Perfect	
werde kommen	werden kommen	war gekommen	waren gekommen
wirst kommen	werdet kommen	warst gekommen	wart gekommen
wird kommen	werden kommen	war gekommen	waren gekommen

Subjunctive (II)		Past Subjunctive	
käme	kämen	wäre gekommen	wären gekommen
kämest	kämet	wärest gekommen	wäret gekommen
käme	kämen	wäre gekommen	wären gekommen

Conditional		Special Subjunctive (I)	
würde kommen	würden kommen	komme	kommen
würdest kommen	würdet kommen	kommest	kommet
würde kommen	würden kommen	komme	kommen

20. COMMON IRREGULAR VERBS

INFINITIVE	PRESENT	SIMPLE PAST	PAST PARTICIPLE
backen (*to bake*)	backt	backte	gebacken
befehlen (*to order*)	befiehlt	befahl	befohlen
beginnen (*to begin*)	beginnt	begann	begonnen
beißen (*to bite*)	beißt	biss	gebissen
bewegen (*to move*)	bewegt	bewog	bewogen
biegen (*to bend, turn*)	biegt	bog	ist gebogen
bieten (*to offer*)	bietet	bot	geboten
binden (*to tie*)	bindet	band	gebunden
bitten (*to request*)	bittet	bat	gebeten
blasen (*to blow*)	bläst	blies	geblasen
bleiben (*to stay*)	bleibt	blieb	ist geblieben
brechen (*to break*)	bricht	brach	gebrochen
brennen (*to burn*)	brennt	brannte	gebrannt
bringen (*to bring*)	bringt	brachte	gebracht
denken (*to think*)	denkt	dachte	gedacht
dürfen (*may*)	darf	durfte	gedurft
empfehlen (*to recommend*)	empfiehlt	empfahl	empfohlen
essen (*to eat*)	isst	aß	gegessen
fahren (*to go, drive*)	fährt	fuhr	ist gefahren
fallen (*to fall*)	fällt	fiel	ist gefallen
fangen (*to catch*)	fängt	fing	gefangen

INFINITIVE	PRESENT	SIMPLE PAST	PAST PARTICIPLE
finden (*to find*)	findet	fand	gefunden
fliegen (*to fly*)	fliegt	flog	ist geflogen
fließen (*to flow*)	fließt	floss	geflossen
frieren (*to freeze*)	friert	fror	ist gefroren
geben (*to give*)	gibt	gab	gegeben
gehen (*to go, walk*)	geht	ging	ist gegangen
genießen (*to enjoy*)	genießt	genoss	genossen
geschehen (*to happen*)	geschieht	geschah	ist geschehen
gewinnen (*to win*)	gewinnt	gewann	gewonnen
gießen (*to pour*)	gießt	goss	gegossen
gleichen (*to resemble*)	gleicht	glich	geglichen
gleiten (*to glide*)	gleitet	glitt	ist geglitten
graben (*to dig*)	gräbt	grub	gegraben
greifen (*to grasp*)	greift	griff	gegriffen
haben (*to have*)	hat	hatte	gehabt
halten (*to hold*)	hält	hielt	gehalten
hängen (*to be hanging*)	hängt	hing	gehangen
heißen (*to be called*)	heißt	hieß	geheißen
helfen (*to help*)	hilft	half	geholfen
kennen (*to know*)	kennt	kannte	gekannt
kommen (*to come*)	kommt	kam	ist gekommen
können (*can*)	kann	konnte	gekonnt
lassen (*to let*)	lässt	ließ	gelassen

INFINITIVE	PRESENT	SIMPLE PAST	PAST PARTICIPLE
laufen (to run)	läuft	lief	ist gelaufen
leihen (to lend)	leiht	lieh	geliehen
lesen (to read)	liest	las	gelesen
liegen (to lie, be lying)	liegt	lag	gelegen
lügen (to lie, tell lies)	lügt	log	gelogen
mögen (to like)	mag	mochte	gemocht
müssen (must)	muss	musste	gemusst
nehmen (to take)	nimmt	nahm	genommen
nennen (to name)	nennt	nannte	genannt
raten (to advise)	rät	riet	geraten
reißen (to rip)	reißt	riss	gerissen
reiten (to ride)	reitet	ritt	ist geritten
rennen (to run)	rennt	rannte	ist gerannt
riechen (to smell)	riecht	roch	gerochen
rufen (to call, shout)	ruft	rief	gerufen
scheinen (to seem, shine)	scheint	schien	geschienen
schießen (to shoot)	schießt	schoss	geschossen
schlafen (to sleep)	schläft	schlief	geschlafen
schlagen (to hit, beat)	schlägt	schlug	geschlagen
schließen (to shut)	schließt	schloss	geschlossen
schneiden (to cut)	schneidet	schnitt	geschnitten
schreiben (to write)	schreibt	schrieb	geschrieben
schreien (to yell)	schreit	schrie	geschrieen

INFINITIVE	PRESENT	SIMPLE PAST	PAST PARTICIPLE
schwimmen (to swim)	schwimmt	schwamm	ist geschwommen
sehen (to see)	sieht	sah	gesehen
sein (to be)	ist	war	ist gewesen
senden (to send)	sendet	sandte	gesandt
singen (to sing)	singt	sang	gesungen
sinken (to sink)	sinkt	sank	ist gesunken
sitzen (to sit, be sitting)	sitzt	saß	gesessen
sollen (should)	soll	sollte	gesollt
sprechen (to speak)	spricht	sprach	gesprochen
springen (to jump)	springt	sprang	ist gesprungen
stehen (to stand)	steht	stand	gestanden
stehlen (to steal)	stiehlt	stahl	gestohlen
steigen (to rise, mount)	steigt	stieg	ist gestiegen
sterben (to die)	stirbt	starb	ist gestorben
stinken (to stink)	stinkt	stank	gestunken
stoßen (to push, kick)	stößt	stieß	gestoßen
tragen (to wear, carry)	trägt	trug	getragen
treffen (to meet)	trifft	traf	getroffen
treiben (to drive, force)	treibt	trieb	getrieben
trinken (to drink)	trinkt	trank	getrunken
tun (to do)	tut	tat	getan

INFINITIVE	PRESENT	SIMPLE PAST	PAST PARTICIPLE
verbergen (to hide, conceal)	verbirgt	verbarg	verborgen
verderben (to ruin, spoil)	verdirbt	verdarb	verdorben
vergessen (to forget)	vergisst	vergaß	vergessen
verlassen (to leave, quit someone/thing)	verlässt	verließ	verlassen
verlieren (to lose)	verliert	verlor	verloren
vermeiden (to avoid)	vermeidet	vermied	vermieden
verschwinden (to disappear)	verschwindet	verschwand	ist verschwunden
verzeihen (to excuse, to forgive)	verzeiht	verzieh	verziehen
wachsen (to grow, get bigger)	wächst	wuchs	ist gewachsen
waschen (to wash)	wäscht	wusch	gewaschen
wenden (to turn)	wendet	wandte	gewandt
werden (to get, become)	wird	wurde	ist geworden
werfen (to throw)	wirft	warf	geworfen
wiegen (to weigh)	wiegt	wog	gewogen
wissen (to know)	weiß	wusste	gewusst
wollen (to want)	will	wollte	gewollt
ziehen (to pull)	zieht	zog	gezogen
zwingen (to force, compel)	zwingt	zwang	gezwungen

Glossary

Note that the following abbreviations will be used in this glossary: (m.) = masculine, (f.) = feminine, (sg.) = singular, (pl.) = plural, (fml.) = formal/polite, (infml.) = informal/familiar. If a word has two grammatical genders, (m./f.) or (f./m.) is used.

German-English

A

abbiegen *to turn*
  links abbiegen *to turn left*
  rechts abbiegen *to turn right*
Abend (m.) (Abende) *evening*
  am Abend *in the evening*
  gestern Abend *last night*
  Guten Abend. *Good evening.*
  heute Abend *tonight, this evening*
Abendessen (n.) (Abendessen) *dinner*
abends *in the evening*
aber *but*
  Aber gern! *With pleasure!*
  Das klingt aber gut. *That sounds good.*
  schon, aber … *yes, but …*
abfahren *to leave*
Abitur (n.) (Abiture) *high school exam*
  das Abitur machen *to take the high school exam*
abnehmen *to remove, to decrease, to lose weight*
absagen *to cancel*
abschicken *to send off, to mail*
Absicht (f.) (Absichten) *intention*
ach *oh*
  Ach so. *I see.*
acht *eight*
achtundzwanzig *twenty-eight*
achtzehn *eighteen*
achtzig *eighty*
Adresse (f.) (Adressen) *address*
Afrika (n.) *Africa*
Äh … *Uh …*
Aha! *I see.*
akademisch *academic*

akademische Viertel (n.) *academic quarter*
alle *all*
allergisch *allergic*
  gegen Katzen allergisch sein *to be allergic to cats*
alles *everything*
  Alles Gute zum Geburtstag! *Happy birthday!*
  Alles zusammen? *One check? (at a restaurant)*
  Das ist alles. *That's everything.*
  Ist alles in Ordnung? *Is everything okay?*
als *as, than, when*
also *so, therefore*
  Na also! *See!/There you have it!*
alt *old*
  Ich bin zwanzig Jahre alt. *I am twenty years old.*
  Wie alt sind Sie? *How old are you?*
Alter (n.) (Alter) *age*
  im Alter von *at the age of*
am (an + dem) *at/to/on the, at the side of the*
  am Abend *in the evening*
  am größten *biggest* (adverb)
  am höchsten *highest* (adverb)
  am meisten *most* (adverb)
  am Montag *on Monday*
  am Morgen *in the morning*
  am Nachmittag *in the afternoon*
  am Stück *in one piece*
Amateur-Filmemacher/-in (m./f.) (Amateur-Filmemacher/-innen) *amateur filmmaker*
Amerika (n.) *America*
Amerikaner/-in (m./f.) (Amerikaner/-innen) *American*
Ampel (f.) (Ampeln) *traffic light*
  an der Ampel *at the traffic light*
an *at, at the side of, to, on*
andere *other, another*
  die anderen *the others*

ändern *to change, to alter*
anders *differently*
anfangen *to begin*
Angebot (n.) (Angebote) *offer*
  im Angebot *on sale*
Angestellte (m./f.) (Angestellten) *employee*
ankommen *to arrive*
anlegen *to put, to lay on*
  einen Verband anlegen *to put on a bandage*
Annonce (f.) (Annoncen) *classified ad*
anprobieren *to try on*
Anrufbeantworter (m.)
  (Anrufbeantworter) *answering machine*
anrufen *to call (on the telephone)*
ans (an + das) *at/to/on the, at the side of the*
ansagen *to announce*
anstatt *instead of*
anstecken *to infect*
  sich anstecken *to catch something (somebody else's illness)*
ansteckend *contagious*
Antwort (f.) (Antworten) *answer*
  Wie lautet die richtige Antwort? *What's the right answer?*
antworten *to answer*
Anwalt/Anwältin (m./f.) (Anwälte/
  Anwältinnen) *lawyer*
anziehen *to dress, to wear, to put on*
Anzug (m.) (Anzüge) *suit*
Apfel (m.) (Äpfel) *apple*
Apfelsaft (m.) (Apfelsäfte) *apple juice*
Apotheke (f.) (Apotheken) *pharmacy*
Apparat (m.) (Apparate) *apparatus*
  am Apparat *on the phone, speaking*
  Honberg am Apparat. *Honberg speaking.*
  Wer ist am Apparat? *Who is speaking?*
Appetit (m.) (no pl.) *appetite*
  Guten Appetit! *Enjoy your meal!*
April (m.) (Aprile) *April*
Arbeit (f.) (Arbeiten) *work*
arbeiten *to work*
  freiberuflich arbeiten *to freelance*
Arbeiter/-in (m./f.) (Arbeiter/-innen) *worker*
Arbeitnehmer/-in (m./f.) (Arbeitnehmer/-
  innen) *employee*
Arbeitskollege/Arbeitskollegin
  (m./f.) (Arbeitskollegen/
  Arbeitskolleginnen) *colleague*

arbeitslos *unemployed*
Arbeitslose (m./f.) (Arbeitslosen) *unemployed (people)*
Arbeitslosenquote (f.) (Arbeitslosenquoten) *unemployment rate*
Arbeitsplatz (m.) (Arbeitsplätze) *workplace*
Arbeitsstelle (f.) (Arbeitsstellen) *workplace, job*
Arbeitszeit (f.) (Arbeitszeiten) *work hours, working hours*
  gleitende Arbeitszeit *flexible working hours*
Arbeitszimmer (n.) (Arbeitszimmer) *office*
Architekt/-in (m./f.) (Architekten/
  Architektinnen) *architect*
ärgern *to annoy*
  sich ärgern *to be annoyed*
arm *poor*
Arm (m.) (Arme) *arm*
Artikel (m.) (Artikel) *article*
Arzt/Ärztin (m./f.) (Ärzte/Ärztinnen) *doctor*
Aspirin (n.) (no pl.) *aspirin*
Assistent/-in (m./f.) (Assistenten/
  Assistentinnen) *assistant*
Au ja. *Oh yes.*
auch *too, also, as well, even*
auf *on, on top of, onto*
  Auf welchen Namen? *Under which name? (reservation)*
  Auf Wiederhören. *Until next time. (on the phone)*
  Auf Wiedersehen. *Goodbye.*
  Auf Wiedersehen bis dann. *Good-bye until then.*
  warten auf *to wait for*
Aufgabe (f.) (Aufgaben) *job, task*
aufgeregt *excited; excitedly*
auflegen *to hang up*
  den Hörer auflegen *to hang up the receiver*
aufmachen *to open*
aufpassen *to watch, to keep an eye on*
  Pass auf! *Pay attention!*
  Pass gut auf dich auf! *Take good care of yourself!/Be careful!*
aufrecht *upright*
aufrunden *to round up (the amount)*
aufs (auf + das) *on/onto the, on top of the*
aufstehen *to get up*
  früh aufstehen *to get up early*

spät aufstehen *to get up late*
Auge (n.) (Augen) *eye*
August (m.) (Auguste) *August*
aus *from, out of*
Ausbildung (f.) (Ausbildungen) *professional training, apprenticeship, education*
  eine Ausbildung machen *to apprentice*
Ausbildungsstelle (f.) (Ausbildungsstellen) *apprenticeship*
Ausdruck (m.) (Ausdrücke) *expression*
Ausfahrt (f.) (Ausfahrten) *exit, departure*
ausgebucht *booked out*
ausgehen *to go out*
ausgezeichnet *excellent*
auskennen *to know one's way around*
  sich auskennen *to know one's way around*
aussehen *to look, to appear*
  Sie sehen schlecht aus. *You look bad/sick.*
außer *except for*
außerdem *in addition*
auswaschen *to wash out*
  Wunde (f.) auswaschen *to clean the wound*
Auszubildende (m./f.) (Auszubildenden) *apprentice*
Auto (n.) (Autos) *car*
  das Auto nehmen *to take the car*
  mit dem Auto *by car*
Autobahn (f.) (Autobahnen) *highway (interstate)*
Azubi (m./f.) (Azubis) *apprentice*

B

backen *to bake*
Bäcker/-in (m./f.) (Bäcker/Bäckerinnen) *baker*
Bäckerei (f.) (Bäckereien) *bakery*
Bad (n.) (Bäder) *bathroom*
Badezimmer (n.) (Badezimmer) *bathroom*
Bahnhof (m.) (Bahnhöfe) *train station*
bald *soon*
  Bis bald. *See you soon.*
Balkon (m.) (Balkone) *balcony*
Ball (m.) (Bälle) *ball*
Ballettunterricht (m.) (no pl.) *ballet classes*
Banane (f.) (Bananen) *banana*
Bank (f.) (Banken) *bank (financial institution)*
Bank (f.) (Bänke) *bench*
Basketball (m.) (no pl.) *basketball (game)*
  Basketball spielen *to play basketball*

Bauch (m.) (Bäuche) *belly, stomach*
Bauchschmerzen (pl.) *stomachache*
Bauchweh (n.) (no pl.) *stomachache*
beantworten *to reply to*
Bedienung (f.) (no pl.) *waitress*
beeilen *to hurry, to hasten*
  sich beeilen *to hurry*
beeindruckend *impressive*
befördern *to promote*
Beförderung (f.) (Beförderungen) *promotion*
beginnen *to begin*
behandeln *to treat*
bei *with, by, at*
  bei gutem Wetter *in good weather*
  bei Regenwetter *in rainy weather*
  bei schlechtem Wetter *in bad weather*
  bei Schneewetter *in snowy weather*
beide *both*
beim (bei + dem) *at/by the*
Bein (n.) (Beine) *leg*
beitreten *to join*
  einem Verein beitreten *to join a club*
bekommen *to get, to receive*
  ein Kind bekommen *to have a baby*
  eine Erkältung bekommen *to catch a cold*
belegen *to cover*
  belegte Brote (pl.) *open-faced sandwiches*
beliebt *popular*
benutzen *to use*
Berg (m.) (Berge) *mountain*
  Berg steigen *to go mountain climbing*
Beruf (m.) (Berufe) *occupation, profession, job*
  von Beruf *by profession*
beruflich *job-oriented, professionally*
  Sie sind beruflich hier. *You are here on business.*
Berufsaussicht (f.) (Berufsaussichten) *professional outlook*
Berufschance (f.) (Berufsschancen) *job opportunity, chance*
Berufserfahrung (f.) (Berufserfahrungen) *professional experience*
Berufsschule (f.) (Berufsschulen) *vocational school*
Beschäftigung (f.) (Beschäftigungen) *employment*
beschreiben *to describe*
besetzt *busy (phone line), being used*

Besprechung (f.) (**Besprechungen**) *meeting*
besser *better*
beste *best* (adjective)
  am besten *best* (adverb)
Besteck (n.) (**Bestecke**) *silverware*
bestellen *to order*
  einen Tisch bestellen *to reserve a table, to make reservations*
bestimmen *to decide, to determine*
bestimmt *certain, definite; certainly, definitely*
  Bestimmt! *Sure!*
Besuch (m.) (**Besuche**) *visit*
  zu Besuch sein *to be on a visit*
besuchen *to visit*
Bett (n.) (**Betten**) *bed*
  ins Bett gehen *to go to bed*
Beurteilung (f.) (**Beurteilungen**) *evaluation*
beweisen *to prove*
bewerben *to apply*
  sich auf eine Stelle bewerben *to apply for a job, to apply for a position*
bewundern *to admire*
bezahlen *to pay*
Bier (n.) (**Biere**) *beer*
Bild (n.) (**Bilder**) *photo, picture*
billig *cheap*
Biologie (f.) (no pl.) *biology*
bis *until*
  Bis bald. *See you soon.*
  Bis zum nächsten Mal. *Till next time.*
  von … bis *from … to*
bitte *please, you're welcome*
  Bitte sehr. *Here you go.*
  Wie bitte? *Excuse me/I'm sorry?*
blau *blue*
bleiben *to stay, to remain*
  fit bleiben *to stay in shape*
Blitz (m.) (**Blitze**) *lightning*
Blume (f.) (**Blumen**) *flower*
  Vielen Dank für die Blumen! *Thanks for the compliment! (lit., Thanks for the flowers. [often used ironically])*
Bluse (f.) (**Blusen**) *blouse*
böse *angry, bad*
Boss (m.) (**Bosse**) *boss*
Boutique (f.) (**Boutiquen**) *boutique*
brauchen *to need*
braun *brown*

Bravo! *Well done!*
brechen *to break*
Brief (m.) (**Briefe**) *letter*
Briefmarke (f.) (**Briefmarken**) *stamp*
bringen *to bring*
Brot (n.) (**Brote**) *bread*
  belegte Brote (pl.) *open-faced sandwiches*
  ein Laib Brot *a loaf of bread*
Brötchen (n.) (**Brötchen**) *breakfast roll*
Bruder (m.) (**Brüder**) *brother*
Brüderchen (n.) (**Brüderchen**) *little brother*
Brunch (m.) (**Brunches/Brunche**) *brunch*
Buch (n.) (**Bücher**) *book*
Buchhalter/-in (m./f.) (**Buchhalter/-innen**) *accountant*
Buchseite (f.) (**Buchseiten**) *book page*
Büro (n.) (**Büros**) *office*
  im Büro *in an office, at the office*
  ins Büro *to the office*
bummeln *to stroll*
  bummeln gehen *to go (window-)shopping*
Bus (m.) (**Busse**) *bus*
  den Bus nehmen *to take the bus*
  mit dem Bus *by bus*
Bushaltestelle (f.) (**Bushaltestellen**) *bus stop*
Butter (f.) (no pl.) *butter*

C

Champagner (m.) (no pl.) *champagne*
Chance (f.) (**Chancen**) *chance*
Chef/-in (m./f.) (**Chefs/Chefinnen**) *boss*
Computer (m.) (**Computer**) *computer*
Computermaus (f.) (**Computermäuse**) *computer mouse*
Couch (f.) (**Couches**) *couch*
Cousin/Cousine (m./f.) (**Cousins/Cousinen**) *cousin*

D

da *there, then*
dabei *at the same time, with it, near, near by*
dadurch *thereby, through it*
dafür *for it, for that, instead*
dagegen *against it, on the other hand*
dahin *to there, to that place*
Dame (f.) (**Damen**) *lady*
Damenpullover (m.) (**Damenpullover**) *woman's sweater*

damit *with it*

danach *afterwards*

Dank (m.) (no pl.) *thanks* (pl.)
 Vielen Dank. *Many thanks.*
 Vielen Dank für die Blumen! *Thanks for the compliment! (lit., Thanks for the flowers. [often used ironically])*

danken *to thank*
 Danke. *Thank you.*
 Danke schön. *Thank you.*

dann *then*
 Na dann . . . *Well, in that case . . .*

daran (dran) *on it, alongside it, by it*

darauf *on that, on there, on it*
 Das kommt darauf an. *That depends.*

darin (drin) *in it*

darüber *over it, about it, concerning that*

darum *about it, about that; therefore*

das *the* (n.) (nominative); *the* (n.) (accusative); *that, those* (demonstrative pronoun); *who* (n.), *whom* (n.) (relative pronoun)
 Das ist . . . *This is . . .*
 Das sind . . . *Those are . . .*

dass *that*

davor *in front of it, before that*

dazu *to it, for it*

dazwischen *in between*

dein *your* (sg. infml.)

dem *the* (m./n.) (dative); *to whom* (m./n.) (relative pronoun)

den *the* (m.) (accusative); *the* (pl.) (dative); *whom* (m.) (relative pronoun)

denen *to whom* (pl.) (relative pronoun)

denken *to think*

denn *because, since, then*
 Was ist denn los? *What's the matter?*

der *the* (m.) (nominative); *the* (f.) (dative); *of the* (f./pl.) (genitive); *who* (m.), *to whom* (f.) (relative pronoun)

deren *whose* (f./pl.) (relative pronoun)

des *of the* (m./n.) (genitive)

deshalb *therefore*

dessen *whose* (m./n.) (relative pronoun)

Deutsch (n.) (no pl.) *German (language)*
 auf Deutsch *in German*

Deutscher/Deutsche (m./f.) **(Deutschen)** *German (person)*

Deutschland (n.) (no pl.) *Germany*

Dezember (m.) **(Dezember)** *December*

dich *you* (sg. infml.) (accusative); *yourself* (sg. infml.)

dick *fat*
 dick machen *to be fattening*

die *the* (f./pl.) (nominative); *the* (f./pl.) (accusative); *who* (f./pl.), *whom* (f./pl.) (relative pronoun)

Diele (f.) **(Dielen)** *foyer*

Dienstag (m.) **(Dienstage)** *Tuesday*

dieser *this*

dir *you, to you* (sg. infml.) (dative)

direkt *straight, directly*

doch *"flavoring" word*
 Ja, doch! *Yes, absolutely!*
 Kommst du nicht mit? -Doch! *Aren't you coming along? -Yes, I am!*
 Nimm doch den Fisch. *Have the fish, why don't you?*

Doktor (m.) **(Doktoren)** *Ph.D.*
 einen Doktor machen *to study for a Ph.D.*

Donner (m.) (no pl.) *thunder*

Donnerstag (m.) **(Donnerstage)** *Thursday*
 jeden Donnerstag *every Thursday*

Dorf (n.) **(Dörfer)** *village*

dort *there*

dran (daran) *on it, alongside it, by it*

draußen *outside*

drei *three*

dreimal *three times*

dreißig *thirty*
 Es ist vier Uhr dreißig. *It is four thirty.*

dreiundzwanzig *twenty-three*

dreizehn *thirteen*

drin (darin) *in it*

dringend *urgent; urgently*

Drogerie (f.) **(Drogerien)** *drugstore*

du *you* (sg. infml.) (nominative)

dürfen *to be allowed to*
 Darf's sonst noch etwas sein? *Anything else? (at a store)*
 Was darf's (denn) sein? *What can I get you?*

durch *through, by*

E

eben *just, simply*

Ecke (f.) **(Ecken)** *corner*
 an der Ecke *at the corner*
 um die Ecke *around the corner*

egal *the same*
  Es ist mir egal. *I don't care./It makes no difference to me.*
Ehefrau (f.) (Ehefrauen) *wife*
Ehemann (m.) (Ehemänner) *husband*
ehrlich *honest*
eilig *urgent*
ein *a/an*
  ein bisschen *a little bit*
Einbahnstraße (f.) (Einbahnstraßen) *one-way street*
einfach *simple; simply, just*
Einfahrt (f.) (Einfahrten) *entrance*
einkaufen *to shop*
  einkaufen gehen *to go (grocery) shopping*
Einkaufsliste (f.) (Einkaufslisten) *shopping list*
einladen *to invite*
Einladung (f.) (Einladungen) *invitation*
einmal *once*
  noch einmal *once more*
eins *one*
einschlafen *to fall asleep*
einstellen *to hire*
einunddreißig *thirty-one*
einundzwanzig *twenty-one*
Eis (n.) (no pl.) *ice cream*
Elektriker/-in (m./f.) (Elektriker/-innen) *electrician*
elf *eleven*
Ellbogen (m.) (Ellbogen) *elbow*
Eltern (pl.) *parents*
E-Mail (f.) (E-Mails) *e-mail*
empfehlen *to recommend*
Ende (n.) (Enden) *end*
enden *to end*
endlich *finally*
  Na endlich! *Finally!/At last!*
eng *tight*
Enkel/-in (m./f.) (Enkel/-innen) *grandson/granddaughter*
Enkelkind (n.) (Enkelkinder) *grandchild*
entlassen *to let go, to fire*
Entlassung (f.) (Entlassungen) *layoff*
entschuldigen *to excuse*
  Entschuldige. *Excuse me.*
  sich entschuldigen *to apologize*
Entschuldigung (f.) (Entschuldigungen) *excuse*

Entschuldigung. *Excuse me./Sorry./Forgive me.*
entweder *either*
  entweder ... oder ... *either ... or ...*
er *he*
Erbsensuppe (f.) (Erbsensuppen) *pea soup*
Erfahrung (f.) (Erfahrungen) *experience*
erfolgreich *successful*
erhalten *to receive, to maintain*
erhöhen *to raise, to increase*
  erhöhte Temperatur (f.) *elevated temperature*
Erhöhung (f.) (Erhöhungen) *raise*
erkälten (reflexive) *to catch a cold*
  sich erkälten *to catch a cold*
Erkältung (f.) (Erkältungen) *cold*
  eine Erkältung bekommen *to catch a cold*
erklären *to explain*
eröffnen *to open*
  neu eröffnen *to reopen*
erreichen *to reach*
erst *only, not until, at first*
  erst mal *first*
  zum ersten Mal *for the first time*
erstaunlich *amazing*
es *it* (nominative); *it* (accusative)
essen *to eat*
  zu Mittag essen *to have lunch*
Essen (n.) (Essen) *meal*
Esstisch (m.) (Esstische) *dining table*
Esszimmer (n.) (Esszimmer) *dining room*
etwa *about, approximately, by chance*
etwas *something, some, somewhat*
  Darf's sonst noch etwas sein? *Anything else?* (at a store)
  noch etwas *some more*
  so etwas *something like that*
euch *you* (pl. infml.) (accusative); *you, to you* (pl. infml.) (dative); *yourselves* (pl. infml.)
euer *your* (pl. infml.)
Euro (m.) (Euros) *euro*

F

Fach (n.) (Fächer) *subject*
  Lieblingsfach (n.) *favorite subject*
fahren *to drive, to go, to leave, to take*
  die Tochter in die Schule fahren *to take the daughter to school*
  Fahrrad fahren *to ride a bicycle*

fahren mit … *to go by means of …*
Rad fahren *to bicycle*
Ski fahren *to go skiing*
Fahrgast (n.) (Fahrgäste) *passenger*
Fahrgeld (n.) (no pl.) *fare*
Fahrkarte (f.) (Fahrkarten) *ticket*
Fahrrad (n.) (Fahrräder) *bicycle*
Fahrrad fahren *to ride a bicycle*
Fahrt (f.) (Fahrten) *trip*
Gute Fahrt! *Drive safely!*
falsch *wrong*
Familie (f.) (Familien) *family*
eine Familie gründen *to start a family*
Familienfotos (pl.) *family photographs*
Familienleben (n.) (no pl.) *family life*
fantastisch *fantastic*
Farbe (f.) (Farben) *color*
fast *almost*
Februar (m.) (Februare) *February*
fehlen *to be missing, to be lacking*
feiern *to celebrate*
Fenster (n.) (Fenster) *window*
Ferien (pl.) *vacation*
Ferienwohnung (f.)
(Ferienwohnungen) *vacation apartment*
Fernsehen (n.) (no pl.) *television*
im Fernsehen *on TV*
Fernseher (m.) (Fernseher) *television (set)*
fertig *finished*
Fieber (n.) (Fieber) *fever*
Fieber messen *to take someone's temperature*
hohes Fieber *high fever*
Film (m.) (Filme) *movie*
finden *to find*
Das finde ich auch. *I think so, too.*
Finger (m.) (Finger) *finger*
Firma (f.) (Firmen) *company*
Fisch (m.) (Fische) *fish*
fit *fit*
fit bleiben *to stay in shape*
Fitnessclub (m.) (Fitnessclubs) *fitness club*
Flasche (f.) (Flaschen) *bottle*
eine Flasche Mineralwasser *a bottle of mineral water*
eine Flasche Wein *a bottle of wine*
Fleisch (n.) (no pl.) *meat*
Flughafen (m.) (Flughäfen) *airport*
folgen *to follow*

Foto (n.) (Fotos) *photograph*
Familienfotos (pl.) *family photographs*
fotografieren *to photograph*
Frage (n.) (Fragen) *question, issue*
fragen *to ask, to wonder*
Fragestunde (f.) (Fragestunden) *question time*
Frankreich (n.) (no pl.) *France*
Franzose (m.) (Franzosen) *Frenchman*
Frau (f.) (Frauen) *woman, wife, Mrs., Ms.*
meine Frau *my wife*
Willst du meine Frau werden? *Will you marry me? (lit., Will you be my wife?)*
Fräulein (n.) (Fräulein) *Miss*
frei *vacant*
freiberuflich *freelance (adjective/adverb)*
freiberuflich arbeiten *to freelance*
freiberuflich tätig sein *to freelance*
Freitag (m.) (Freitage) *Friday*
Freizeit (f.) (no pl.) *leisure time*
Freizeitbeschäftigung (f.) (Freizeitbeschäfti-gungen) *leisure time activity*
fremd *foreign, strange*
freuen (reflexive) *to be glad*
sich auf … freuen *to look forward to …*
Freund (m.) (Freunde) *friend (male), boyfriend*
Freundin (f.) (Freundinnen) *friend (female), girlfriend*
freundlich *kind, friendly*
frisch *fresh*
früh *early*
früh aufstehen *to get up early*
früher *earlier*
Frühling (m.) (Frühlinge) *spring*
Frühstück (n.) (Frühstücke) *breakfast*
fühlen *to feel*
sich fühlen *to feel*
sich gesund fühlen *to feel healthy*
sich krank fühlen *to feel sick*
sich wohl fühlen *to feel well*
fünf *five*
fünfundzwanzig *twenty-five*
fünfzehn *fifteen*
Es ist sechs Uhr fünfzehn. *It is 6:15.*
fünfzig *fifty*
aus den Fünfzigern *from the fifties ('50s)*
für *for*
fürs (für + das) *for the*
Fuß (m.) (Füße) *foot*

zu Fuß gehen *to go by foot, to walk*
Fußball (m.) (no pl.) *soccer (game), soccer ball*
  Fußball spielen *to play soccer*
Fußgänger (m.) (Fußgänger) *pedestrian*
Fußgängerüberweg (m.)
  (Fußgängerüberwege) *crosswalk*
  Gehen Sie über den
    Fußgängerüberweg. *Take the crosswalk.*
Fußgängerzone (f.)
  (Fußgängerzonen) *pedestrian zone*

G

Gabel (f.) (Gabeln) *fork*
ganz *entire, whole, complete; completely*
  den ganzen Tag *all day*
  ganz neu *brand-new*
gar *fully, quite*
  gar nicht *not at all*
Garten (m.) (Gärten) *garden*
  im Garten arbeiten *to work in the garden*
Gartenarbeit (f.) (Gartenarbeiten) *garden
  work*
Gast (m.) (Gäste) *guest*
Gatte (m.) (Gatten) *husband*
geben *to give*
  eine Party geben *have a party*
  es gibt *there is/are*
  Was gibt's Neues? *What's new?*
Geburtstag (m.) (Geburtstage) *birthday*
  Alles Gute zum Geburtstag! *Happy birthday!*
gefährlich *dangerous*
gefallen *to please, to be to one's liking*
  Das gefällt mir. *I like it.*
  Das gefällt mir nicht. *I don't like it.*
gegen *against, toward*
  gegen Katzen allergisch sein *to be allergic
    to cats*
Gegenstand (m.) (Gegenstände) *thing*
gegenüber *across from*
Gehalt (n.) (Gehälter) *salary*
Gehaltserhöhung (f.)
  (Gehaltserhöhungen) *raise (in salary)*
gehen *to go*
  bummeln gehen *to go (window-)shopping*
  einkaufen gehen *to go (grocery) shopping*
  in Rente gehen *to retire*
  ins Bett gehen *to go to bed*
  schwimmen gehen *to go swimming*

spazieren gehen *to go for a walk*
  Wie geht es Ihnen? *How are you?* (fml.)
  Wie geht's? *How are you?* (infml.)
gehören *to belong to*
Gehweg (m.) (Gehwege) *sidewalk*
gelb *yellow*
Geld (n.) (Gelder) *money*
Geldbeutel (m.) (Geldbeutel) *wallet*
Gelee (m.) (Gelees) *jam, jelly*
Gemüse (n.) (no pl.) *vegetables*
Gemüseladen (m.) (Gemüseläden) *grocery store*
genehmigen *to approve*
  Genehmigt! *Accepted!, Approved!*
genug *enough*
gerade *at the moment, just*
geradeaus *straight (ahead)*
  geradeaus gehen *to continue straight ahead*
gern(e) *gladly, willingly, happily (expresses likes
  and preferences)*
  Aber gern! *With pleasure!*
  Gern geschehen! *You're welcome!/My
    pleasure!*
  gern haben *to like*
  gern Ski fahren *to enjoy skiing*
  Ich hätte gern … *I would like to have …*
  Ja, gern. *Yes, please.*
Gesamtschule (f.)
  (Gesamtschulen) *comprehensive school*
Geschäft (n.) (Geschäfte) *store*
Geschäftsmann (m.)
  (Geschäftsmänner) *businessman*
Geschäftsreise (f.) (Geschäftsreisen) *business
  trip*
geschehen *to happen*
  Gern geschehen! *You're welcome!/My
    pleasure!*
Geschenk (n.) (Geschenke) *gift*
  als Geschenk für … *as a gift for …*
geschieden *divorced*
  geschieden werden *to get divorced*
Geschwister (pl.) *siblings*
gestern *yesterday*
  gestern Abend *last night*
gestreift *striped*
gesund *healthy*
  sich gesund fühlen *to feel healthy*
Getränk (n.) (Getränke) *drink, beverage*
gewinnen *to win*

Gewürz (n.) (Gewürze) *spice*
Gitarre (f.) (Gitarren) *guitar*
 Gitarre spielen *to play the guitar*
Glas (n.) (Gläser) *glass*
 ein Glas Wein *a glass of wine*
glauben *to believe, to think*
 Ich glaube nicht. *I don't think so.*
gleich *same; right, just, immediately*
 gleich hier *right here*
gleitend *gliding, sliding*
 gleitende Arbeitszeit (f.) *flexible working
 hours*
Glück (n.) (no pl.) *luck*
 Viel Glück! *Good luck!*
Glückwunsch (m.)
 (Glückwünsche) *congratulation, wish*
 Herzlichen Glückwunsch! *Congratulations!*
Golf (m.) *golf*
 Golf spielen *to play golf*
Golfplatz (m.) (Golfplätze) *golf course*
Grad (m.) (Grade) *degree*
Gramm (n.) (Gramme; no pl. after
 numbers) *gram*
Gras (n.) (Gräser) *grass*
grau *gray*
Grippe (f.) (Grippen) *flu*
 Die Grippe geht um. *The flu is going around.*
 Grippe haben *to have the flu*
groß *big*
 am größten *biggest* (adverb)
 größer *bigger*
 größte *biggest* (adjective)
Größe (f.) (Größen) *size*
 welche Größe *what size*
Großeltern (pl.) *grandparents*
Großmutter (f.) (Großmütter) *grandmother*
Großvater (m.) (Großväter) *grandfather*
grün *green*
gründen *to found*
 eine Familie gründen *to start a family*
Grüß Gott. *Hello.*
Grundschule (f.) (Grundschulen) *elementary
 school (first grade through fourth grade)*
gucken *to look*
 Guck mal! *Look!*
Gürtel (m.) (Gürtel) *belt*
Gurke (f.) (Gurken) *cucumber*
gut *good, well*

gut kochen *to cook well*
gut passen *to fit well*
gut passen zu *to go well with*
gut stehen *to look good on (somebody)*
Alles Gute zum Geburtstag! *Happy birthday!*
Guten Abend. *Good evening.*
Guten Appetit! *Enjoy your meal!*
Guten Morgen. *Good morning.*
Guten Tag. *Hello./Good day.*
Gute Fahrt! *Drive safely!*
Mach's gut. *Take care.*
Pass gut auf dich auf! *Take good care of
 yourself!/Be careful!*
Schon gut. *It's okay.*
Sehr gut. *Very well.*
Wie kann ich das wieder gut machen? *How
 can I make this up to you?*
gutaussehend *handsome, good-looking*
Gymnasium (n.) (Gymnasien) *high school (fifth
 grade through twelfth grade)*

H

Haar (n.) (Haare) *hair*
haben *to have*
 gern haben *to like*
 Hunger haben *to be hungry*
 Ich hätte gern … *I would like to have …*
 keine Lust haben *to not feel like*
 lieb haben *to like (among family members)*
 Lust haben *to feel like*
 Recht haben *to be right*
 Schmerzen haben *to be in pain*
 zu etwas Lust haben *to feel like doing
 something*
häkeln *to crochet*
halb *half*
 Es ist halb acht. *It is half past seven.*
Hallo. *Hi.*
Halsschmerzen (pl.) *sore throat*
halten *to hold*
Haltestelle (f.) (Haltestellen) *stop (bus, tram,
 subway)*
Hand (f.) (Hände) *hand*
Handball (m.) (no pl.) *handball (game)*
 Handball spielen *to play handball*
Handschuhe (pl.) *gloves*
Handwerk (n.) (Handwerke) *trade*
Handy (n.) (Handys) *cell phone*

Handynummer (f.) (Handynummern) *cell phone number*
hängen *to hang*
hart *hard*
Hauptgericht (n.) (Hauptgerichte) *main course*
Hauptschulabschluß (m.)
  (Hauptschulabschlüsse) *school-leaving exam (lower level)*
Hauptschule (f.) (Hauptschulen) *junior high school (fifth grade through ninth grade)*
Hauptspeise (f.) (Hauptspeisen) *main course*
  als Hauptspeise *as a main course*
Haus (n.) (Häuser) *house*
  nach Hause *home*
  zu Hause *home*
Hausaufgaben (pl.) *homework*
  die Hausaufgaben machen *to do homework*
heiraten *to get married*
  Heirate mich! *Marry me!*
heiß *hot*
  Es ist heiß. *It is hot.*
heißen *to be named, to be called*
  Ich heiße ... *My name is ...*
  Wie heißen Sie? *What's your name?* (fml.)
helfen *to help*
  Kann ich Ihnen helfen? *Can I help you?*
Hemd (n.) (Hemden) *shirt*
her *here, from*
  Wo kommen Sie her? *Where are you from?*
herangehen *to approach*
Herbst (m.) (Herbste) *fall*
Herr (m.) (Herren) *Mr.*
Herrenabteilung (f.)
  (Herrenabteilungen) *men's department*
herum *around*
hervorragend *outstanding, excellent; very well*
herzlich *warm, sincere*
  Herzlichen Glückwunsch! *Congratulations!*
heute *today*
  heute Abend *tonight, this evening*
heutzutage *these days*
hier *here*
  gleich hier *right here*
  Hier Philipp. *Hello, this is Philipp. (on the phone)*
Hilfe (f.) (Hilfen) *help*
hinausgehen *to go out*
hinter *in back of, behind*

hinterlassen *to leave (behind)*
  Nachricht (f.) hinterlassen *to leave a message*
Hobby (n.) (Hobbys) *hobby*
  einem Hobby nachgehen *to have a hobby*
Hobbyfotograf/-in (m./f.) (Hobbyfotografen/-grafinnen) *amateur photographer*
hoch *high*
  am höchsten *highest* (adverb)
  hohes Fieber (n.) *high fever*
  höchste *highest* (adjective)
  höher *higher*
Hochsaison (f.) (Hochsaisons) *peak season*
Hochzeit (f.) (Hochzeiten) *wedding*
hoffen *to hope*
holen *to get, to fetch*
hören *to listen, to hear*
  Hör mal. *Listen.*
Hörer (m.) (Hörer) *receiver*
  den Hörer auflegen *to hang up the receiver*
Hose (f.) (Hosen) *pair of pants*
Hotel (n.) (Hotels) *hotel*
Hotelzimmer (n.) (Hotelzimmer) *hotel room*
Hühnchen (n.) (Hühnchen) *chicken*
Huhn (n.) (Hühner) *chicken*
Hund (m.) (Hunde) *dog*
hundert *hundred*
  einhundert *one hundred*
  einhundert(und)eins *one hundred one*
  einhundert(und)einundzwanzig *one hundred twenty-one*
  hunderttausend *one hundred thousand*
Hunger (m.) (no pl.) *hunger*
  Hunger haben *to be hungry*
Husten (m.) (no pl.) *cough*
  Husten haben *to have a cough*
Hut (m.) (Hüte) *hat*

I

ich *I*
  Ich bin's. *It's me.*
Idee (f.) (Ideen) *idea*
ihm *him/it, to him/it* (dative)
ihn *him* (accusative)
ihnen *them, to them* (dative)
Ihnen *you, to you* (sg. fml./pl. fml.) (dative)
ihr *you* (pl. infml.) (nominative); *her, to her* (dative); *her, their* (possessive)
Ihr *your* (sg. fml./pl. fml.)

im (in + dem) *in/inside/into the*
  im Büro *in an/the office*
  im Januar *in January*
immer *always*
  wie immer *as always*
in *in, inside, into*
inklusive *inclusive*
  Ist das Trinkgeld inklusive? *Is the tip included?*
Innenstadt (f.) **(Innenstädte)** *city center*
ins (in + das) *in/inside/into the*
  ins Büro *to the office*
intelligent *intelligent*
interessieren *to interest*
inzwischen *in the meantime*

J

Ja. *Yes.*
  Au ja. *Oh yes.*
  Na ja … *Well …*
Jacke (f.) **(Jacken)** *jacket*
Jahr (n.) **(Jahre)** *year*
  Ich bin zwanzig Jahre alt. *I am twenty years old.*
  letztes Jahr *last year*
  nächstes Jahr *next year*
  vor vielen Jahren *many years ago*
  Wie alt sind Sie? *How old are you?*
Januar (m.) **(Januare)** *January*
  im Januar *in January*
Japan (n.) *Japan*
je *ever, each*
  Oh je! *Oh dear!*
Jeans (pl.) *jeans*
jede *each, every*
  jeden Donnerstag *every Thursday*
  jeden Tag *every day*
jemand *someone*
jetzt *now*
joggen *to jog*
Joghurt (m.) **(Joghurts)** *yogurt*
Journalist/-in (m./f.) **(Journalisten/ Journalistinnen)** *journalist*
Juli (m.) **(Julis)** *July*
jung *young*
Junge (m.) **(Jungen)** *boy*
Juni (m.) **(Junis)** *June*
Jura (pl.) *the study of law*

K

Kaffee (m.) **(Kaffees)** *coffee*
  ein Kännchen Kaffee *a portion (lit., a small pot) of coffee*
  eine Tasse Kaffee *a cup of coffee*
Kaffeetasse (f.) **(Kafeetassen)** *coffee cup*
Kalbfleisch (n.) (no pl.) *veal*
Kalifornien (n.) *California*
kalt *cold*
  Es ist kalt. *It is cold.*
kämmen *to comb*
  sich kämmen *to comb one's hair*
Kanada (n.) *Canada*
Kännchen (n.) **(Kännchen)** *pot*
  ein Kännchen Kaffee *a portion/a small pot of coffee*
kaputt *broken*
Karate (n.) (no pl.) *karate*
Karatelehrer (m.) **(Karatelehrer)** *karate teacher*
kariert *checkered*
Karotte (f.) **(Karotten)** *carrot*
Karriere (f.) **(Karrieren)** *career*
  Karriere machen *to advance (to make a career)*
Karte (f.) **(Karten)** *card, map*
  Karten spielen *to play cards*
Kartenspiel (n.) **(Kartenspiele)** *card game*
Kartoffel (f.) **(Kartoffeln)** *potato*
Kartoffelsalat (m.) **(Kartoffelsalate)** *potato salad*
Käse (m.) (no pl.) *cheese*
Kasse (f.) **(Kassen)** *cashier, checkout*
  an der Kasse *at the cashier, at the checkout*
Katze (f.) **(Katzen)** *cat*
kaufen *to buy*
Kaufhaus (n.) **(Kaufhäuser)** *department store*
kein *no, none, not any*
  Keine Sorge. *No worries./Don't worry.*
Keks (m.) **(Kekse)** *cookie*
Kellner/-in (m./f.) **(Kellner/-innen)** *waiter/ waitress*
kennen *to know (people, animals, places, and things)*
kennenlernen *to become acquainted with, to meet*
  Leute kennenlernen *to meet people*

Kilogramm (n.) **(Kilogramme; no pl. after numbers)** *kilogram*
Kilometer (m.) **(Kilometer)** *kilometer*
Kind (n.) **(Kinder)** *child*
  ein Kind bekommen *to have a baby*
Kinderzimmer (n.) **(Kinderzimmer)** *children's room*
Kino (n.) **(Kinos)** *movie theater*
Klavier (n.) **(Klaviere)** *piano*
  Klavier spielen *to play the piano*
Kleid (n.) **(Kleider)** *dress*
  Kleider (pl.) *clothes*
Kleidung (f.) **(no pl.)** *clothing*
klein *small*
Klient/-in (m./f.) **(Klienten/Klientinnen)** *client*
klingeln *to ring the doorbell*
klingen *to sound*
  Das klingt aber gut. *That sounds good.*
Kneipe (f.) **(Kneipen)** *neighborhood bar*
Knie (n.) **(Knie)** *knee*
Knöchel (m.) **(Knöchel)** *ankle*
Koch/Köchin (m./f.) **(Köche/Köchinnen)** *cook*
kochen *to cook*
  gut kochen *to cook well*
Koffer (m.) **(Koffer)** *suitcase*
Kollege/Kollegin (m./f.) **(Kollegen/Kolleginnen)** *colleague*
Köln (n.) *Cologne*
kommen *to come*
  Ich komme aus … *I'm from …*
  Das kommt darauf an. *That depends.*
  Wie komme ich … ? *How do I get to … ?*
  Wo kommen Sie her?/Woher kommen Sie? *Where are you from?*
Kommilitone/Kommilitonin (m./f.) **(Kommilitonen/Kommilitoninnen)** *fellow university student*
Kompliment (n.) **(Komplimente)** *compliment*
können *can, to be able to*
  Kann ich Ihnen helfen? *Can I help you?*
Kopf (m.) **(Köpfe)** *head*
Kopfschmerzen (pl.) *headache*
Kopfschmerztablette (f.) **(Kopfschmerztabletten)** *headache tablet*
Kopfweh (n.) **(no pl.)** *headache*
  Kopfweh/Kopfschmerzen haben *to have a headache*
kosten *to cost*

krank *sick*
  sich krank fühlen *to feel sick*
Krankenhaus (n.) **(Krankenhäuser)** *hospital*
Krankenpfleger/Krankenschwester (m./f.) **(Krankenpfleger/Krankenschwestern)** *nurse*
Krawatte (f.) **(Krawatten)** *tie*
Kreditkarte (f.) **(Kreditkarten)** *credit card*
Kreuzung (f.) **(Kreuzungen)** *intersection*
Kuchen (m.) **(Kuchen)** *cake*
  ein Stück Kuchen *a piece of cake*
Küche (f.) **(Küchen)** *kitchen*
kümmern *to concern*
  sich kümmern um … *to take care of …*
küssen *to kiss*
Kunde/Kundin (m./f.) *client, customer*
kurz *short*

L

Laib (m.) **(Laibe)** *loaf*
  ein Laib Brot *a loaf of bread*
Lamm (n.) **(Lämmer)** *lamb*
Lampe (f.) **(Lampen)** *lamp*
Landstraße (f.) **(Landstraßen)** *country road*
lang *long*
langsam *slow*
lassen *to let, to allow*
lästig *annoying*
Lauf (m.) **(Läufe)** *course, run*
laufen *to run*
  einen Marathon laufen *to run a marathon*
  Schlittschuh laufen *to go ice-skating*
laut *loud; according to*
lauten *to be*
  meine Nummer lautet … *my (phone) number is …*
  Wie lautet die richtige Antwort? *What's the right answer?*
läuten *to ring the doorbell*
leben *to live*
Leben (n.) **(Leben)** *life*
  tägliches Leben *everyday life*
Lebenslauf (m.) **(Lebensläufe)** *résumé*
  den Lebenslauf schreiben *to prepare one's résumé*
Lebensmittel (n.) **(Lebensmittel)** *food, groceries*
ledig *single*

ledig sein *to be single*
leer *empty*
legen *to put, to place*
  auf die Waage legen *to put on the scale*
Lehrer/-in (m./f.) **(Lehrer/-innen)** *teacher*
leid *sorry*
  (Es) tut mir leid. *I'm sorry.*
leider *unfortunately*
leihen *to borrow*
leise *quiet*
leisten *to achieve, to manage*
leiten *to lead, to run (a business)*
  ein Geschäft leiten *to run a business*
Leitung (f.) **(Leitungen)** *line*
  auf der anderen Leitung (sprechen) *(to speak) on the other line*
Lektion (f.) **(Lektionen)** *lesson*
lernen *to learn*
  viel zu lernen haben *to have a lot to learn*
lesen *to read*
letzte *last*
  letztes Jahr *last year*
  letzten Monat *last month*
  letzte Woche *last week*
Leute (pl.) *people*
  Leute kennenlernen *to meet people*
lieb *nice*
  lieb haben *to like, to love (among family members)*
lieben *to love*
lieber *rather, better*
Liebling (m.) **(Lieblinge)** *favorite, darling*
  Lieblingsfach (n.) *favorite subject*
liebste *best* (adjective)
  am liebsten *best* (adverb)
liegen *to lie* (location)
lila *violet*
Linie (f.) **(Linien)** *line*
links *left, to the left*
  links abbiegen *to turn left*
Liter (m.) **(Liter)** *liter*
  ein Liter Milch *a liter of milk*
loben *to praise*
Löffel (m.) **(Löffel)** *spoon*
los *loose*
  Was ist denn los? *What's the matter?*
Lust (f.) **(Lüste)** *pleasure, delight*
  keine Lust haben *to not feel like*

Lust haben *to feel like*
  zu etwas Lust haben *to feel like doing something*
Lyoner (f.) (no pl.) *bologna*

M

machen *to do, to make, to amount to*
  Das macht acht Euro fünfzig. *That's eight euros and fifty cents.*
  Das macht nichts. *It doesn't matter.*
  die Hausaufgaben machen *to do homework*
  eine Pause machen *to take a break*
  ein Picknick machen *to have a picnic*
  eine Verabredung machen *to make an appointment*
  Mach's gut. *Take care.*
  Pläne machen *to make plans*
  Spaß machen *to be fun*
  Urlaub machen *to go on vacation*
  Wie kann ich das wieder gut machen? *How can I make this up to you?*
Mädchen (n.) **(Mädchen)** *girl*
Magen (m.) **(Mägen)** *stomach*
Magister (m.) **(magister)** *master's degree*
  einen Magister machen *to study for a master's degree*
Mai (m.) **(Maien)** *May*
Mais (m.) (no pl.) *corn*
mal *time* (occasion)
  Bis zum nächsten Mal. *Till next time.*
  Guck mal! *Look!*
  Hör mal. *Listen.*
  jedes Mal *every time*
  zum ersten Mal *for the first time*
malen *to paint*
Mama (f.) **(Mamas)** *mom*
man *one, they* (indefinite pronoun)
Manager/-in (m./f.) **(Manager/-innen)** *manager*
manchmal *sometimes*
Mann (m.) **(Männer)** *man, husband*
  mein Mann *my husband*
  Willst du mein Mann werden? *Will you marry me? (lit., Will you be my husband?)*
Mantel (m.) **(Mäntel)** *coat*
Marathon (m.) **(Marathons)** *marathon*
  einen Marathon laufen *to run a marathon*
Marktplatz (m.) **(Marktplätze)** *market place*
Marmelade (f.) **(Marmeladen)** *marmalade,*

jam, jelly

Marmorkuchen (m.) (**Marmorkuchen**) *marble cake*

März (m.) (**Märze**) *March*

Maus (f.) (**Mäuse**) *mouse*

Medikament (n.) (**Medikamente**) *medicine, medication*

Medizin (f.) (no pl.) *medicine*

mehr *more*

  nicht mehr *any more, no more*

mein *my*

meinen *to mean, to think*

  So war das nicht gemeint. *That's not what this was supposed to mean./I didn't mean it that way.*

Meinung (f.) (**Meinungen**) *opinion*

meiste *most* (adjective)

  am meisten *most* (adverb)

melden *to report, to notify*

messen *to measure*

  Fieber (n.) **messen** *to take someone's temperature*

Messer (n.) (**Messer**) *knife*

Meter (m.) (**Meter**) *meter*

Metzger/-in (m./f.) (**Metzger/-innen**) *butcher*

mich *me* (accusative)*; myself*

mieten *to rent*

Milch (f.) (no pl.) *milk*

  ein Liter Milch *a liter of milk*

Milliarde (f.) (**Milliarden**) *billion*

Million (f.) (**Millionen**) *million*

Mineralwasser (n.) (**Mineralwässer/Mineralwasser**) *mineral water*

  eine Flasche Mineralwasser *a bottle of mineral water*

minus *minus*

Minute (f.) (**Minuten**) *minute*

  in zehn Minuten *in ten minutes*

mir *me, to me* (dative)

missen *to miss*

mit *with, in*

  mit dem Bus *by bus*

  Wie wär's mit ... *How about ...*

Mitarbeiter/-in (m./f.) (**Mitarbeiter/-innen**) *employee, colleague*

Mitbewohner/-in (m./f.) (**Mitbewohner/-innen**) *roommate*

mitbringen *to bring along*

Mitglied (n.) (**Mitglieder**) *member*

mitkommen *to come along*

mitnehmen *to take along*

Mitschüler/-in (m./f.) (**Mitschüler/-innen**) *classmate*

mitspielen *to play along*

Mittag (m.) (**Mittage**) *noon*

  zu Mittag essen *to have lunch*

Mittagessen (n.) (**Mittagessen**) *lunch*

Mitte (f.) (**Mitten**) *middle*

Mittwoch (m.) (**Mittwoche**) *Wednesday*

Möbel (pl.) *furniture*

möchten *to like to*

  Ich möchte gern ... *I'd like ...*

mögen *to like (people, things, food, drinks)*

Moment (m.) (**Momente**) *moment*

  Einen Moment bitte. *One moment please.*

Monat (m.) (**Monate**) *month*

  letzten Monat *last month*

  nächsten Monat *next month*

Montag (m.) (**Montage**) *Monday*

  am Montag *on Monday*

  nächsten Montag *next Monday*

morgen *tomorrow*

Morgen (m.) (**Morgen**) *morning*

  am Morgen *in the morning*

  Guten Morgen. *Good morning.*

morgens *in the morning*

Motorrad (n.) (**Motorräder**) *motorcycle*

  Motorrad fahren *to ride a motorcycle*

müde *tired*

München *Munich*

müssen *to have to*

Mütze (f.) (**Mützen**) *cap, hat*

Mund (m.) (**Münder**) *mouth*

Museum (n.) (**Museen**) *museum*

Musik (f.) (no pl.) *music*

Muster (n.) (**Muster**) *pattern*

Mutter (f.) (**Mütter**) *mother*

N

na *well*

  Na also! *See!/There you have it!*

  Na dann ... *Well, in that case ...*

  Na endlich! *Finally!/At last!*

  Na ja ... *Well ...*

  Na und? *So what?*

nach *to, after, past*

Es ist viertel nach drei. *It is quarter past three.*

Es ist zehn nach zwölf. *It is ten after twelve.*

nach Hause *home*

Nachbar/-in (m./f.) **(Nachbarn/ Nachbarinnen)** *neighbor*

nachgehen *to pursue, to practice*

einem Hobby nachgehen *to have a hobby*

Nachmittag (m.) **(Nachmittage)** *afternoon*

am Nachmittag *in the afternoon*

nachmittags *in the afternoon*

Nachprüfung (f.) **(Nachprüfungen)** *review*

Nachricht (f.) **(Nachrichten)** *message, (a piece of) news*

Das ist eine gute Nachricht. *That's good news.*

Nachricht hinterlassen *to leave a message*

Nachspeise (f.) **(Nachspeisen)** *dessert*

als Nachspeise *for dessert*

nächste *next*

Bis zum nächsten Mal. *Till next time.*

nächste Woche *next week*

nächsten Monat *next month*

nächsten Montag *next Monday*

nächstes Jahr *next year*

Nacht (n.) **(Nächte)** *night*

Nachtisch (m.) **(Nachtische)** *dessert*

nachts *at night*

nahe *near*

am nächsten *nearest* (adverb)

nächste *nearest* (adjective)

näher *nearer*

Nähe (f.) **(Nähen)** *closeness*

in der Nähe *nearby*

Name (m.) **(Namen)** *name*

Auf welchen Namen? *Under which name?* (reservation)

Nase (f.) **(Nasen)** *nose*

naseweis *meddling, nosy*

nass *wet*

natürlich *naturally, of course*

neben *beside, next to*

Nebenzimmer (n.) **(Nebenzimmer)** *side room*

Neffe (m.) *nephew*

nehmen *to take*

das Auto nehmen *to take the car*

den Bus nehmen *to take the bus*

die Straßenbahn nehmen *to take the tram*

Nein. *No.*

nett *nice*

neu *new*

ganz neu *brand-new*

neu eröffnen *to reopen*

Was gibt's Neues? *What's new?*

neugierig *curious*

neun *nine*

neunundzwanzig *twenty-nine*

neunzehn *nineteen*

neunzig *ninety*

nicht *not*

gar nicht *not at all*

Nein, noch nicht. *No, not yet.*

nicht mehr *any more, no more*

Nicht wahr? *Isn't that right?*

Nichts passiert. *No harm done.*

Nichte (f.) **(Nichten)** *niece*

nie *never*

noch *still, yet*

Darf's sonst noch etwas sein? *Anything else?* (at a store)

Nein, noch nicht. *No, not yet.*

noch ein *another*

noch einmal *once more*

noch etwas *some more*

Was brauchen Sie sonst noch? *What else do you need?*

Notaufnahme (f.) **(Notaufnahmen)** *emergency room*

Note (f.) **(Noten)** *mark*

Notfall (m.) **(Notfälle)** *emergency*

nötig *necessary*

November (m.) **(November)** *November*

Nudeln (pl.) *noodles, pasta*

null *zero*

null Uhr *midnight*

Nummer (f.) **(Nummern)** *number, size*

meine Nummer lautet … *my (phone) number is …*

nun *now, then*

Nun … *Well …*

nur *only*

O

ob *if, whether*

Ober (m.) **(Ober)** *waiter*

Obst (n.) (no pl.) *fruit*

oder *or*
 entweder ... oder ... *either ... or ...*
öffnen *to open*
oft *often*
ohne *without*
Ohrring (m.) (Ohrringe) *earring*
Oktober (m.) (Oktober) *October*
Oma (f.) (Omas) *grandma*
Onkel (m.) (Onkel) *uncle*
Opa (m.) (Opas) *grandpa*
Orange (f.) (Orangen) *orange*
Orangensaft (m.) (Orangensäfte) *orange juice*
Ordnung (f.) (Ordnungen) *order*
 Ist alles in Ordnung? *Is everything okay?*
Österreich (n.) *Austria*

P

Paar (n.) (Paare) *pair, couple*
 ein Paar Schuhe *a pair of shoes*
 ein paar Tage *a couple of days, a few days*
Papa (m.) (Papas) *dad(dy)*
Paprika (m.) (Paprikas) *pepper (vegetable)*
Park (m.) (Parks) *park*
parken *to park*
Parkhaus (n.) (Parkhäuser) *parking garage*
 im Parkhaus parken *to park in a parking garage*
Partner/-in (m./f.) (Partner/-innen) *partner*
Party (f.) (Partys) *party*
 eine Party geben *to have a party*
passen *to fit*
 gut passen *to fit well*
 gut passen zu *to go well with*
passend *matching*
passieren *to happen*
 Nichts passiert. *No harm done.*
Patient/-in (m./f.) (Patienten/ Patientinnen) *patient*
Pause (f.) (Pausen) *break*
 eine Pause machen *to take a break*
Pausenbrot (n.) (Pausenbrote) *something to eat at break*
Pech (n.) (no pl.) *bad luck*
 So ein Pech. *Too bad.*
peinlich *embarrassing*
Penizillin (n.) (no pl.) *penicillin*
Pension (f.) (Pensionen) *pension*
 in Pension gehen *to retire*

pensioniert *retired*
perfekt *perfect*
persönlich *personally*
Pfeffer (m.) (no pl.) *pepper (spice)*
Pferd (n.) (Pferde) *horse*
pflanzen *to plant*
Pflaster (n.) (Pflaster) *adhesive bandage*
Pfund (n.) (Pfunde) *pound*
 ein Pfund Tomaten *a pound of tomatoes*
Pianist/-in (m./f.) (Pianisten/ Pianistinnen) *pianist*
Picknick (n.) (Picknicke) *picnic*
 ein Picknick machen *to have a picnic*
Plan (m.) (Pläne) *plan*
 Pläne machen *to make plans*
Polizei (f.) (no pl.) *police*
Post (f.) (no pl.) *post office*
Praktikum (n.) (Praktika) *internship*
Praxis (f.) (Praxen) *practice, doctor's office*
Preis (m.) (Preise) *price*
prima *great, top-quality*
 Prima! *Great!*
pro *per*
probieren *to try*
Problem (n.) (Probleme) *problem*
 Kein Problem. *No problem.*
Programm (n.) (Programme) *program*
Projekt (n.) (Projekte) *project*
Prozent (n.) (Prozente) *percent*
Prüfung (f.) (Prüfungen) *exam*
Psychologie (f.) (Psychologien) *psychology*
pünktlich *punctual*
Pullover (m.) (Pullover) *sweater*

R

Rad (n.) (Räder) *bike*
 Rad fahren *to bike*
Radio (n.) (Radios) *radio*
Radiosprecher/-in (m./f.) (Radiosprecher/- innen) *radio announcer*
Radtour (f.) (Radtouren) *bike tour*
Rat (m.) (Räte) *advice*
Rate (f.) (Raten) *rate*
Rathaus (n.) (Rathäuser) *town hall*
rauchen *to smoke*
raus *out*
Realschule (f.) (Realschulen) *middle school (fifth grade through tenth grade)*

Realschulprüfung (f.)
  (Realschulprüfungen) *middle school exam*
  die Realschulprüfung machen *to take the
    middle school exam*
Rechnung (f.) **(Rechnungen)** *bill, check, invoice*
Recht (n.) **(Rechte)** *right*
  Recht haben *to be right*
rechts *right, to the right*
  rechts abbiegen *to turn right*
Rechtsanwalt/Rechtsanwältin (m./f.)
  (Rechtsanwälte/Rechtsanwältinnen) *lawyer*
Redakteur/-in (m./f.) **(Redakteure/
  Redakteurinnen)** *editor*
reden *to talk*
Regal (n.) **(Regale)** *shelf*
Regen (m.) (no pl.) *rain*
Regenwetter (n.) **(Regenwetter)** *rainy weather*
  bei Regenwetter *in rainy weather*
regnen *to rain*
  Es regnet. *It is raining.*
reich *rich*
Reis (m.) (no pl.) *rice*
rennen *to run*
Rente (f.) **(Renten)** *retirement*
  in Rente gehen *to retire*
reservieren *to reserve*
  einen Tisch reservieren *to reserve a table, to
    make reservations*
Reservierung (f.)
  (Reservierungen) *reservation*
Restaurant (n.) **(Restaurants)** *restaurant*
Retrospektive (f.)
  (Retrospektiven) *retrospective*
Rezept (n.) **(Rezepte)** *prescription*
richtig *right, correct; really*
Richtung (f.) **(Richtungen)** *direction*
  Fahren Sie in Richtung München. *Drive
    towards/in the direction of Munich.*
Rinderbraten (m.) **(Rinderbraten)** *roast beef*
Rindfleisch (n.) (no pl.) *beef*
Rivale/Rivalin (m./f.) **(Rivalen/
  Rivalinnen)** *rival*
Rock (m.) **(Röcke)** *skirt*
Roman (m.) **(Romane)** *novel*
rosa *pink*
Rose (f.) **(Rosen)** *rose*
Rostbraten (m.) **(Rostbraten)** *roast*
rot *red*

Rotwein (m.) **(Rotweine)** *red wine*
rufen *to call, to yell*
  den Arzt rufen *to call a doctor*

S

Saft (m.) **(Säfte)** *juice*
sagen *to say*
Salami (f.) **(Salamis)** *salami*
Salat (m.) **(Salate)** *salad, lettuce*
Salz (n.) **(Salze)** *salt*
sammeln *to collect*
Samstag (m.) **(Samstage)** *Saturday*
Satz (m.) **(Sätze)** *sentence*
sauer *sour*
Sauerbraten (m.) **(Sauerbraten)** *braised beef*
Sauerkraut (n.) (no pl.) *sauerkraut*
Schal (m.) **(Schale, Schals)** *scarf*
Schatz (m.) **(Schätze)** *treasure, darling,
  sweetheart*
scheinen *to shine*
schenken *to give (as a gift)*
schicken *to send*
Schiff (n.) **(Schiffe)** *ship*
Schifffahrt (f.) **(Schifffahrten)** *cruise*
Schild (n.) **(Schilder)** *sign, signpost*
Schinken (m.) **(Schinken)** *ham*
Schirm (m.) **(Schirme)** *umbrella*
schlafen *to sleep*
Schlafzimmer (n.) **(Schlafzimmer)** *bedroom*
Schläger (m.) **(Schläger)** *racquet*
schlank *slim*
schlecht *bad*
  Sie sehen schlecht aus. *You look bad/sick.*
schließlich *after all*
Schlittschuh (m.) **(Schlittschuhe)** *ice skate*
  Schlittschuh laufen *to go ice-skating*
Schlüssel (m.) **(Schlüssel)** *key*
Schluss (m.) **(Schlüsse)** *end*
Schlusssatz (m.) **(Schlusssätze)** *final sentence*
schmecken *to taste, to be to one's taste*
Schmerz (m.) **(Schmerzen)** *pain*
  Schmerzen haben *to be in pain*
Schnee (m.) (no pl.) *snow*
Schneewetter (n.) (no pl.) *snowy weather*
  bei Schneewetter *in snowy weather*
schneiden *to cut*
schneien *to snow*
  Es schneit. *It is snowing.*

schnell *fast, quick*
schnelllebig *fast-paced*
Schnitzel (n.) (Schnitzel) *cutlet*
Schnupfen (m.) (Schnupfen) *cold*
  Schnupfen haben *to have a runny nose, to*
  have a cold
Schokolade (f.) (Schokoladen) *chocolate*
schon *already, yet, even, certainly*
  schon, aber ... *yes, but ...*
  Schon gut. *It's okay.*
schön *beautiful, nice*
  Danke schön. *Thank you.*
schonen *to save, to conserve*
  sich schonen *to take it easy*
Schrank (m.) (Schränke) *closet*
schreiben *to write*
  den Lebenslauf schreiben *to prepare one's*
  résumé
Schreibtisch (m.) (Schreibtische) *desk*
Schüler/-in (m./f.) (Schüler/-innen) *pupil,*
  schoolboy/girl
Schuh (m.) (Schuhe) *shoe*
  ein Paar Schuhe *a pair of shoes*
Schuhabteilung (f.) (Schuhabteilungen) *shoe*
  department
Schuhgeschäft (n.) (Schuhgeschäfte) *shoe*
  store
schulden *to owe*
Schule (f.) (Schulen) *school*
Schulter (f.) (Schultern) *shoulder*
Schwager (m.) (Schwäger) *brother-in-law*
Schwägerin (f.) (Schwägerinnen) *sister-in-law*
schwanger *pregnant*
  schwanger sein *to be pregnant*
schwarz *black*
Schweinefleisch (n.) (no pl.) *pork*
Schwester (f.) (Schwestern) *sister*
Schwesterchen (n.) (Schwesterchen) *little*
  sister
Schwiegermutter (f.)
  (Schwiegermütter) *mother-in-law*
Schwiegervater (m.) (Schwiegerväter) *father-*
  in-law
schwierig *difficult*
Schwimmbad (n.) (Schwimmbäder) *public pool*
schwimmen *to swim*
sechs *six*
sechsundzwanzig *twenty-six*

sechzehn *sixteen*
sechzig *sixty*
sehen *to see*
sehr *very*
  Bitte sehr. *Here you go.*
  Sehr gut. *Very well.*
sein *to be; his, its*
  Ich bin's. *It's me.*
  tätig sein *to work*
  Wie wär's mit ... *How about ...*
seit *since, for*
Seite (f.) (Seiten) *page*
Sekt (m.) (Sekte) *champagne, sparkling wine*
selbstständig *self-employed*
selbstverständlich *of course*
September (m.) (September) *September*
Service (n.) (no pl.) *service*
servieren *to serve*
Serviette (f.) (Servietten) *napkin*
Servus. *Hello.*
setzen *to sit, to place, to put*
  sich setzen *to sit down*
Show (f.) (Shows) *show*
sich *yourself* (sg. fml.), *himself, herself, itself,*
  yourselves (pl. fml.), *themselves*
  sich schonen *to take it easy*
  sich setzen *to sit down*
  sich treffen *to meet*
sicher *sure, certain*
Sie *you* (sg. fml./pl. fml.) (nominative); *you* (sg. fml./
  pl. fml.) (accusative)
sie *she, they* (nominative); *her, them* (accusative)
sieben *seven*
siebenundzwanzig *twenty-seven*
siebzehn *seventeen*
siebzig *seventy*
singen *to sing*
sitzen *to sit*
Ski (m.) (Ski, Skier) *ski*
  Ski fahren *to go skiing*
Skifahren (n.) *skiing*
Skigebiet (n.) (Skigebiete) *ski resort*
Snowboard (n.) (Snowboards) *snowboard*
snowboarden *to snowboard*
so *so*
  Ach so. *I see.*
  so ... wie *as ... as*
  So ein Pech. *Too bad.*

Stimmt so. *That's correct./Keep the change.*
Socken (pl.) *socks*
Sofa (n.) **(Sofas)** *couch*
sofort *at once, right away*
sogar *even*
Sohn (m.) **(Söhne)** *son*
sollen *ought to*
Sommer (m.) **(Sommer)** *summer*
  im Sommer *in the summer*
Sommerurlaub (m.) **(Sommerurlaube)** *summer vacation*
Sonderangebot (n.) **(Sonderangebote)** *special offer*
  im Sonderangebot *on sale*
Sonne (f.) **(Sonnen)** *sun*
Sonntag (m.) **(Sonntage)** *Sunday*
sonst *else*
  Sonst noch etwas? *Anything else?*
  Was brauchen Sie sonst noch? *What else do you need?*
Sorge (f.) *worry*
  Keine Sorge. *No worries./Don't worry.*
Spaß (m.) **(Späße)** *fun*
  Spaß machen *to be fun*
  Viel Spaß! *Enjoy!/Have fun!*
spät *late*
  Wie spät ist es? *What is the time?*
  spät aufstehen *to get up late*
später *later*
spazieren *to stroll*
  spazieren gehen *to go for a walk*
Speisekarte (f.) **(Speisekarten)** *menu*
Spezialität (f.) **(Spezialitäten)** *specialty*
Spiegel (m.) **(Spiegel)** *mirror*
Spiel (n.) **(Spiele)** *game*
spielen *to play*
  Fußball spielen *to play soccer*
  Gitarre spielen *to play the guitar*
  Karten spielen *to play cards*
Spielzeug (n.) **(Spielzeuge)** *toy*
Spinat (m.) (no pl.) *spinach*
Sport (m.) (no pl.) *sport*
  Sport treiben *to play sports*
Sportart (f.) **(Sportarten)** *sport*
Sportler/-in (m./f.) **(Sportler/-innen)** *athlete*
Sportstudio (n.) **(Sportstudios)** *sports center*
sprechen *to speak*
Spritze (f.) **(Spritzen)** *shot (medical), syringe*

Squash (n.) (no pl.) *squash*
  Squash spielen *to play squash*
Stadion (n.) **(Stadien)** *stadium*
Stadt (f.) **(Städte)** *city, town*
  in der Stadt *around town*
Stadtplan (m.) **(Stadtpläne)** *(city) map*
Stadtrundfahrt (f.) **(Stadtrundfahrten)** *city tour*
  eine Stadtrundfahrt machen *to take a city tour*
ständig *constantly*
stark *strong*
Statistik (f.) **(Statistiken)** *statistics*
statt *instead of*
Stau (m.) **(Staus)** *traffic jam, stopped traffic*
  im Stau stecken *to be stuck in traffic*
  im Stau stehen *to be stopped in traffic*
Steak (n.) **(Steaks)** *steak*
stecken *to be stuck*
  im Stau stecken *to be stuck in traffic*
stehen *to stand, to suit*
  gut stehen *to look good on (somebody)*
  im Stau stehen *to be stopped in traffic*
steigen *to climb, to rise, to increase*
  Berg steigen *to go mountain climbing*
Stelle (f.) **(Stellen)** *place, position, job*
  sich auf eine Stelle bewerben *to apply for a job, to apply for a position*
stellen *to place, to put*
Stellenanzeige (f.) **(Stellenanzeigen)** *job announcement, help-wanted ad*
Stellenmarkt (m.) **(Stellenmärkte)** *job announcements, help-wanted ads; job market*
Stiefel (m.) **(Stiefel)** *boots*
still *quiet*
Stimme (f.) **(Stimmen)** *voice*
stimmen *to be right*
  Das stimmt! *That's true!*
  Stimmt so. *That's correct./Keep the change.*
stolz *proud*
Straße (f.) **(Straßen)** *street*
  zwei Straßen weiter *two blocks farther*
Straßenbahn (f.) **(Straßenbahnen)** *street car*
  die Straßenbahn nehmen *to take the tram*
  mit der Straßenbahn *by tram*
stricken *to knit*
Student/-in (m./f.) **(Studenten/-innen)** *student*
studieren *to study (at a university)*

Studium (n.) **(Studien)** *study, studies*
Stück (n.) **(Stücke)** *piece*
  am Stück *in one piece*
  ein Stück Kuchen *a piece of cake*
Stuhl (m.) **(Stühle)** *chair*
Stunde (f.) **(Stunden)** *hour*
  in einer Stunde *in an hour*
  vor einer Stunde *an hour ago*
suchen *to search, to look for*
Südafrika (n.) *South Africa*
süß *sweet*
süßsauer *sweet-and-sour*
Süßspeise (f.) **(Süßspeisen)** *sweets, dessert*
super *super, great*
Supermarkt (m.) **(Supermärkte)** *grocery store*
Suppe (f.) **(Suppen)** *soup*
  ein Teller Suppe *a bowl of soup*

T

Tablette (f.) **(Tabletten)** *pill*
Tag (m.) **(Tage)** *day*
  den ganzen Tag *all day*
  ein paar Tage *a couple of days, a few days*
  Guten Tag. *Hello./Good day.*
  jeden Tag *every day*
Tageszeitung (f.) **(Tageszeitungen)** *daily newspaper*
täglich *daily*
  tägliches Leben *everyday life*
Tango (m.) **(Tangos)** *tango*
tanken *to get gas*
Tankstelle (f.) **(Tankstellen)** *gas station*
Tankwart/-in (m./f.) **(Tankwarte/-innen)** *gas station attendant*
Tante (f.) **(Tanten)** *aunt*
tanzen *to dance*
Tasche (f.) **(Taschen)** *bag*
Taschengeld (n.) **(Taschengelder)** *allowance*
Tasse (f.) **(Tassen)** *cup*
  eine Tasse Kaffee *a cup of coffee*
tätig *active*
  freiberuflich tätig sein *to freelance*
  tätig sein *to work*
tauchen *to (scuba) dive*
tausend *thousand*
  eintausend *one thousand*
  eintausendeinhundert *one thousand one hundred*

hunderttausend *one hundred thousand*
zehntausend *ten thousand*
zweitausend *two thousand*
Taxi (n.) **(Taxis; Taxen)** *taxi*
  ein Taxi rufen *to call a cab*
  mit dem Taxi fahren *to go by cab*
Taxifahrer (m.) **(Taxifahrer)** *taxi driver*
Teilzeit (f.) **(no pl.)** *part-time*
Teilzeitbeschäftigung (f.) **(Teilzeitbeschäftigungen)** *part-time employment*
Telefon (n.) **(Telefone)** *telephone*
telefonieren *to call*
Telefonnummer (f.) **(Telefonnummern)** *phone number*
Teller (m.) **(Teller)** *plate, bowl*
  ein Teller Suppe *a bowl of soup*
Temperatur (f.) **(Temperaturen)** *temperature*
  erhöhte Temperatur *elevated temperature*
Tennis (n.) **(no pl.)** *tennis*
  Tennis spielen *to play tennis*
Tennisschläger (m.) **(Tennisschläger)** *tennis racquet*
Tennisschuhe (pl.) *tennis shoes*
Termin (m.) **(Termine)** *appointment*
Terrasse (f.) **(Terrassen)** *terrace*
teuer *expensive*
Tisch (m.) **(Tische)** *table*
  einen Tisch bestellen *to reserve a table, to make reservations*
  einen Tisch reservieren *to reserve a table, to make reservations*
Tischler/-in (m./f.) **(Tischler/-innen)** *carpenter*
Tochter (f.) **(Töchter)** *daughter*
Toilette (f.) **(Toiletten)** *bathroom, toilet*
Tomate (f.) **(Tomaten)** *tomato*
  ein Pfund Tomaten *a pound of tomatoes*
Ton (m.) **(no pl.)** *clay*
töpfern *to make pottery*
Tourist/-in (m./f.) **(Touristen/Touristinnen)** *tourist*
tragen *to wear*
Traube (f.) **(Trauben)** *bunch of grapes*
Traum (m.) **(Träume)** *dream*
traurig *sad*
treffen *to hit*
  sich treffen *to meet*
treiben *to drive, to do*

Sport treiben *to play sports*
trinken *to drink*
Trinkgeld (n.) (Trinkgelder) *tip*
  ein Trinkgeld geben *to leave a tip, to tip*
  Ist das Trinkgeld inklusive? *Is the tip included?*
Tropfen (m.) (Tropfen) *drop*
trotz *despite*
trotzdem *nevertheless*
Tschüss. *Bye.*
Tür (f.) (Türen) *door*
tun *to do*
  (Es) tut mir leid. *I'm sorry.*
  viel zu tun haben *to have a lot to do*

U

über *over, above, across, about*
übermorgen *the day after tomorrow*
Überstunde (f.) (Überstunden) *overtime*
  Überstunden machen *to work overtime*
Uhr (f.) (Uhren) *clock, watch, o'clock*
  Es ist sechs Uhr fünfzehn. *It is six fifteen.*
  Es ist vier Uhr dreißig. *It is four thirty.*
  Es ist zehn Uhr. *It's ten o'clock.*
  null Uhr *midnight*
  um ein Uhr *at one o'clock*
  um fünf Uhr *at five o' clock*
  Wieviel Uhr ist es? *What time is it?*
Uhrzeit (f.) (Uhrzeiten) *time, time of day*
  Um welche Uhrzeit? *For what time? (reservation)*
um *at, around, about*
  um ein Uhr *at one o'clock*
  um fünf Uhr *at five o' clock*
umdrehen *to make a U-turn, to turn around*
umgehen *to circulate, to be going around*
  Die Grippe geht um. *The flu is going around.*
Umkleidekabine (f.) (Umkleidekabinen) *fitting room*
umsteigen *to change trains/buses*
umtauschen *to (ex)change*
und *and*
  Na und? *So what?*
Universität (f.) (Universitäten) *university*
uns *us* (accusative); *us, to us* (dative); *ourselves*
unser *our*
unter *under, beneath, among*
unterbrechen *to interrupt*

Unterhaltung (f.) (Unterhaltungen) *entertainment*
Unterricht (m.) (no pl.) *lessons*
unterrichten *to teach*
untersuchen *to examine*
unterwegs *on the way*
  unterwegs sein *to be on the way (baby)*
Urlaub (m.) (Urlaube) *vacation*
  (sich) Urlaub nehmen *to take a vacation, take leave*
  Urlaub machen *to go on vacation*
Urlaubsplan (m.) (Urlaubspläne) *vacation plans*
Ursache (f.) (Ursachen) *cause, reason, motive*
  Keine Ursache! *Don't mention it!*

V

Vase (f.) (Vasen) *vase*
Vater (m.) (Väter) *father*
verabreden *to arrange*
Verabredung (f.) (Verabredungen) *appointment, date*
  eine Verabredung machen (Verabredungen machen) *to make an appointment*
Verband (m.) (Verbände) *bandage*
  einen Verband anlegen *to put on a bandage*
verbessern *to improve*
verbinden *to connect*
Verbindung (f.) (Verbindungen) *connection*
Verein (m.) (Vereine) *club*
  einem Verein beitreten *to join a club*
vereinbaren *to arrange*
vergessen *to forget*
verheiratet *married*
  verheiratet sein *to be married*
verkaufen *to sell*
Verkäufer/-in (m./f.) (Verkäufer/-innen) *salesperson*
Verkehr (m.) (no pl.) *traffic*
Verkehrsdurchsage (f.) (Verkehrsdurchsagen) *traffic announcement*
verleihen *to lend*
verletzen *to hurt, to injure*
  sich verletzen *to hurt oneself*
verlobt *engaged*
  verlobt sein *to be engaged*
verpassen *to miss*
verschieben *to move, to postpone*
verschreiben *to prescribe*

verstehen *to understand*
Verzeihung (f.) (Verzeihungen) *forgiveness*
  Verzeihung. *Forgive me.*
viel *much, a lot*
  Viel Glück! *Good luck!*
  Viel Spaß! *Enjoy!/Have fun!*
  viel zu lernen haben *to have a lot to learn*
  viel zu tun haben *to have a lot to do*
viele *many*
  Vielen Dank. *Many thanks.*
  Vielen Dank für die Blumen! *Thanks for
    the compliment! (lit., Thanks for the flowers.
    [often used ironically])*
vielleicht *maybe*
vier *four*
viertel *quarter*
  Es ist viertel nach drei. *It is quarter past
    three.*
  Es ist viertel vor drei. *It is quarter to three.*
Viertel (n.) (Viertel) *quarter*
  akademische Viertel *academic quarter*
Viertelstunde (f.) (Viertelstunden) *quarter of
  an hour*
  nur noch ein Viertelstündchen *just another
    fifteen minutes*
vierundzwanzig *twenty-four*
vierzehn *fourteen*
vierzig *forty*
violet *purple*
voll *full*
Volleyball (m.) (no pl.) *volleyball (game)*
  Volleyball spielen *to play volleyball*
Vollzeitbeschäftigug (f.)
  (Vollzeitbeschäftigungen) *full-time
  employment*
Volontariat (n.) (Valontariate) *internship
  (newspaper)*
  ein Volontariat machen *to intern at a
    newspaper*
vom (von + dem) *from/by the*
von *from, by*
  von … bis *from … to*
vor *in front of, before, ago*
  Es ist viertel vor drei. *It is quarter to three.*
  Es ist zehn vor zwölf. *It is ten to twelve.*
  vor einer Stunde *an hour ago*
vorbei *over, finished*
vorbereiten *to prepare*

Vorgesetzte (m./f.) (Vorgesetzten) *superior*
vorgestern *the day before yesterday*
vorhin *a little while ago*
vorlesen *to read to, to read out loud*
vorletzte *the … before last*
Vorsicht (f.) (no pl.) *caution, attention*
  Vorsicht! *Careful!*
Vorspeise (f.) (Vorspeisen) *appetizer*
  als Vorspeise *as an appetizer*

W

Waage (f.) (Waagen) *scale*
  auf die Waage legen *to put on the scale*
Wahl (f.) (Wahlen) *choice*
wahr *true, real*
  Nicht wahr? *Isn't that right?*
während *during*
wandern *to hike*
wann *when*
warm *warm*
  Es ist warm. *It is warm.*
warten *to wait*
  warten auf *to wait for*
warum *why*
was *what*
waschen *to wash*
  sich waschen *to wash oneself*
Wasser (n.) (Wasser; Wässer) *water*
wechseln *to (ex)change*
Weg (m.) (Wege) *way, path*
wegen *because*
weh tun *to hurt*
Weihnachten (n.) (Weihnachten) *Christmas*
weil *because*
Wein (m.) (Weine) *wine*
  eine Flasche Wein *a bottle of wine*
  ein Glas Wein *a glass of wine*
weinen *to cry (tears)*
Weinkarte (f.) (Weinkarten) *wine list*
weiß *white*
Weißwein (m.) (Weißweine) *white wine*
weit *far*
  Wie weit … ? *How far … ?*
weiter *farther*
  zwei Straßen weiter *two blocks farther*
welcher *which*
  welche Größe (f.) *what size*
Welt (f.) (Welten) *world*

wenig *little*
wenige *few*
weniger *less*
wenn *if, when*
wer *who*
werden *to become, to happen*
  geschieden werden *to get divorced*
  Willst du mein Mann werden? *Will you marry me? (lit., Will you be my husband?)*
  Willst du meine Frau werden? *Will you marry me? (lit., Will you be my wife?)*
wessen *whose*
Wetter (n.) **(Wetter)** *weather*
  bei gutem Wetter *in good weather*
  bei schlechtem Wetter *in bad weather*
WG (f.) **(WGs)** *shared flat*
wichtig *important*
wie *how, as*
  Wie alt sind Sie? *How old are you?*
  Wie bitte? *Excuse me/I'm sorry?*
  Wie geht es Ihnen? *How are you?* (fml.)
  Wie geht's? *How are you?* (infml.)
  Wie heißen Sie? *What's your name?* (fml.)
  Wie wär's mit … *How about …*
  wie immer *as always*
  Wie wär's mit … *How about …*
wieder *again*
  Wie kann ich das wieder gut machen? *How can I make this up to you?*
wiederholen *to repeat*
wiedersehen *to see again*
  Auf Wiedersehen. *Goodbye.*
  Auf Wiedersehen bis dann. *Good-bye until then.*
wiegen *to weigh*
wie viel *how much*
  Wie viel Uhr ist es? *What time is it?*
wie viele *how many*
Willkommen. *Welcome.*
  Willkommen zurück. *Welcome back.*
Winter (m.) **(Winter)** *winter*
  im Winter *in the winter*
Winterurlaub (m.) **(Winterurlaube)** *winter vacation*
wir *we*
wirklich *really*
  Wirklich? *Really?*
wissen *to know (facts)*

  Nicht dass ich wüsste. *Not that I know of.*
  Woher wusstest du das? *How did you know that?*
Wissenschaftler/-in (m./f.) **(Wissenschaftler/-innen)** *scientist, academic*
wo *where*
  Wo kommen Sie her? *Where are you from?*
Woche (f.) **(Wochen)** *week*
  letzte Woche *last week*
  nächste Woche *next week*
  pro Woche *per week*
Wochenende (n.) **(Wochenenden)** *weekend*
  am Wochenende *on the weekend*
woher *where from*
  Woher kommen Sie? *Where are you from?*
  Woher wusstest du das? *How did you know that?*
wohl *well*
  Auf dein Wohl! *To your health!*
  sich wohl fühlen *to feel well*
  Zum Wohl! *Cheers! (lit., To wellness!)*
wohlhabend *wealthy, prosperous*
wohnen *to reside, to live*
  Ich wohne in Berlin. *I live in Berlin.*
  Wo wohnen Sie? *Where do you live?*
Wohngemeinschaft (f.) **(Wohngemeinschaften)** *shared flat*
Wohnung (f.) **(Wohnungen)** *apartment*
Wohnzimmer (n.) **(Wohnzimmer)** *living room*
wollen *to want to*
wünschen *to wish*
Wunde (f.) **(Wunden)** *wound*
  Wunde auswaschen *to clean the wound*
Wurstaufschnitt (m.) (no pl.) *cold cuts*

Y

Yoga (m./n.) (no pl.) *yoga*
Yogastudio (n.) **(Yogastudios)** *Yoga studio*

Z

Zahn (m.) **(Zähne)** *tooth*
Zahnarzt/Zahnärztin (m./f.) **(Zahnärzte/Zahnärztinnen)** *dentist*
Zahnschmerzen (pl.) *toothache*
Zahnweh (n.) (no pl.) *toothache*
  Zahnweh haben *to have a toothache*
Zehe (f.) **(Zehen)** *toe*
zehn *ten*

zeichnen *to draw*
zeigen *to show*
Zeit (f.) (Zeiten) *time*
Zeitung (f.) (Zeitungen) *newspaper*
Zeitungsartikel (m.)
(Zeitungsartikel) *newspaper article*
Zeugnis (n.) (Zeugnisse) *report card*
ziehen *to pull*
Zimmer (n.) (Zimmer) *room*
zu *to, towards* (preposition); *too* (adverb)
um ... zu *in order to*
zu etwas Lust haben *to feel like doing something*
zu Mittag essen *to have lunch*
Zucker (m.) (no pl.) *sugar*
zuckersüß *sugar sweet*
zuerst *first*
Zufall (m.) (Zufälle) *coincidence*
Zug (m.) (Züge) *train*
Zuhause (n.) (no pl.) *home*
zuhören *to listen*
zum (zu + dem) *to/toward the*
Zum Wohl! *Cheers! (lit., To wellness!)*
zumachen *to close*
zur (zu + der) *to/toward the*
zurück *back*
Willkommen zurück. *Welcome back.*
zurückrufen *to call back*
zusammen *together*
Alles zusammen? *One check? (at a restaurant)*
Zuschauer/-in (m./f.) (Zuschauer/-innen) *viewer*
zwanzig *twenty*
zwei *two*
zweiundzwanzig *twenty-two*
Zwiebel (f.) (Zwiebeln) *onion*
zwischen *between*
zwölf *twelve*

English-German

A

a/an *ein*
able to (to be) *können*
about *etwa, um, über*
above *über*
academic *akademisch*
academic quarter *akademische Viertel* (n.)
according to *laut*
accountant *Buchhalter/-in* (m./f.) (*Buchhalter/-innen*)
achieve (to) *leisten*
acquainted with (to become) *kennenlernen*
across *über*
across from *gegenüber*
active *tätig*
addition (in addition) *außerdem*
address *Adresse* (f.) (*Adressen*)
admire (to) *bewundern*
advice *Rat* (m.) (*Räte*)
Africa *Afrika* (n.)
after *nach*
after all *schließlich*
It is ten after twelve. *Es ist zehn nach zwölf.*
afternoon *Nachmittag* (m.) (*Nachmittage*)
in the afternoon *am Nachmittag, nachmittags*
afterwards *danach*
again *wieder*
see again (to) *wiedersehen*
against *gegen*
age *Alter* (n.) (*Alter*)
at the age of *im Alter von*
ago *vor*
a little while ago *vorhin*
an hour ago *vor einer Stunde*
many years ago *vor vielen Jahren*
airport *Flughafen* (m.) (*Flughäfen*)
all *alle*
all day *den ganzen Tag*
allergic *allergisch*
allergic to cats (to be) *gegen Katzen allergisch sein*
allow (to) *lassen*
allowed to (to be) *dürfen*
allowance *Taschengeld* (n.) (*Taschengelder*)
almost *fast*

already *schon*
also *auch*
alter (to) *ändern*
always *immer*
　as always *wie immer*
amateur filmmaker *Amateur-Filmemacher/-in* (m./f.) *(Amateur-Filmemacher/-innen)*
amateur photographer *Hobbyfotograf/-in* (m./f.) *(Hobbyfotografen/Hobbyfotografinnen)*
amazing *erstaunlich*
America *Amerika* (n.)
American *Amerikaner/-in* (m./f.) *(Amerikaner/-innen)*
among *unter*
amount to (to) *machen*
and *und*
angry *böse*
ankle *Knöchel* (m.) *(Knöchel)*
announce (to) *ansagen*
annoy (to) *ärgern*
　annoyed (to be) *sich ärgern*
annoying *lästig*
another *andere, noch ein*
answer *Antwort* (f.) *(Antworten)*
　What's the right answer? *Wie lautet die richtige Antwort?*
answer (to) *antworten*
answering machine *Anrufbeantworter* (m.) *(Anrufbeantworter)*
apartment *Wohnung* (f.) *(Wohnungen)*
apologize (to) *entschuldigen*
apparatus *Apparat* (m.) *(Apparate)*
appear (to) *aussehen*
appetite *Appetit* (m.) (no pl.)
appetizer *Vorspeise* (f.) *(Vorspeisen)*
　as an appetizer *als Vorspeise*
apple *Apfel* (m.) *(Äpfel)*
apple juice *Apfelsaft* (m.) *(Apfelsäfte)*
apply (to) *bewerben*
　apply for a job/position (to) *sich auf eine Stelle bewerben*
appointment *Termin* (m.) *(Termine), Verabredung* (f.) *(Verabredungen)*
　make an appointment (to) *eine Verabredung machen (Verabredungen machen)*
apprentice *Auszubildende* (m./f.) *(Auszubildenden), Azubi* (m./f.) *(Azubis)*
apprentice (to) *eine Ausbildung machen*

apprenticeship *Ausbildungsstelle* (f.) *(Ausbildungsstellen), Ausbildung* (f.) *(Ausbildungen)*
approach (to) *herangehen*
approve (to) *genehmigen*
approximately *etwa*
April *April* (m.) *(Aprile)*
architect *Architekt/-in* (m./f.) *(Architekten/Architektinnen)*
arm *Arm* (m.) *(Arme)*
around *um, herum*
　around the corner *um die Ecke*
　around town *in der Stadt*
　going around (to be) *umgehen*
　know one's way around (to) *sich auskennen*
　turn around (to) (U-turn) *umdrehen*
arrange (to) *verabreden, vereinbaren*
arrive (to) *ankommen*
article *Artikel* (m.) *(Artikel)*
as *wie, als*
　as … as *so … wie*
　as always *wie immer*
ask (to) *fragen*
aspirin *Aspirin* (n.) (no pl.)
assistant *Assistent/-in* (m./f.) *(Assistenten/Assistentinnen)*
at *um, bei, an*
　at five o' clock *um fünf Uhr*
　at once *sofort*
　at one o'clock *um ein Uhr*
　at the corner *an der Ecke*
athlete *Sportler/-in* (m./f.) *(Sportler/-innen)*
attention *Vorsicht* (f.) (no pl.)
　Pay attention! *Pass auf!*
August *August* (m.) *(Auguste)*
aunt *Tante* (f.) *(Tanten)*
Austria *Österreich* (n.)

B

baby *Kind* (n.) *(Kinder)*
　have a baby (to) *ein Kind bekommen*
back *zurück*
　in back of *hinter*
　Welcome back. *Willkommen zurück.*
bad *schlecht, böse*
　bad luck *Pech* (n.) (no pl.)
　Too bad. *So ein Pech.*
　You look bad/sick. *Sie sehen schlecht aus.*

bag *Tasche* (f.) *(Taschen)*
bake (to) *backen*
baker *Bäcker/-in* (m.) *(Bäcker/Bäckerinnen)*
bakery *Bäckerei* (f.) *(Bäckereien)*
balcony *Balkon* (m.) *(Balkone)*
ball *Ball* (m.) *(Bälle)*
ballet classes *Ballettunterricht* (m.) (no pl.)
banana *Banane* (f.) *(Bananen)*
bandage *Verband* (m.) *(Verbände)*
  bandage (adhesive bandage) *Pflaster* (n.)
    (Pflaster)
  put on a bandage (to) *Verband anlegen*
bank (financial institution) *Bank* (f.) *(Banken)*
bar (neighborhood bar) *Kneipe* (f.) *(Kneipen)*
basketball (game) *Basketball* (m.) (no pl.)
  play basketball (to) *Basketball spielen*
bathroom *Bad* (n.) *(Bäder)*, *Badezimmer* (n.)
    (Badezimmer), *Toilette* (f.) *(Toiletten)*
be (to) *sein, lauten*
beautiful *schön*
because *wegen, weil, denn*
become (to) *werden*
bed *Bett* (n.) *(Betten)*
  go to bed (to) *ins Bett gehen*
bedroom *Schlafzimmer* (n.) *(Schlafzimmer)*
beef *Rindfleisch* (n.) (no pl.)
  braised beef *Sauerbraten* (m.) *(Sauerbraten)*
beer *Bier* (n.) *(Biere)*
before *vor*
begin (to) *anfangen, beginnen*
behind *hinter*
believe (to) *glauben*
belly *Bauch* (m.) *(Bäuche)*
belong to (to) *gehören*
belt *Gürtel* (m.) *(Gürtel)*
bench *Bank* (f.) *(Bänke)*
beneath *unter*
beside *neben*
best (adjective) *liebste, beste*
  best (adverb) *am liebsten, am besten*
better *lieber, besser*
between *zwischen*
  in between *dazwischen*
beverage *Getränk* (n.) *(Getränke)*
bicycle *Fahrrad* (n.) *(Fahrräder)*
  ride a bicycle (to) *Fahrrad fahren*
big *groß*
  bigger *größer*

biggest (adjective) *größte*
biggest (adverb) *am größten*
bike *Rad* (n.) *(Räder)*
  bike (to) *Rad fahren*
bike tour *Radtour* (f.) *(Radtouren)*
bill *Rechnung* (f.) *(Rechnungen)*
billion *Milliarde* (f.) *(Milliarden)*
biology *Biologie* (f.) (no pl.)
birthday *Geburtstag* (m.) *(Geburtstage)*
  Happy birthday! *Alles Gute zum Geburtstag!*
black *schwarz*
blouse *Bluse* (f.) *(Blusen)*
blue *blau*
bologna *Lyoner* (f.) (no pl.)
book *Buch* (n.) *(Bücher)*
book page *Buchseite* (f.) *(Buchseiten)*
booked out *ausgebucht*
boots *Stiefel* (m.) *(Stiefel)*
borrow (to) *leihen*
boss *Boss* (m.) *(Bosse)*, *Chef/-in* (m./f.) *(Chefs/*
    Chefinnen)
both *beide*
bottle *Flasche* (f.) *(Flaschen)*
  a bottle of mineral water *eine Flasche*
    Mineralwasser
  a bottle of wine *eine Flasche Wein*
boutique *Boutique* (f.) *(Boutiquen)*
bowl *Teller* (m.) *(Teller)*
  a bowl of soup *ein Teller Suppe*
boy *Junge* (m.) *(Jungen)*
boyfriend *Freund* (m.) *(Freunde)*
braised beef *Sauerbraten* (m.) *(Sauerbraten)*
brand-new *ganz neu*
bread *Brot* (n.) *(Brote)*
  a loaf of bread *ein Laib Brot*
break *Pause* (f.) *(Pausen)*
  take a break (to) *eine Pause machen*
break (to) *brechen*
breakfast *Frühstück* (n.) *(Frühstücke)*
breakfast roll *Brötchen* (n.) *(Brötchen)*
bring (to) *bringen*
  bring along (to) *mitbringen*
broken *kaputt*
brother *Bruder* (m.) *(Brüder)*
brother-in-law *Schwager* (m.) *(Schwäger)*
brown *braun*
brunch *Brunch* (m.) *(Brunches/Brunche)*
bus *Bus* (m.) *(Busse)*

by bus *mit dem Bus*
take the bus (to) *den Bus nehmen*
bus stop *Bushaltestelle* (f.) *(Bushaltestellen)*
business *Geschäft* (n.) *(Geschäfte)*
  run a business (to) *ein Geschäft leiten*
business trip *Geschäftsreise* (f.)
  (Geschäftsreisen)
businessman *Geschäftsmann* (m.)
  (Geschäftsmänner)
busy (phone line) *besetzt*
but *aber*
  yes, but … *schon, aber …*
butcher *Metzger/-in* (m./f.) *(Metzger/-innen)*
butter *Butter* (f.) *(no pl.)*
buy (to) *kaufen*
by *von, bei, durch*
  by bus *mit dem Bus*
  by car *mit dem Auto*
  by chance *etwa*
  by profession *von Beruf*
  by tram *mit der Straßenbahn*
  go by cab/taxi (to) *mit dem Taxi fahren*
  go by foot (to) *zu Fuß gehen*
  go by means of … (to) *fahren mit …*
Bye. *Tschüss.*

C

cab *Taxi* (n.) *(Taxis; Taxen)*
  call a cab (to) *ein Taxi rufen*
  go by cab (to) *mit dem Taxi fahren*
cab driver *Taxifahrer* (m.) *(Taxifahrer)*
cake *Kuchen* (m.) *(Kuchen)*
  a piece of cake *ein Stück Kuchen*
California *Kalifornien* (n.)
call (to) *rufen, anrufen, telefonieren*
  called (to be) *heißen*
  call a doctor (to) *den Arzt rufen*
call back (to) *zurückrufen*
can *können*
  Can I help you? *Kann ich Ihnen helfen?*
Canada *Kanada* (n.)
cancel (to) *absagen*
cap (hat) *Mütze* (f.) *(Mützen)*
car *Auto* (n.) *(Autos)*
  by car *mit dem Auto*
  take the car (to) *das Auto nehmen*
card *Karte* (f.) *(Karten)*
  play cards (to) *Karten spielen*

card game *Kartenspiel* (n.) *(Kartenspiele)*
career *Karriere* (f.) *(Karrieren)*
  advance (to make a career) (to) *Karriere*
  machen
Careful! *Vorsicht!*
  Be careful! *Pass gut auf dich auf!*
carpenter *Tischler/-in* (m./f.) *(Tischler/-innen)*
carrot *Karotte* (f.) *(Karotten)*
cashier *Kasse* (f.) *(Kassen)*
  at the cashier *an der Kasse*
cat *Katze* (f.) *(Katzen)*
catch a cold (to) *sich erkälten, eine Erkältung*
  bekommen
catch something (somebody else's illness)
  (to) *sich anstecken*
cause *Ursache* (f.) *(Ursachen)*
caution *Vorsicht* (f.) *(no pl.)*
celebrate (to) *feiern*
cell phone *Handy* (n.) *(Handys)*
cell phone number *Handynummer* (f.)
  (Handynummern)
certain *bestimmt, sicher*
certainly *bestimmt, schon*
chair *Stuhl* (m.) *(Stühle)*
champagne *Champagner* (m.) *(no pl.)*
chance *Chance* (f.) *(Chancen)*
  by chance *etwa*
change (to) *umtauschen, wechseln, ändern*
change (trains/buses) (to) *umsteigen*
cheap *billig*
check *Rechnung* (f.) *(Rechnungen)*
  One check? (at a restaurant) *Alles*
  zusammen?
checkered *kariert*
Cheers! (lit., To wellness!) *Zum Wohl!*
cheese *Käse* (m.) *(no pl.)*
chicken *Hühnchen* (n.) *(Hühnchen), Huhn* (n.)
  (Hühner)
child *Kind* (n.) *(Kinder)*
children's room *Kinderzimmer* (n.)
  (Kinderzimmer)
chocolate *Schokolade* (f.) *(Schokoladen)*
choice *Wahl* (f.) *(Wahlen)*
Christmas *Weihnachten* (n.) *(Weihnachten)*
circulate (to) *umgehen*
city *Stadt* (f.) *(Städte)*
city center *Innenstadt* (f.) *(Innenstädte)*
city tour *Stadtrundfahrt* (f.) *(Stadtrundfahrten)*

take a city tour (to) *eine Stadtrundfahrt machen*
classified ad *Annonce* (f.) *(Annoncen)*
classmate *Mitschüler/-in* (m./f.) *(Mitschüler/-innen)*
clay *Ton* (m.) (no pl.)
clean (to) *reinigen, auswaschen*
clean the wound (to) *Wunde auswaschen*
client *Klient/-in* (m./f.) *(Klienten/Klientinnen), Kunde/Kundin* (m./f.)
climb (to) *steigen*
clock *Uhr* (f.) *(Uhren)*
close (to) *zumachen*
closeness *Nähe* (f.) *(Nähen)*
closet *Schrank* (m.) *(Schränke)*
clothes *Kleider* (pl.)
clothing *Kleidung* (f.) *(Kleidungen)*
club *Verein* (m.) *(Vereine)*
join a club (to) *einem Verein beitreten*
coat *Mantel* (m.) *(Mäntel)*
coffee *Kaffee* (m.) *(Kaffees)*
a cup of coffee *eine Tasse Kaffee*
a portion (lit., a small pot) of coffee *ein Kännchen Kaffee*
coffee cup *Kaffeetasse* (f.) *(Kafeetassen)*
coincidence *Zufall* (m.) *(Zufälle)*
cold *kalt; Erkältung* (f.) *(Erkältungen), Schnupfen* (m.) *(Schnupfen)*
catch a cold (to) *eine Erkältung bekommen*
have a cold (to) *Schnupfen haben*
It is cold. *Es ist kalt.*
cold cuts *Wurstaufschnitt* (m.) (no pl.)
colleague *Arbeitskollege/Arbeitskollegin* (m./f.) *(Arbeitskollegen/Arbeitskolleginnen), Kollege/Kollegin* (m./f.) *(Kollegen/Kolleginnen), Mitarbeiter/-in* (m./f.) *(Mitarbeiter/-innen)*
collect (to) *sammeln*
Cologne *Köln* (n.)
color *Farbe* (f.) *(Farben)*
comb (to) *kämmen*
comb one's hair (to) *sich kämmen*
come (to) *kommen*
come along (to) *mitkommen*
company *Firma* (f.) *(Firmen)*
complete *ganz*
completely *ganz*
compliment *Kompliment* (n.) *(Komplimente)*
computer *Computer* (m.) *(Computer)*

concern (to) *kümmern, betreffen*
congratulation *Glückwunsch* (m.) *(Glückwünsche)*
Congratulations! *Herzlichen Glückwunsch!*
connect (to) *verbinden*
connection *Verbindung* (f.) *(Verbindungen)*
conserve (to) *schonen*
constantly *ständig*
contagious *ansteckend*
continue straight ahead (to) *geradeaus gehen*
cook *Koch/Köchin* (m./f.) *(Köche/Köchinnen)*
cook (to) *kochen*
cook well (to) *gut kochen*
cookie *Keks* (m.) *(Kekse)*
corn *Mais* (m.) (no pl.)
corner *Ecke* (f.) *(Ecken)*
around the corner *um die Ecke*
at the corner *an der Ecke*
correct *richtig*
cost (to) *kosten*
couch *Couch* (f.) *(Couches), Sofa* (n.) *(Sofas)*
cough *Husten* (m.) (no pl.)
have a cough (to) *Husten haben*
couple *Paar* (n.) *(Paare)*
a couple of days *ein paar Tage*
course *Lauf* (m.) *(Läufe)*
cousin *Cousin/Cousine* (m./f.) *(Cousins/Cousinen)*
cover (to) *belegen*
credit card *Kreditkarte* (f.) *(Kreditkarten)*
crochet (to) *häkeln*
crosswalk *Fußgängerüberweg* (m.) *(Fußgängerüberwege)*
Take the crosswalk. *Gehen Sie über den Fußgängerüberweg.*
cruise *Schifffahrt* (f.) *(Schifffahrten)*
cry (tears) (to) *weinen*
cucumber *Gurke* (f.) *(Gurken)*
cup *Tasse* (f.) *(Tassen)*
a cup of coffee *eine Tasse Kaffee*
curious *neugierig*
customer *Kunde/Kundin* (m./f.)
cut (to) *schneiden*
cutlet *Schnitzel* (n.) *(Schnitzel)*

D

dad(dy) *Papa* (m.) *(Papas)*
daily *täglich*

dance (to) *tanzen*
dangerous *gefährlich*
darling *Schatz* (m.) *(Schätze), Liebling* (m.)
  (Lieblinge)
date *Verabredung* (f.) *(Verabredungen)*
daughter *Tochter* (f.) *(Töchter)*
day *Tag* (m.) *(Tage)*
  a couple of days, a few days *ein paar Tage*
  all day *den ganzen Tag*
  every day *jeden Tag*
  Good day. *Guten Tag.*
  the day after tomorrow *übermorgen*
  the day before yesterday *vorgestern*
  these days *heutzutage*
December *Dezember* (m.) *(Dezember)*
decide (to) *bestimmen, entscheiden*
decrease (to) *abnehmen*
definite *bestimmt*
definitely *bestimmt*
degree *Grad* (m.) *(Grade)*
delight *Lust* (f.) *(Lüste)*
dentist *Zahnarzt/Zahnärztin* (m./f.)
  (Zahnärzte/Zahnärztinnen)
department store *Kaufhaus* (n.) *(Kaufhäuser)*
  men's department *Herrenabteilung* (f.)
    (Herrenabteilungen)
  shoe department *Schuhabteilung* (f.)
    (Schuhabteilungen)
departure *Abfahrt* (f.) *(Abfahrten), Abreise* (f.)
  (Abreisen)
describe (to) *beschreiben*
desk *Schreibtisch* (m.) *(Schreibtische)*
despite *trotz*
dessert *Nachspeise* (f.) *(Nachspeisen), Nachtisch*
  (m.) *(Nachtische), Süßspeise* (f.) *(Süßspeisen)*
  for dessert *als Nachspeise*
determine (to) *bestimmen*
differently *anders*
difficult *schwierig*
dining room *Esszimmer* (n.) *(Esszimmer)*
dining table *Esstisch* (m.) *(Esstische)*
dinner *Abendessen* (n.) *(Abendessen)*
direction *Richtung* (f.) *(Richtungen)*
  Drive towards/in the direction of
    Munich. *Fahren Sie in Richtung München.*
directly *direkt*
dive (scuba dive) (to) *tauchen*
divorced *geschieden*

get divorced (to) *geschieden werden*
do (to) *machen, tun, treiben*
  have a lot to do (to) *viel zu tun haben*
doctor *Arzt/Ärztin* (m./f.) *(Ärzte/Ärztinnen)*
doctor's office *Praxis* (f.) *(Praxen)*
dog *Hund* (m.) *(Hunde)*
door *Tür* (f.) *(Türen)*
draw (to) *zeichnen*
dream *Traum* (m.) *(Träume)*
dress *Kleid* (n.) *(Kleider)*
dress (to) *anziehen*
drink *Getränk* (n.) *(Getränke)*
drink (to) *trinken*
drive (to) *fahren, treiben*
  Drive safely! *Gute Fahrt!*
drop *Tropfen* (m.) *(Tropfen)*
drugstore *Drogerie* (f.) *(Drogerien)*
during *während*

E

each *jede, je*
earlier *früher*
early *früh*
earring *Ohrring* (m.) *(Ohrringe)*
eat (to) *essen*
editor *Redakteur/-in* (m./f.) *(Redakteure/*
  Redakteurinnen)
education *Ausbildung* (f.) *(Ausbildungen)*
eight *acht*
eighteen *achtzehn*
eighty *achtzig*
either *entweder*
  either … or … *entweder … oder …*
elbow *Ellbogen* (m.) *(Ellbogen)*
electrician *Elektriker/-in* (m./f.) *(Elektriker/-*
  innen)
elementary school (first grade through fourth
  grade) *Grundschule* (f.) *(Grundschulen)*
eleven *elf*
else *sonst*
  Anything else? *Sonst noch etwas?/Darf's*
    sonst noch etwas sein?
  What else do you need? *Was brauchen Sie*
    sonst noch?
e-mail *E-Mail* (f.) *(E-Mails)*
embarrassing *peinlich*
emergency *Notfall* (m.) *(Notfälle)*
emergency room *Notaufnahme* (f.)

(Notaufnahmen)

employee *Arbeitnehmer/-in* (m./f.)
(*Arbeitnehmer/-innen*), *Angestellte* (m./f.)
(*Angestellten*), *Mitarbeiter/-in* (m./f.)
(*Mitarbeiter/-innen*)

employment *Beschäftigung* (f.)
(*Beschäftigungen*)

full-time employment *Vollzeitbeschäftigug*
(f.) (*Vollzeitbeschäftigungen*)

part-time employment *Teilzeitbeschäftigung*
(f.) (*Teilzeitbeschäftigungen*)

self-employed *selbstständig*

empty *leer*

end *Ende* (n.) (*Enden*), *Schluss* (m.) (*Schlüsse*)

end (to) *beenden*

engaged *verlobt*

engaged (to be) *verlobt sein*

Enjoy! *Viel Spaß!*

Enjoy your meal! *Guten Appetit!*

enough *genug*

entertainment *Unterhaltung* (f.)
(*Unterhaltungen*)

entire *ganz*

entrance *Einfahrt* (f.) (*Einfahrten*)

euro *Euro* (m.) (*Euros*)

evaluation *Beurteilung* (f.) (*Beurteilungen*)

even *schon, sogar, auch*

evening *Abend* (m.) (*Abende*)

Good evening. *Guten Abend.*

in the evening *am Abend, abends*

this evening *heute Abend*

ever *je*

every *jede*

every day *jeden Tag*

every Thursday *jeden Donnerstag*

every time *jedes Mal*

everyday life *tägliches Leben*

everything *alles*

Is everything okay? *Ist alles in Ordnung?*

That's everything. *Das ist alles.*

exam *Prüfung* (f.) (*Prüfungen*)

high school exam *Abitur* (n.) (*Abiture*)

middle school exam *Realschulprüfung* (f.)
(*Realschulprüfungen*)

school-leaving exam (lower
level) *Hauptschulabschluß* (m.)
(*Hauptschulabschlüsse*)

take the high school exam (to) *das Abitur*

machen

take the middle school exam (to) *die
Realschulprüfung machen*

examine (to) *untersuchen*

excellent *ausgezeichnet, hervorragend*

except for *außer*

exchange (to) *umtauschen, wechseln*

excited *aufgeregt*

excitedly *aufgeregt*

excuse *Entschuldigung* (f.) (*Entschuldigungen*)

Excuse me. *Entschuldigung.*

excuse (to) *entschuldigen*

Excuse me. *Entschuldige.*

Excuse me?/I'm sorry? *Wie bitte?*

exit *Ausfahrt* (f.) (*Ausfahrten*)

expensive *teuer*

experience *Erfahrung* (f.) (*Erfahrungen*)

explain (to) *erklären*

expression *Ausdruck* (m.) (*Ausdrücke*)

eye *Auge* (n.) (*Augen*)

keep an eye on (to) *aufpassen*

F

fall *Herbst* (m.) (*Herbste*)

fall (to) *fallen*

fall asleep (to) *einschlafen*

family *Familie* (f.) (*Familien*)

family life *Familienleben* (n.) (no pl.)

family photographs *Familienfotos* (pl.)

start a family (to) *eine Familie gründen*

fantastic *fantastisch*

far *weit*

How far … ? *Wie weit … ?*

fare *Fahrgeld* (n.) (no pl.)

farther *weiter*

two blocks farther *zwei Straßen weiter*

fast *schnell*

fast-paced *schnelllebig*

fat *dick*

fattening (to be) *dick machen*

father *Vater* (m.) (*Väter*)

father-in-law *Schwiegervater* (m.)
(*Schwiegerväter*)

favorite *Liebling* (m.) (*Lieblinge*)

favorite subject *Lieblingsfach* (n.)

February *Februar* (m.) (*Februare*)

feel (to) *fühlen, sich fühlen*

feel healthy (to) *sich gesund fühlen*

feel like (to) *Lust haben*
feel like doing something (to) *zu etwas Lust haben*
feel sick (to) *sich krank fühlen*
feel well (to) *sich wohl fühlen*
not feel like (to) *keine Lust haben*
fetch (to) *holen*
fever *Fieber* (n.) *(Fieber)*
  high fever *hohes Fieber*
  take someone's temperature (to) *Fieber messen*
few *wenige*
fifteen *fünfzehn*
  It is six fifteen. (time) *Es ist sechs Uhr fünfzehn.*
fifty *fünfzig*
  from the fifties ('50s) *aus den Fünfzigern*
final sentence *Schlusssatz* (m.) *(Schlusssätze)*
finally *endlich*
  Finally! *Na endlich!*
find (to) *finden*
finger *Finger* (m.) *(Finger)*
finished *fertig, vorbei*
fire (to) *entlassen*
first *zuerst, erst mal*
  at first *erst*
  for the first time *zum ersten Mal*
fish *Fisch* (m.) *(Fische)*
fit *fit*
fit (to) *passen*
  fit well (to) *gut passen*
fitness club *Fitnessclub* (m.) *(Fitnessclubs)*
fitting room *Umkleidekabine* (f.) *(Umkleidekabinen)*
five *fünf*
flexible working hours *gleitende Arbeitszeit* (f.)
flower *Blume* (f.) *(Blumen)*
flu *Grippe* (f.) *(Grippen)*
  have the flu (to) *Grippe haben*
  The flu is going around. *Die Grippe geht um.*
follow (to) *folgen*
food *Lebensmittel* (n.) *(Lebensmittel)*
foot *Fuß* (m.) *(Füße)*
  go by foot (to) *zu Fuß gehen*
for *für, seit*
foreign *fremd*
forget (to) *vergessen*
Forgive me. *Entschuldigung./Verzeihung.*

forgiveness *Verzeihung* (f.) *(Verzeihungen)*
fork *Gabel* (f.) *(Gabeln)*
forty *vierzig*
found (to) *gründen*
four *vier*
fourteen *vierzehn*
foyer *Diele* (f.) *(Dielen)*
France *Frankreich* (n.) *(no pl.)*
freelance (adjective/adverb) *freiberuflich*
freelance (to) *freiberuflich arbeiten, freiberuflich tätig sein*
Frenchman *Franzose* (m.) *(Franzosen)*
fresh *frisch*
Friday *Freitag* (m.) *(Freitage)*
friend *Freund/Freundin* (m./f.) *(Freunde/ Freundinnen)*
friendly *freundlich*
from *von, aus, her*
  from … to *von … bis*
  I'm from … *Ich komme aus …*
  Where are you from? *Wo kommen Sie her?/ Woher kommen Sie?*
front (in front of) *vor*
fruit *Obst* (n.) *(no pl.)*
full *voll*
full-time employment *Vollzeitbeschäftigug* (f.) *(Vollzeitbeschäftigungen)*
fully *ganz*
fun *Spaß* (m.) *(Späße)*
  fun (to be) *Spaß machen*
  Have fun! *Viel Spaß!*
furniture *Möbel* (pl.)

G

game *Spiel* (n.) *(Spiele)*
garden *Garten* (m.) *(Gärten)*
  work in the garden (to) *im Garten arbeiten*
garden work *Gartenarbeit* (f.) *(Gartenarbeiten)*
gas (to get) *tanken*
gas station *Tankstelle* (f.) *(Tankstellen)*
gas station attendant *Tankwart/-in* (m./f.) *(Tankwarte/-innen)*
German (language) *Deutsch* (n.) *(no pl.)*
  in German *auf Deutsch*
German (person) *Deutscher/Deutsche* (m./f.) *(Deutschen)*
Germany *Deutschland* (n.) *(no pl.)*
get (to) *holen, bekommen*

How do I get to ... ? *Wie komme ich ... ?*
get up (to) *aufstehen*
  get up early (to) *früh aufstehen*
  get up late (to) *spät aufstehen*
gift *Geschenk* (n.) *(Geschenke)*
  as a gift for ... *als Geschenk für ...*
girl *Mädchen* (n.) *(Mädchen)*
girlfriend *Freundin* (f.) *(Freundinnen)*
give (as a gift) (to) *schenken*
give (to) *geben*
glad (to be) *freuen*
glass *Glas* (n.) *(Gläser)*
  a glass of wine *ein Glas Wein*
gliding *gleitend*
gloves *Handschuhe* (pl.)
go (to) *gehen, fahren*
  go by means of ... (to) *fahren mit ...*
  go by cab (to) *mit dem Taxi fahren*
  go by foot (to) *zu Fuß gehen*
  go for a walk (to) *spazieren gehen*
  go ice-skating (to) *Schlittschuh laufen*
  go on vacation (to) *Urlaub machen*
  go to bed (to) *ins Bett gehen*
  go skiing (to) *Ski fahren*
  go swimming (to) *schwimmen gehen*
  go well with (to) *gut passen zu*
go out (to) *ausgehen, hinausgehen*
going around (to be) *umgehen*
  The flu is going around. *Die Grippe geht um.*
golf *Golf* (n.)
  play golf (to) *Golf spielen*
golf course *Golfplatz* (m.) *(Golfplätze)*
good *gut*
  Good day. *Guten Tag.*
  Good evening. *Guten Abend.*
  good-looking *gutaussehend*
  Good luck! *Viel Glück!*
  Good morning. *Guten Morgen.*
Goodbye. *Auf Wiedersehen.*
  Good-bye until then. *Auf Wiedersehen bis dann.*
gram *Gramm* (n.) *(Gramme; but no pl. after numbers)*
grandchild *Enkelkind* (n.) *(Enkelkinder)*
granddaughter *Enkelin* (f.) *(Enkelinnen)*
grandfather *Großvater* (m.) *(Großväter)*
grandma *Oma* (f.) *(Omas)*
grandmother *Großmutter* (f.) *(Großmütter)*

grandpa *Opa* (m.) *(Opas)*
grandparents *Großeltern* (pl.)
grandson *Enkel* (m.) *(Enkel)*
grapes (bunch of) *Traube* (f.) *(Trauben)*
grass *Gras* (n.) *(Gräser)*
gray *grau*
great *prima, super*
  Great! *Prima!*
green *grün*
groceries *Lebensmittel* (f.) *(Lebensmittel)*
grocery store *Gemüseladen* (m.) *(Gemüseläden)*, *Supermarkt* (m.) *(Supermärkte)*
guest *Gast* (m.) *(Gäste)*
guitar *Gitarre* (f.) *(Gitarren)*
  play the guitar (to) *Gitarre spielen*

H

hair *Haar* (n.) *(Haare)*
half *halb*
  It is half past seven. *Es ist halb acht.*
ham *Schinken* (m.) *(Schinken)*
hand *Hand* (f.) *(Hände)*
  on the other hand *dagegen*
handball (game) *Handball* (m.) *(no pl.)*
  play handball (to) *Handball spielen*
handsome *gutaussehend*
hang (to) *hängen*
hang up (to) *auflegen*
  hang up the receiver (to) *den Hörer auflegen*
happen (to) *werden, geschehen, passieren*
Happy birthday! *Alles Gute zum Geburtstag!*
hard *hart*
hasten (to) *beeilen*
hat *Hut* (m.) *(Hüte)*, *Mütze* (f.) *(Mützen)*
have (to) *haben*
  have a baby (to) *ein Kind bekommen*
  have a hobby (to) *einem Hobby nachgehen*
  have a picnic (to) *ein Picknick machen*
  I would like to have ... *Ich hätte gern ...*
  There you have it! *Na also!*
have to (to) *müssen*
he *er*
head *Kopf* (m.) *(Köpfe)*
headache *Kopfweh* (n.) *(no pl.)*, *Kopfschmerzen* (pl.)
  have a headache (to) *Kopfweh/ Kopfschmerzen haben*
headache tablet *Kopfschmerztablette* (f.)

(Kopfschmerztabletten)
healthy *gesund*
  feel healthy (to) *sich gesund fühlen*
  To your health! *Auf dein Wohl!*
hear (to) *hören*
Hello. *Guten Tag./Grüß Gott./Servus.*
  Hello, this is Philipp. (on the phone) *Hier Philipp.*
help *Hilfe* (f.) *(Hilfen)*
help (to) *helfen*
  Can I help you? *Kann ich Ihnen helfen?*
help-wanted ad *Stellenanzeige* (f.) *(Stellenanzeigen), Stellenmarkt* (m.) *(Stellenmärkte)*
her (accusative) *sie*
  her, to her (dative) *ihr*
  her (possessive) *ihr*
here *hier, her*
  Here you go. *Bitte sehr.*
  right here *gleich hier*
herself *sich*
Hi. *Hallo.*
high *hoch*
  high fever *hohes Fieber* (n.)
  higher *höher*
  highest (adjective) *höchste*
  highest (adverb) *am höchsten*
highway (interstate) *Autobahn* (f.) *(Autobahnen)*
  state highway *Landstraße* (f.) *(Landstraßen)*
hike (to) *wandern*
him (accusative) *ihn*
  him, to him (dative) *ihm*
himself *sich*
hire (to) *einstellen*
his *sein*
hit (to) *treffen*
hobby *Hobby* (n.) *(Hobbys)*
  have a hobby (to) *einem Hobby nachgehen*
hold (to) *halten*
home *Zuhause* (n.) (no pl.), *zu Hause, nach Hause*
homework *Hausaufgaben* (pl.)
  do homework (to) *die Hausaufgaben machen*
honest *ehrlich*
hope (to) *hoffen*
horse *Pferd* (n.) *(Pferde)*
hospital *Krankenhaus* (n.) *(Krankenhäuser)*
hot *heiß*

  It is hot. *Es ist heiß.*
hotel *Hotel* (n.) *(Hotels)*
hotel room *Hotelzimmer* (n.) *(Hotelzimmer)*
hour *Stunde* (f.) *(Stunden)*
  an hour ago *vor einer Stunde*
  in an hour *in einer Stunde*
  quarter of an hour *Viertelstunde* (f.) *(Viertelstunden)*
house *Haus* (n.) *(Häuser)*
how *wie*
  How about … *Wie wär's mit …*
  How are you? (fml.) *Wie geht es Ihnen?*
  How are you? (infml.) *Wie geht's?*
  how many *wie viele*
  how much *wie viel*
hundred *hundert*
  one hundred *einhundert*
  one hundred one *einhundert(und)eins*
  one hundred thousand *hunderttausend*
  one hundred twenty-one *einhundert(und) einundzwanzig*
hunger *Hunger* (m.) (no pl.)
hungry (to be) *Hunger haben*
hurry (to) *beeilen, sich beeilen*
hurt (to) *verletzen, weh tun*
  hurt oneself (to) *sich verletzen*
husband *Ehemann* (m.) *(Ehemänner), Gatte* (m.) *(Gatten), Mann* (m.) *(Männer)*
  my husband *mein Mann*

I ──────────────────────────────

I *ich*
  I'm sorry. *(Es) tut mir leid.*
ice cream *Eis* (n.) (no pl.)
ice skate *Schlittschuh* (m.) *(Schlittschuhe)*
  go ice-skating (to) *Schlittschuh laufen*
idea *Idee* (f.) *(Ideen)*
if *wenn, ob*
immediately *gleich*
important *wichtig*
impressive *beeindruckend*
improve (to) *verbessern*
in *in, mit*
in order to *um … zu*
inclusive *inklusive*
increase (to) *steigen, erhöhen*
infect (to) *anstecken*
injure (to) *verletzen*

inside *in*
instead *dafür*
instead of *statt, anstatt*
intelligent *intelligent*
intention *Absicht* (f.) (*Absichten*)
interest (to) *interessieren*
internship *Volontariat* (n.) (*Valontariate*)
 internship (newspaper) *Praktikum* (n.)
  (*Praktika*)
 intern at a newspaper (to) *ein Volontariat
  machen*
interrupt (to) *unterbrechen*
intersection *Kreuzung* (f.) (*Kreuzungen*)
into *in*
invitation *Einladung* (f.) (*Einladungen*)
invite (to) *einladen*
invoice *Rechnung* (f.) (*Rechnungen*)
issue *Frage* (f.) (*Fragen*)
it (nominative) *es*
 it (accusative) *es*
 it, to it (dative) *ihm*
its *sein*
itself *sich*

J

jacket *Jacke* (f.) (*Jacken*)
jam *Marmelade* (f.) (*Marmeladen*)
January *Januar* (m.) (*Januare*)
 in January *im Januar*
Japan *Japan* (n.)
jeans *Jeans* (pl.)
jelly *Gelee* (m.) (*Gelees*)
job *Aufgabe* (f.) (*Aufgaben*), *Beruf* (m.)
 (*Berufe*), *Stelle* (f.) (*Stellen*), *Arbeitsstelle* (f.)
 (*Arbeitsstellen*)
job announcement *Stellenanzeige* (f.)
 (*Stellenanzeigen*), *Stellenmarkt* (m.)
 (*Stellenmärkte*)
job opportunity *Berufsaussicht* (f.)
 (*Berufsaussichten*); *Berufschance* (f.)
 (*Berufsschancen*)
job-oriented *beruflich*
jog (to) *joggen*
join (to) *beitreten*
 join a club (to) *einem Verein beitreten*
journalist *Journalist/-in* (m./f.) (*Journalisten/
 Journalistinnen*)
juice *Saft* (m.) (*Säfte*)

July *Juli* (m.) (*Julis*)
June *Juni* (m.) (*Junis*)
junior high school (fifth grade through ninth
 grade) *Hauptschule* (f.) (*Hauptschulen*)
just *gerade, eben, gleich, einfach*

K

karate *Karate* (n.) (no pl.)
karate teacher *Karatelehrer* (m.) (*Karatelehrer*)
keep an eye on (to) *aufpassen*
Keep the change. *Stimmt so.*
key *Schlüssel* (m.) (*Schlüssel*)
kilogram *Kilogramm* (n.) (*Kilogramme; but no
 pl. after numbers*)
kilometer *Kilometer* (m.) (*Kilometer*)
kind *freundlich*
kiss (to) *küssen*
kitchen *Küche* (f.) (*Küchen*)
knee *Knie* (n.) (*Knie*)
knife *Messer* (n.) (*Messer*)
knit (to) *stricken*
know (facts) (to) *wissen*
 know (people, animals, places, and things)
  (to) *kennen*
 How did you know that? *Woher wußtest du
  das?*
 know one's way around (to) *sich auskennen*
 Not that I know of. *Nicht dass ich wüsste.*

L

lacking (to be) *fehlen*
lady *Dame* (f.) (*Damen*)
lamb *Lamm* (n.) (*Lämmer*)
lamp *Lampe* (f.) (*Lampen*)
last *letzte*
 At last! *Na endlich!*
 last month *letzten Monat*
 last night *gestern Abend*
 last week *letzte Woche*
 last year *letztes Jahr*
 the … before last *vorletzte*
late *spät*
later *später*
law (the study of law) *Jura* (pl.)
lawyer *Anwalt/Anwältin* (m./f.) (*Anwälte/
 Anwältinnen*), *Rechtsanwalt/Rechtsanwältin*
 (m./f.) (*Rechtsanwälte/Rechtsanwältinnen*)
lay on (to) *anlegen*

layoff *Entlassung* (f.) *(Entlassungen)*
lead (to) *leiten*
learn (to) *lernen*
  have a lot to learn (to) *viel zu lernen haben*
leave (to) *fahren, abfahren, hinterlassen*
  leave a message (to) *Nachricht* (f.)
    hinterlassen
left, to the left *links*
  turn left (to) *links abbiegen*
leg *Bein* (n.) *(Beine)*
leisure time *Freizeit* (f.) (no pl.)
leisure time activity *Freizeitbeschäftigung* (f.)
  (Freizeitbeschäftigungen)
lend (to) *verleihen*
less *weniger*
lesson *Lektion* (f.) *(Lektionen)*
  lessons *Unterricht* (m.) (no pl.)
let (to) *lassen*
  let go (to) *gehen lassen, entlassen*
letter *Brief* (m.) *(Briefe)*
lettuce *Salat* (m.) *(Salate)*
lie (to) (location) *liegen*
life *Leben* (n.) *(Leben)*
  everyday life *tägliches Leben*
lightning *Blitz* (m.) *(Blitze)*
like (to) *gern haben*
  like (to) (among family members) *lieb haben*
  like (to) (people, things, food, drinks) *mögen*
  like to (would) *möchten*
  I don't like it. *Das gefällt mir nicht.*
  I like it. *Das gefällt mir.*
  I'd like … *Ich möchte gern …*
  I'd like to have … *Ich hätte gern …*
line *Linie* (f.) *(Linien), Leitung* (f.) *(Leitungen)*
  (to speak) on the other line *auf der anderen
    Leitung (sprechen)*
listen (to) *hören, zuhören*
  Listen. *Hör mal.*
liter *Liter* (m.) *(Liter)*
  a liter of milk *ein Liter Milch*
little *wenig*
  a little bit *ein bisschen*
  little brother *Brüderchen* (n.) *(Brüderchen)*
  little sister *Schwesterchen* (n.)
    (Schwesterchen)
live (to) *leben, wohnen*
  I live in Berlin. *Ich wohne in Berlin.*
  Where do you live? *Wo wohnen Sie?*

living room *Wohnzimmer* (n.) *(Wohnzimmer)*
loaf *Laib* (m.) *(Laibe)*
  a loaf of bread *ein Laib Brot*
long *lang*
look (to) *gucken, aussehen*
  Look! *Guck mal!*
  look good on (somebody) (to) *gut stehen*
  You look bad/sick. *Sie sehen schlecht aus.*
look for (to) *suchen*
look forward to … (to) *sich auf … freuen*
loose *los*
lose weight (to) *abnehmen*
lot (a lot) *viel*
  have a lot to learn (to) *viel zu lernen haben*
  have a lot to do (to) *viel zu tun haben*
loud *laut*
love (to) *lieben*
luck *Glück* (n.) (no pl.)
  bad luck *Pech* (n.) (no pl.)
  Good luck! *Viel Glück!*
lunch *Mittagessen* (n.) *(Mittagessen)*
  have lunch (to) *zu Mittag essen*

M

mail (to) *abschicken*
main course *Hauptgericht* (n.) *(Hauptgerichte),
  Hauptspeise* (f.) *(Hauptspeisen)*
  as a main course *als Hauptspeise*
maintain (to) *erhalten*
make (to) *machen*
  How can I make this up to you? *Wie kann ich
    das wieder gut machen?*
  make plans (to) *Pläne machen*
man *Mann* (m.) *(Männer)*
  men's department *Herrenabteilung* (f.)
    (Herrenabteilungen)
manage (to) *leisten*
manager *Manager/-in* (m./f.) *(Manager/-innen)*
many *viele*
  how many *wieviele*
  many years ago *vor vielen Jahren*
map *Karte* (f.) *(Karten)*
  map (city map) *Stadtplan* (m.) *(Stadtpläne)*
marathon *Marathon* (m.) *(Marathons)*
  run a marathon (to) *einen Marathon laufen*
marble cake *Marmorkuchen* (m.)
  (Marmorkuchen)
March *März* (m.) *(Märze)*

mark *Note* (f.) *(Noten)*
market place *Marktplatz* (m.) *(Marktplätze)*
marmalade *Marmelade* (f.) *(Marmeladen)*
married *verheiratet*
　married (to be) *verheiratet sein*
　get married (to) *heiraten*
Marry me! *Heirate mich!*
　Will you marry me? (lit., Will you be my
　　husband?) *Willst du mein Mann werden?*
　Will you marry me? (lit., Will you be my
　　wife?) *Willst du meine Frau werden?*
master's degree *Magister* (m.) *(Magister)*
　study for a master's degree (to) *einen*
　　Magister machen
matching *passend*
May *Mai* (m.) *(Maie)*
maybe *vielleicht*
me (accusative) *mich*
　me, to me (dative) *mir*
　It's me. *Ich bin's.*
meal *Essen* (n.) *(Essen)*
mean (to) *meinen, beabsichtigen*
　That's not what this was supposed to
　　mean./I didn't mean it that way. *So war*
　　das nicht gemeint.
meantime (in the meantime) *inzwischen*
measure (to) *messen*
meat *Fleisch* (n.) (no pl.)
meddling *naseweis*
medication *Medikament* (n.) *(Medikamente)*
medicine *Medizin* (f.) (no pl.), *Medikament* (n.)
　(Medikamente)
meet (to) *kennenlernen, sich treffen*
　meet people (to) *Leute kennenlernen*
meeting *Besprechung* (f.) *(Besprechungen)*
member *Mitglied* (n.) *(Mitglieder)*
menu *Speisekarte* (f.) *(Speisekarten)*
message *Nachricht* (f.) *(Nachrichten)*
　leave a message (to) *Nachricht hinterlassen*
meter *Meter* (m.) *(Meter)*
middle *Mitte* (f.) *(Mitten)*
midnight *null Uhr*
milk *Milch* (f.) (no pl.)
　a liter of milk *ein Liter Milch*
million *Million* (f.) *(Millionen)*
mineral water *Mineralwasser* (n.)
　(Mineralwässer/Mineralwasser)
　a bottle of mineral water *eine Flasche*
　　Mineralwasser
minus *minus*
minute *Minute* (f.) *(Minuten)*
　in ten minutes *in zehn Minuten*
mirror *Spiegel* (m.) *(Spiegel)*
Miss *Fräulein* (n.) *(Fräulein)*
miss (to) *missen, verpassen*
missing (to be) *fehlen*
mom *Mama* (f.) *(Mamas)*
moment *Moment* (m.) *(Momente)*
　at the moment *gerade*
　One moment please. *Einen Moment bitte.*
Monday *Montag* (m.) *(Montage)*
　next Monday *nächsten Montag*
　on Monday *am Montag*
money *Geld* (n.) *(Gelder)*
month *Monat* (m.) *(Monate)*
　last month *letzten Monat*
　next month *nächsten Monat*
more *mehr*
　not any more, no more *nicht mehr*
　once more *noch einmal*
　some more *noch etwas*
morning *Morgen* (m.) *(Morgen)*
　Good morning. *Guten Morgen.*
　in the morning *am Morgen, morgens*
most (adjective) *meiste*
　most (adverb) *am meisten*
mother *Mutter* (f.) *(Mütter)*
mother-in-law *Schwiegermutter* (f.)
　(Schwiegermütter)
motive *Beweggrund* (m.) *(Beweggründe)*
motorcycle *Motorrad* (n.) *(Motorräder)*
　ride a motorcycle (to) *Motorrad fahren*
mountain *Berg* (m.) *(Berge)*
　go mountain climbing (to) *Berg steigen*
mouse *Maus* (f.) *(Mäuse)*
　computer mouse *Computermaus* (f.)
　　(Computermäuse)
mouth *Mund* (m.) *(Münder)*
move (to) *verschieben*
movie *Film* (m.) *(Filme)*
movie theater *Kino* (n.) *(Kinos)*
Mr. *Herr* (m.) *(Herren)*
Mrs./Ms. *Frau* (f.) *(Frauen)*
much *viel*
　how much *wie viel*
Munich *München*

museum *Museum* (n.) *(Museen)*
music *Musik* (f.) (no pl.)
my *mein*
  My name is … *Ich heiße …*
  My pleasure! *Gern geschehen!*
myself *mich*

N

name *Name* (m.) *(Namen)*
  My name is … *Ich heiße …*
  Under which name? (reservation) *Auf*
    welchen Namen?
  What's your name? (fml.) *Wie heißen Sie?*
named (to be) *heißen*
napkin *Serviette* (f.) *(Servietten)*
naturally *natürlich*
near *nahe, dabei*
  nearby *in der Nähe*
  nearer *näher*
  nearest (adjective) *nächste*
  nearest (adverb) *am nächsten*
necessary *nötig*
need (to) *brauchen*
neighbor *Nachbar/-in* (m./f.) *(Nachbarn/*
  Nachbarinnen)
nephew *Neffe* (m.)
never *nie*
nevertheless *trotzdem*
new *neu*
  brand-new *ganz neu*
  What's new? *Was gibt's Neues?*
news (a piece of news) *Nachricht* (f.)
  (Nachrichten)
  That's good news. *Das ist eine gute Nachricht.*
newspaper *Zeitung* (f.) *(Zeitungen)*
  daily newspaper *Tageszeitung* (f.)
    (Tageszeitungen)
  newspaper article *Zeitungsartikel* (m.)
    (Zeitungsartikel)
next *nächste*
  next Monday *nächsten Montag*
  next month *nächsten Monat*
  next week *nächste Woche*
  next year *nächstes Jahr*
  Till next time. *Bis zum nächsten Mal.*
  Until next time. (on the phone) *Auf*
    Wiederhören.
next to *neben*

nice *nett, schön*
nicely *lieb*
niece *Nichte* (f.) *(Nichten)*
night *Nacht* (n.) *(Nächte)*
  at night *nachts*
  last night *gestern Abend*
nine *neun*
nineteen *neunzehn*
ninety *neunzig*
no *kein*
  No. *Nein.*
none *kein*
noodles *Nudeln* (pl.)
noon *Mittag* (m.) *(Mittage)*
nose *Nase* (f.) *(Nasen)*
nosy *naseweis*
not *nicht*
  not any *kein*
  not at all *gar nicht*
  not feel like (to) *keine Lust haben*
  No, not yet. *Nein, noch nicht.*
notify (to) *melden*
novel *Roman* (m.) *(Romane)*
November *November* (m.) *(November)*
now *jetzt, nun*
number *Nummer* (f.) *(Nummern)*
  my (phone) number is … *meine Nummer*
    lautet …
nurse *Krankenpfleger/Krankenschwester* (m./f.)
  (Krankenpfleger/Krankenschwestern)

O

o'clock *Uhr* (f.) *(in time expressions)*
  at five o' clock *um fünf Uhr*
  at one o'clock *um ein Uhr*
  It's ten o'clock. *Es ist zehn Uhr.*
occupation *Beruf* (m.) *(Berufe)*
October *Oktober* (m.) *(Oktober)*
of course *natürlich, selbstverständlich*
offer *Angebot* (n.) *(Angebote)*
  special offer *Sonderangebot* (n.)
    (Sonderangebote)
office *Büro* (n.) *(Büros), Arbeitszimmer* (n.)
  (Arbeitszimmer)
  in an office *im Büro*
  to the office *ins Büro*
often *oft*
oh *ach*

okay (It's okay.) *Schon gut.*
   Is everything okay? *Ist alles in Ordnung?*
old *alt*
   How old are you? *Wie alt sind Sie?*
   I am twenty years old. *Ich bin zwanzig Jahre alt.*
on *an, auf*
   on top of *auf*
once *einmal*
   once more *noch einmal*
one *eins*
   one (indefinite pronoun) *man*
one-way street *Einbahnstraße* (f.) *(Einbahnstraßen)*
onion *Zwiebel* (f.) *(Zwiebeln)*
only *nur, erst*
onto *auf*
open (to) *aufmachen, öffnen, eröffnen*
opinion *Meinung* (f.) *(Meinungen)*
or *oder*
orange *Orange* (f.) *(Orangen)*
orange juice *Orangensaft* (m.) *(Orangensäfte)*
order *Ordnung* (f.) *(Ordnungen)*
order (to) *bestellen*
other *andere*
   the others *die anderen*
ought to *sollen*
our *unser*
ourselves *uns*
out *raus*
   out of *aus*
outside *draußen*
outstanding *hervorragend*
over *über, vorbei*
overtime *Überstunde* (f.) *(Überstunden)*
   work overtime (to) *Überstunden machen*
owe (to) *schulden*

P

page *Seite* (f.) *(Seiten)*
   book page *Buchseite* (f.) *(Buchseiten)*
pain *Schmerz* (m.) *(Schmerzen)*
   in pain (to be) *Schmerzen haben*
paint (to) *malen*
pair *Paar* (n.) *(Paare)*
   a pair of shoes *ein Paar Schuhe*
pants (pair of pants) *Hose* (f.) *(Hosen)*
parents *Eltern* (pl.)

park *Park* (m.) *(Parks)*
park (to) *parken*
   park in a parking garage (to) *im Parkhaus parken*
parking garage *Parkhaus* (n.) *(Parkhäuser)*
partner *Partner/-in* (m./f.) *(Partner/-innen)*
part-time *Teilzeit* (f.) (no pl.)
   part-time employment *Teilzeitbeschäftigung* (f.) *(Teilzeitbeschäftigungen)*
party *Party* (f.) *(Partys)*
   have a party (to) *eine Party geben*
passenger *Fahrgast* (n.) *(Fahrgäste)*
past *nach*
   It is quarter past three. *Es ist viertel nach drei.*
pasta *Nudeln* (pl.)
path *Weg* (m.) *(Wege)*
patient *Patient/-in* (m./f.) *(Patienten/ Patientinnen)*
pattern *Muster* (n.) *(Muster)*
pay (to) *bezahlen*
   Pay attention! *Pass auf!*
pea soup *Erbsensuppe* (f.) *(Erbsensuppen)*
peak season *Hochsaison* (f.) *(Hochsaisons)*
pedestrian *Fußgänger* (m.) *(Fußgänger)*
   pedestrian zone *Fußgängerzone* (f.) *(Fußgängerzonen)*
penicillin *Penizillin* (n.) (no pl.)
pension *Pension* (f.) *(Pensionen)*
people *Leute* (pl.)
   meet people (to) *Leute kennenlernen*
pepper (spice) *Pfeffer* (m.) (no pl.)
pepper (vegetable) *Paprika* (m.) *(Paprikas)*
per *pro*
percent *Prozent* (n.) *(Prozente)*
perfect *perfekt*
personally *persönlich*
Ph.D. *Doktor* (m.) *(Doktoren)*
   study for a Ph.D. (to) *einen Doktor machen*
pharmacy *Apotheke* (f.) *(Apotheken)*
photo *Bild* (n.) *(Bilder)*
photograph *Foto* (n.) *(Fotos)*
   family photographs *Familienfotos* (pl.)
photograph (to) *fotografieren*
pianist *Pianist/-in* (m./f.) *(Pianisten/ Pianistinnen)*
piano *Klavier* (n.) *(Klaviere)*
   play the piano (to) *Klavier spielen*

picnic *Picknick* (n.) *(Picknicke)*
  have a picnic (to) *ein Picknick machen*
picture *Bild* (n.) *(Bilder)*
piece *Stück* (n.) *(Stücke)*
  a piece of cake *ein Stück Kuchen*
  in one piece *am Stück*
pill *Tablette* (f.) *(Tabletten)*
pink *rosa*
place *Stelle* (f.) *(Stellen)*
place (to) *stellen, legen, setzen*
plan *Plan* (m.) *(Pläne)*
  make plans (to) *Pläne machen*
plant (to) *pflanzen*
plate *Teller* (m.) *(Teller)*
play (to) *spielen*
  play along (to) *mitspielen*
  play basketball (to) *Basketball spielen*
  play cards (to) *Karten spielen*
  play soccer (to) *Fußball spielen*
  play sports (to) *Sport treiben*
  play the guitar (to) *Gitarre spielen*
  play the piano (to) *Klavier spielen*
please *bitte*
  Yes, please. *Ja, gern.*
please (to) *gefallen*
pleasure *Lust* (f.) *(Lüste)*
  My pleasure! *Gern geschehen!*
  With pleasure! *Aber gern!*
police *Polizei* (f.) (no pl.)
pool (public pool) *Schwimmbad* (n.)
  (Schwimmbäder)
poor *arm*
popular *beliebt*
pork *Schweinefleisch* (n.) (no pl.)
position *Stelle* (f.) *(Stellen)*
post office *Post* (f.) (no pl.)
postpone (to) *verschieben*
pot *Kännchen* (n.) *(Kännchen); Topf* (m.) *(Töpfe)*
  a portion (lit., a small pot) of coffee *ein Kännchen Kaffee*
potato *Kartoffel* (f.) *(Kartoffeln)*
potato salad *Kartoffelsalat* (m.) *(Kartoffelsalate)*
pottery (to make) *töpfern*
pound *Pfund* (n.) *(Pfunde)*
  a pound of tomatoes *ein Pfund Tomaten*
practice (doctor's office) *Praxis* (f.) *(Praxen)*
practice (to) *nachgehen*
praise (to) *loben*

pregnant *schwanger*
  pregnant (to be) *schwanger sein*
prepare (to) *vorbereiten*
prescribe (to) *verschreiben*
prescription *Rezept* (n.) *(Rezepte)*
price *Preis* (m.) *(Preise)*
problem *Problem* (n.) *(Probleme)*
  No problem. *Kein Problem.*
profession *Beruf* (m.) *(Berufe)*
  by profession *von Beruf*
  professional experience *Berufserfahrung* (f.) *(Berufserfahrungen)*
  professional outlook *Berufsaussicht* (f.) *(Berufsaussichten)*
  professional training *Ausbildung* (f.) *(Ausbildungen)*
professionally *beruflich*
program *Programm* (n.) *(Programme)*
project *Projekt* (n.) *(Projekte)*
promote (to) *befördern*
promotion *Beförderung* (f.) *(Beförderungen)*
prosperous *wohlhabend*
proud *stolz*
prove (to) *beweisen*
psychology *Psychologie* (f.) *(Psychologien)*
punctual *pünktlich*
pupil *Schüler/-in* (m./f.) *(Schüler/-innen)*
purple *violet*
pursue (to) *nachgehen*
put (to) *stellen, anlegen, legen, setzen*
  put on the scale (to) *auf die Waage legen*
  put on (to) *anlegen, anziehen*
  put on a bandage (to) *Verband anlegen*

 Q

quarter (adjective) *viertel*
  It is quarter past three. *Es ist viertel nach drei.*
  It is quarter to three. *Es ist viertel vor drei.*
quarter (noun) *Viertel* (n.) *(Viertel)*
  academic quarter *akademische Viertel*
  quarter of an hour *Viertelstunde* (f.) *(Viertelstunden)*
question *Frage* (n.) *(Fragen)*
  question time *Fragestunde* (f.) *(Fragestunden)*
quick *schnell*
quiet *leise, still*
quite *ganz*

R

racquet *Schläger* (m.) *(Schläger)*
radio *Radio* (n.) *(Radios)*
  radio announcer *Radiosprecher/-in* (m./f.)
    (Radiosprecher/-innen)
rain *Regen* (m.) *(no pl.)*
rain (to) *regnen*
  It is raining. *Es regnet.*
rainy weather *Regenwetter* (n.) *(Regenwetter)*
  in rainy weather *bei Regenwetter*
raise *Erhöhung* (f.) *(Erhöhungen)*
  raise (in salary) *Gehaltserhöhung* (f.)
    (Gehaltserhöhungen)
raise (to) *erhöhen*
rate *Rate* (f.) *(Raten)*
rather *lieber*
reach (to) *erreichen*
read (to) *lesen*
  read out loud (to) *vorlesen*
real *wahr*
really *wirklich, richtig*
  Really? *Wirklich?*
reason *Ursache* (f.) *(Ursachen)*
receive (to) *bekommen, erhalten*
receiver *Hörer* (m.) *(Hörer)*
  hang up the receiver (to) *den Hörer auflegen*
recommend (to) *empfehlen*
red *rot*
red wine *Rotwein* (m.) *(Rotweine)*
remain (to) *bleiben*
remove (to) *abnehmen*
rent (to) *mieten*
reopen (to) *neu eröffnen*
repeat (to) *wiederholen*
reply to (to) *beantworten*
report (to) *melden*
report card *Zeugnis* (n.) *(Zeugnisse)*
reservation *Reservierung* (f.) *(Reservierungen)*
reserve (to) *reservieren*
  reserve a table (to) *einen Tisch bestellen,*
    einen Tisch reservieren
reside (to) *wohnen*
restaurant *Restaurant* (n.) *(Restaurants)*
résumé *Lebenslauf* (m.) *(Lebensläufe)*
  prepare one's résumé (to) *den Lebenslauf*
    schreiben
retire (to) *in Rente gehen, in Pension gehen*

retired *pensioniert*
retirement *Rente* (f.) *(Renten)*
retrospective *Retrospektive* (f.)
  (Retrospektiven)
review *Nachprüfung* (f.) *(Nachprüfungen)*
rice *Reis* (m.) *(no pl.)*
rich *reich*
ride a bicycle (to) *Fahrrad fahren*
right *richtig, gleich; Recht* (n.) *(Rechte)*
  right (to be) *Recht haben, stimmen*
  Isn't that right? *Nicht wahr?*
  right away *sofort*
  right here *gleich hier*
  to the right *rechts*
  turn right (to) *rechts abbiegen*
ring the doorbell (to) *läuten, klingeln*
rise (to) *steigen*
rival *Rivale/Rivalin* (m./f.) *(Rivalen/Rivalinnen)*
road (country road) *Landstraße* (f.)
  (Landstraßen)
roast *Braten* (m.) *(Braten)*
roast beef *Rinderbraten* (m.) *(Rinderbraten)*
room *Zimmer* (n.) *(Zimmer)*
  children's room *Kinderzimmer* (n.)
    (Kinderzimmer)
  dining room *Esszimmer* (n.) *(Esszimmer)*
roommate *Mitbewohner/-in* (m./f.)
  (Mitbewohner/-innen)
rose *Rose* (f.) *(Rosen)*
round up (the amount) (to) *aufrunden*
run (to) *rennen, laufen, leiten*
  run a business (to) *ein Geschäft leiten*
  run a marathon (to) *einen Marathon laufen*
runny nose (to have a runny nose) *Schnupfen*
  haben

S

sad *traurig*
salad *Salat* (m.) *(Salate)*
salami *Salami* (f.) *(Salamis)*
salary *Gehalt* (n.) *(Gehälter)*
sale (on sale) *im Angebot, im Sonderangebot*
salesperson *Verkäufer/-in* (m./f.) *(Verkäufer/-*
  innen)
salt *Salz* (n.) *(Salze)*
same *gleich, egal*
  at the same time *dabei*
Saturday *Samstag* (m.) *(Samstage)*

sauerkraut *Sauerkraut* (n.) (no pl.)
save (to) *schonen*
say (to) *sagen*
scale *Waage* (f.) *(Waagen)*
  put on the scale (to) *auf die Waage legen*
scarf *Schal* (m.) *(Schale, Schals)*
school *Schule* (f.) *(Schulen)*
  comprehensive school *Gesamtschule* (f.) *(Gesamtschulen)*
  elementary school (first grade through fourth grade) *Grundschule* (f.) *(Grundschulen)*
  high school (fifth grade through twelfth grade) *Gymnasium* (n.) *(Gymnasien)*
  junior high school (fifth grade through ninth grade) *Hauptschule* (f.) *(Hauptschulen)*
  middle school (fifth grade through tenth grade) *Realschule* (f.) *(Realschulen)*
  vocational school *Berufsschule* (f.) *(Berufsschulen)*
  schoolboy/girl *Schüler/-in* (m./f.) *(Schüler/-innen)*
scientist *Wissenschaftler/-in* (m./f.) *(Wissenschaftler/-innen)*
search (to) *suchen*
see (to) *sehen*
  I see. *Ach so./Aha!*
  See! *Na also!*
  see again (to) *wiedersehen*
  See you soon. *Bis bald.*
self-employed *selbstständig*
sell (to) *verkaufen*
send (to) *schicken*
send off (to) *abschicken*
sentence *Satz* (m.) *(Sätze)*
  final sentence *Schlusssatz* (m.) *(Schlusssätze)*
September *September* (m.) *(September)*
serve (to) *servieren*
service *Service* (m.) (no pl.)
seven *sieben*
seventeen *siebzehn*
seventy *siebzig*
shared flat *Wohngemeinschaft* (f.) *(Wohngemeinschaften)*, WG (f.) *(WGs)*
she (nominative) *sie*
shelf *Regal* (n.) *(Regale)*
shine (to) *scheinen*

ship *Schiff* (n.) *(Schiffe)*
shirt *Hemd* (n.) *(Hemden)*
shoe *Schuh* (m.) *(Schuhe)*
  a pair of shoes *ein Paar Schuhe*
  shoe department *Schuhabteilung* (f.) *(Schuhabteilungen)*
  shoe store *Schuhgeschäft* (n.) *(Schuhgschäfte)*
shop (to) *einkaufen*
  go (grocery) shopping (to) *einkaufen gehen*
  go (window-)shopping (to) *bummeln gehen*
  shopping list *Einkaufsliste* (f.) *(Einkaufslisten)*
short *kurz*
shot (medical) *Spritze* (f.) *(Spritzen)*
shoulder *Schulter* (f.) *(Schultern)*
show *Show* (f.) *(Shows)*
show (to) *zeigen*
siblings *Geschwister* (pl.)
sick *krank*
  feel sick (to) *sich krank fühlen*
  You look bad/sick. *Sie sehen schlecht aus.*
side room *Nebenzimmer* (n.) *(Nebenzimmer)*
sidewalk *Gehweg* (m.) *(Gehwege)*
signpost *Schild* (n.) *(Schilder)*
silverware *Besteck* (n.) *(Bestecke)*
simple *einfach*
simply *eben, einfach*
since *denn, seit*
sincere *herzlich*
sing (to) *singen*
single *ledig*
  single (to be) *ledig sein*
sister *Schwester* (f.) *(Schwestern)*
sister-in-law *Schwägerin* (f.) *(Schwägerinnen)*
sit (to) *sitzen, sich setzen*
  sit down (to) *sich setzen*
six *sechs*
sixteen *sechzehn*
sixty *sechzig*
size *Größe* (f.) *(Größen)*, *Nummer* (f.) *(Nummern)*
  what size *welche Größe*
ski *Ski* (m.) *(Ski; Skier)*
  go skiing (to) *Ski fahren*
ski resort *Skigebiet* (n.) *(Skigebiete)*
skiing *skifahren* (n.)
skirt *Rock* (m.) *(Röcke)*
sleep (to) *schlafen*
slim *schlank*
slow *langsam*

small *klein*
smoke (to) *rauchen*
snow *Schnee* (m.) (no pl.)
snow (to) *schneien*
  It is snowing. *Es schneit.*
snowboard *Snowboard* (n.) (*Snowboards*)
snowboard (to) *snowboarden*
snowy weather *Schneewetter* (n.) (no pl.)
  in snowy weather *bei Schneewetter*
so *so, also*
  So what? *Na und?*
soccer *Fußball* (m.) (no pl.)
  play soccer (to) *Fußball spielen*
socks *Socken* (pl.)
some *etwas*
  some more *noch etwas*
someone *jemand*
something *etwas*
  something like that *so etwas*
sometimes *manchmal*
somewhat *etwas*
son *Sohn* (m.) (*Söhne*)
soon *bald*
  See you soon. *Bis bald.*
sore throat *Halsschmerzen* (pl.)
sorry *leid*
  Sorry. *Entschuldigung.*
  I'm sorry. *(Es) tut mir leid.*
sound (to) *klingen*
  That sounds good. *Das klingt aber gut.*
soup *Suppe* (f.) (*Suppen*)
  a bowl of soup *ein Teller Suppe*
  pea soup *Erbsensuppe* (f.) (*Erbsensuppen*)
sour *sauer*
South Africa *Südafrika* (n.)
sparkling wine *Sekt* (m.) (*Sekte*)
speak (to) *sprechen*
speaking *am Apparat*
  Honberg speaking. *Honberg am Apparat.*
  Who is speaking? *Wer ist am Apparat?*
special offer *Sonderangebot* (n.)
  (*Sonderangebote*)
specialty *Spezialität* (f.) (*Spezialitäten*)
spice *Gewürz* (n.) (*Gewürze*)
spinach *Spinat* (m.) (no pl.)
spoon *Löffel* (m.) (*Löffel*)
sport *Sport* (m.) (no pl.), *Sportart* (f.) (*Sportarten*)
  play sports (to) *Sport treiben*

sports center *Sportstudio* (n.) (*Sportstudios*)
spring *Frühling* (m.) (*Frühlinge*)
squash *Squash* (n.) (no pl.)
  play squash (to) *Squash spielen*
stadium *Stadion* (n.) (*Stadien*)
stamp *Briefmarke* (f.) (*Briefmarken*)
stand (to) *stehen*
start a family (to) *eine Familie gründen*
statistics *Statistik* (f.) (*Statistiken*)
stay (to) *bleiben*
  stay in shape (to) *fit bleiben*
steak *Steak* (n.) (*Steaks*)
still *noch*
stomach *Bauch* (m.) (*Bäuche*), *Magen* (m.)
  (*Mägen*)
stomachache *Bauchschmerzen* (pl.), *Bauchweh*
  (n.) (no pl.)
stop *Haltestelle* (f.) (*Haltestellen*)
store *Geschäft* (n.) (*Geschäfte*)
straight *direkt*
  straight (ahead) *geradeaus*
  continue straight ahead (to) *geradeaus gehen*
strange *fremd*
street *Straße* (f.) (*Straßen*)
  one-way street *Einbahnstraße* (f.)
  (*Einbahnstraßen*)
street car *Straßenbahn* (f.) (*Straßenbahnen*)
striped *gestreift*
stroll (to) *bummeln, spazieren*
strong *stark*
stuck (to be) *stecken*
  stuck in traffic (to be) *im Stau stecken*
student *Student/-in* (m./f.) (*Studenten/-innen*)
  fellow university student *Kommilitone/*
    Kommilitonin (m./f.) (*Kommilitonen/*
    Kommilitoninnen)
studies *Studium* (n.) (*Studien*)
study *Studium* (n.) (*Studien*)
study (to) (at a university) *studieren*
  study for a Ph.D. (to) *einen Doktor machen*
subject *Fach* (n.) (*Fächer*)
  favorite subject *Lieblingsfach* (n.)
successful *erfolgreich*
sugar *Zucker* (m.) (no pl.)
sugar sweet *zuckersüß*
suit *Anzug* (m.) (*Anzüge*)
suit (to) *stehen, passen*
suitcase *Koffer* (m.) (*Koffer*)

summer *Sommer* (m.) *(Sommer)*
in the summer *im Sommer*
summer vacation *Sommerurlaub* (m.)
(Sommerurlaube)
sun *Sonne* (f.) *(Sonnen)*
Sunday *Sonntag* (m.) *(Sonntage)*
super *super*
superior *Vorgesetzte* (m./f.) *(Vorgesetzten)*
sure *sicher*
Sure! *Bestimmt!*
sweater *Pullover* (m.) *(Pullover)*
woman's sweater *Damenpullover* (m.)
(Damenpullover)
sweet *süß*
sweet-and-sour *süßsauer*
sweetheart *Schatz* (m.) *(Schätze)*
sweets *Süßspeise* (f.) *(Süßspeisen)*
swim (to) *schwimmen*
go swimming (to) *schwimmen gehen*
syringe *Spritze* (f.) *(Spritzen)*

T

table *Tisch* (m.) *(Tische)*
dining table *Esstisch* (m.) *(Esstische)*
reserve a table (to) *einen Tisch bestellen,
einen Tisch reservieren*
take (to) *fahren, nehmen*
take a city tour (to) *eine Stadtrundfahrt
machen*
take along (to) *mitnehmen*
Take care. *Mach's gut.*
take care of … (to) *sich kümmern um …*
Take good care of yourself! *Pass gut auf dich
auf!*
take it easy (to) *sich schonen*
take the bus (to) *den Bus nehmen*
take the car (to) *das Auto nehmen*
take the daughter to school (to) *die Tochter
in die Schule fahren*
take the high school exam (to) *das Abitur
machen*
take the tram (to) *die Straßenbahn nehmen*
talk (to) *reden*
tango *Tango* (m.) *(Tangos)*
task *Aufgabe* (f.) *(Aufgaben)*
taste (to)/one's taste (to be) *schmecken*
taxi *Taxi* (n.) *(Taxis; Taxen)*
call a taxi (to) *ein Taxi rufen*

go by taxi (to) *mit dem Taxi fahren*
taxi driver *Taxifahrer/-in* (m./f.) *(Taxifahrer/-
innen)*
teach (to) *unterrichten*
teacher *Lehrer/-in* (m./f.) *(Lehrer/-innen)*
telephone *Telefon* (n.) *(Telefone)*
on the phone *am Apparat*
phone number *Telefonnummer* (f.)
(Telefonnummern)
television *Fernsehen* (n.) (no pl.)
television (set) *Fernseher* (m.) *(Fernseher)*
on TV *im Fernsehen*
temperature *Temperatur* (f.) *(Temperaturen)*
elevated temperature *erhöhte Temperatur*
ten *zehn*
tennis *Tennis* (n.) (no pl.)
play tennis (to) *Tennis spielen*
tennis racquet *Tennisschläger* (m.)
(Tennisschläger)
tennis shoes *Tennisschuhe* (pl.)
terrace *Terrasse* (f.) *(Terrassen)*
than *als*
thank (to) *danken*
Thank you. *Danke./Danke schön.*
thanks *Dank* (m.) (no pl.)
Many thanks. *Vielen Dank.*
Thanks for the compliment! *Vielen Dank
für die Blumen! (lit., Thanks for the flowers.
[often used ironically])*
that (conjunction) *dass*
that (demonstrative pronoun) *das*
That sounds good. *Das klingt aber gut.*
the (nominative) *der* (m.), *das* (n.), *die* (f./pl.)
the (accusative) *den* (m.), *das* (n.), *die* (f./pl.)
the (dative) *dem* (m./n.), *der* (f.), *den* (pl.)
of the (genitive) *des* (m./n.), *der* (f./pl.)
their *ihr*
them (accusative) *sie*
them, to them (dative) *ihnen*
themselves *sich*
then *denn, nun, dann, da*
there *dort, da*
there is/are *es gibt*
therefore *also, deshalb*
these days *heutzutage*
they (nominative) *sie* (pl.)
they (indefinite pronoun) *man*
thing *Gegenstand* (m.) *(Gegenstände)*

think (to) *glauben, meinen, denken*
  I don't think so. *Ich glaube nicht.*
  I think so, too. *Das finde ich auch.*
thirteen *dreizehn*
thirty *dreißig*
  It is four thirty. *Es ist vier Uhr dreißig.*
thirty-one *einunddreißig*
this *dieser*
  This is … *Das ist …*
those *jene, die* (pl.)
  Those are … *Das sind …*
thousand *tausend*
  one hundred thousand *hunderttausend*
  one thousand *eintausend*
  one thousand one
    hundred *eintausendeinhundert*
  ten thousand *zehntausend*
  two thousand *zweitausend*
three *drei*
  three times *dreimal*
through *durch*
thunder *Donner* (m.) (no pl.)
Thursday *Donnerstag* (m.) (*Donnerstage*)
  every Thursday *jeden Donnerstag*
ticket *Fahrkarte* (f.) (*Fahrkarten*)
tie *Krawatte* (f.) (*Krawatten*)
tight *eng*
time *Zeit* (f.) (*Zeiten*), *Uhrzeit* (f.) (*Uhrzeiten*)
  time (occasion) *mal*
  every time *jedes Mal*
  for the first time *zum ersten Mal*
  For what time? (reservation) *Um welche Uhrzeit?*
  question time *Fragestunde* (f.) (*Fragestunden*)
  Till next time. *Bis zum nächsten Mal.*
  What is the time? *Wie spät ist es?*
  What time is it? *Wieviel Uhr ist es?*
tip *Trinkgeld* (n.) (*Trinkgelder*)
  Is the tip included? *Ist das Trinkgeld inklusive?*
tip (to) *ein Trinkgeld geben*
tired *müde*
to *an, zu, nach*
  It is quarter to three. *Es ist viertel vor drei.*
  It is ten to twelve. *Es ist zehn vor zwölf.*
  To your health! *Auf dein Wohl!*
today (to) *heute*
toe (to) *Zehe* (f.) (*Zehen*)

together (to) *zusammen*
toilet *Toilette* (f.) (*Toiletten*)
tomato *Tomate* (f.) (*Tomaten*)
  a pound of tomatoes *ein Pfund Tomaten*
tomorrow *morgen*
  the day after tomorrow *übermorgen*
tonight *heute Abend*
too *auch, zu*
  Too bad. *So ein Pech.*
tooth *Zahn* (m.) (*Zähne*)
toothache *Zahnweh* (n.) (no pl.), *Zahnschmerzen* (pl.)
  have a toothache (to) *Zahnweh haben*
tourist *Tourist/-in* (m./f.) (*Touristen/Touristinnen*)
toward *zu, gegen*
town *Stadt* (f.) (*Städte*)
  around town *in der Stadt*
town hall *Rathaus* (n.) (*Rathäuser*)
toy *Spielzeug* (n.) (*Spielzeuge*)
trade *Handwerk* (n.) (*Handwerke*)
traffic *Verkehr* (m.) (no pl.)
traffic announcement *Verkehrsdurchsage* (f.) (*Verkehrsdurchsagen*)
traffic jam *Stau* (m.) (*Staus*)
  stopped in traffic (to be) *im Stau stehen*
  stuck in traffic (to be) *im Stau stecken*
traffic light *Ampel* (f.) (*Ampeln*)
  at the traffic light *an der Ampel*
train *Zug* (m.) (*Züge*)
train station *Bahnhof* (m.) (*Bahnhöfe*)
tram *Straßenbahn* (f.) (*Straßenbahnen*)
  by tram *mit der Straßenbahn*
  take the tram (to) *die Straßenbahn nehmen*
treat (to) *behandeln*
trip *Fahrt* (f.) (*Fahrten*)
true *wahr*
  That's true! *Das stimmt!*
try (to) *probieren*
try on (to) *anprobieren*
Tuesday *Dienstag* (m.) (*Dienstage*)
turn (to) *abbiegen*
  turn left (to) *links abbiegen*
  turn right (to) *rechts abbiegen*
turn around (to) (U-turn) *umdrehen*
twelve *zwölf*
twenty *zwanzig*
twenty-eight *achtundzwanzig*

twenty-five *fünfundzwanzig*
twenty-four *vierundzwanzig*
twenty-nine *neunundzwanzig*
twenty-one *einundzwanzig*
twenty-seven *siebenundzwanzig*
twenty-six *sechsundzwanzig*
twenty-three *dreiundzwanzig*
twenty-two *zweiundzwanzig*
two *zwei*

U

Uh… *Äh…*
umbrella *Schirm* (m.) *(Schirme)*
uncle *Onkel* (m.) *(Onkel)*
under *unter*
  Under which name? (reservation) *Auf welchen Namen?*
understand (to) *verstehen*
unemployed *arbeitslos*
  unemployed (people) *Arbeitslose* (m./f.) *(Arbeitslosen)*
unemployment rate *Arbeitslosenquote* (f.) *(Arbeitslosenquoten)*
unfortunately *leider*
university *Universität* (f.) *(Universitäten)*
  fellow university student *Kommilitone/ Kommilitonin* (m./f.) *(Kommilitonen/ Kommilitoninnen)*
until *bis*
  not until *erst*
  Till next time. *Bis zum nächsten Mal.*
  Until next time. (on the phone) *Auf Wiederhören.*
upright *aufrecht*
urgent *eilig, dringend*
urgently *dringend*
us (accusative); us, to us (dative) *uns*
use (to) *benutzen*
  being used *besetzt*

V

vacant *frei*
vacation *Urlaub* (m.) *(Urlaube), Ferien* (pl.)
  go on vacation (to) *Urlaub machen*
  take a vacation (to) *(sich) Urlaub nehmen*
vacation apartment *Ferienwohnung* (f.) *(Ferienwohnungen)*
vacation plans *Urlaubsplan* (m.) *(Urlaubspläne)*

vase *Vase* (f.) *(Vasen)*
veal *Kalbfleisch* (n.) (no pl.)
vegetables *Gemüse* (n.) (no pl.)
very *sehr*
  Very well. *Sehr gut.*
viewer *Zuschauer/-in* (m./f.) *(Zuschauer/-innen)*
village *Dorf* (n.) *(Dörfer)*
violet *lila*
visit *Besuch* (m.) *(Besuche)*
  on a visit (to be) *zu Besuch sein*
visit (to) *besuchen*
voice *Stimme* (f.) *(Stimmen)*
volleyball (game) *Volleyball* (m.) (no pl.)
  play volleyball (to) *Volleyball spielen*

W

wait (to) *warten*
  wait for (to) *warten auf*
waiter *Ober* (m.) *(Ober), Kellner* (m.) *(Kellner)*
waitress *Bedienung* (f.) (no pl.), *Kellnerin* (f.) *(Kellnerinnen)*
walk (to) *zu Fuß gehen*
  go for a walk (to) *spazieren gehen*
wallet *Geldbeutel* (m.) *(Geldbeutel)*
want to (to) *wollen*
warm *warm, herzlich*
  It is warm. *Es ist warm.*
wash (to) *waschen*
  wash oneself (to) *sich waschen*
wash out (to) *auswaschen*
watch *Uhr* (f.) *(Uhren)*
watch (to) *aufpassen*
water *Wasser* (n.) *(Wasser; Wässer)*
way *Weg* (m.) *(Wege)*
  on the way *unterwegs*
  on the way (to be) (baby) *unterwegs sein*
we *wir*
wealthy *wohlhabend*
wear (to) *anziehen, tragen*
weather *Wetter* (n.) *(Wetter)*
  in bad weather *bei schlechtem Wetter*
  in good weather *bei gutem Wetter*
  in rainy weather *bei Regenwetter*
  in snowy weather *bei Schneewetter*
wedding *Hochzeit* (f.) *(Hochzeiten)*
Wednesday *Mittwoch* (m.) *(Mittwoche)*
week *Woche* (f.) *(Wochen)*
  last week *letzte Woche*

next week *nächste Woche*
per week *pro Woche*
weekend *Wochenende* (n.) *(Wochenenden)*
  on the weekend *am Wochenende*
weigh (to) *wiegen*
Welcome. *Willkommen.*
  Welcome back. *Willkommen zurück.*
  You're welcome! *Bitte./Gern geschehen!*
well *na, wohl*
  feel well (to) *sich wohl fühlen*
  very well *hervorragend*
  Very well. *Sehr gut.*
  Well ... *Na ja ... /Nun ...*
  Well done! *Bravo!*
wet *nass*
what *was*
  So what? *Na und?*
  What's new? *Was gibt's Neues?*
  What's the matter? *Was ist denn los?*
  What's your name? (fml.) *Wie heißen Sie?*
when (question) *wann*
  when (conjunction) *wenn, als*
where *wo*
  where from *woher*
  Where are you from? *Woher kommen Sie?/
  Wo kommen Sie her?*
whether *ob*
which *welch-* (all genders, numbers, cases)
white *weiß*
white wine *Weißwein* (m.) *(Weißweine)*
who (question) *wer*
  who (relative pronoun, nominative) *der* (m.), *das*
    (n.), *die* (f./pl.)
  Who is speaking? *Wer ist am Apparat?*
whole *ganz*
whom (relative pronoun, accusative) *den* (m.), *das*
    (n.), *die* (f./pl.)
  to whom (relative pronoun, dative) *dem* (m./n.),
    der (f.), *denen* (pl.)
whose (question) *wessen*
  whose (relative pronoun) *dessen* (m./n.), *deren*
    (f./pl.)
why *warum*
wife *Ehefrau* (f.) *(Ehefrauen)*, *Frau* (f.) *(Frauen)*
  my wife *meine Frau*
win (to) *gewinnen*
window *Fenster* (n.) *(Fenster)*
wine *Wein* (m.) *(Weine)*

a bottle of wine *eine Flasche Wein*
a glass of wine *ein Glas Wein*
red wine *Rotwein* (m.) *(Rotweine)*
sparkling wine *Sekt* (m.) *(Sekte)*
white wine *Weißwein* (m.) *(Weißweine)*
wine list *Weinkarte* (f.) *(Weinkarten)*
winter *Winter* (m.) *(Winter)*
  in the winter *im Winter*
winter vacation *Winterurlaub* (m.)
  (Winterurlaube)
wish *Glückwunsch* (m.) *(Glückwünsche)*
wish (to) *wünschen*
with *mit, bei*
  With pleasure! *Aber gern!*
without *ohne*
woman *Frau* (f.) *(Frauen)*
wonder (to) *fragen*
work *Arbeit* (m.) *(Arbeiten)*
  flexible working hours *gleitende Arbeitszeit*
    (f.)
work (to) *arbeiten, tätig sein*
  work overtime (to) *Überstunden machen*
work hours *Arbeitszeit* (f.) *(Arbeitszeiten)*
  flexible working hours *gleitende Arbeitszeit*
worker *Arbeiter/-in* (m./f.) *(Arbeiter/-innen)*
workplace *Arbeitsplatz* (m.) *(Arbeitsplätze)*,
  Arbeitsstelle (f.) *(Arbeitsstellen)*
world *Welt* (f.) *(Welten)*
worry *Sorge* (f.) *(Sorgen)*
  No worries./Don't worry. *Keine Sorge.*
wound *Wunde* (f.) *(Wunden)*
  clean the wound (to) *Wunde auswaschen*
write (to) *schreiben*
wrong *falsch*

Y

year *Jahr* (n.) *(Jahre)*
  I am twenty years old. *Ich bin zwanzig Jahre
  alt.*
  last year *letztes Jahr*
  many years ago *vor vielen Jahren*
  next year *nächstes Jahr*
yell (to) *rufen*
yellow *gelb*
Yes. *Ja.*
  Oh yes. *Au ja.*
  yes, but ... *schon, aber ...*
yesterday *gestern*

the day before yesterday *vorgestern*
yet *noch, schon*
No, not yet. *Nein, noch nicht.*
yoga *Yoga* (m./n.) (no pl.)
yoga studio *Yogastudio* (n.) *(Yogastudios)*
yogurt *Joghurt* (m.) *(Joghurts)*
you (nominative) *du* (sg. infml.), *Sie* (sg. fml./pl. fml.), *ihr* (pl. infml.)
you (accusative) *dich* (sg. infml.), *Sie* (sg. fml./pl. fml.), *euch* (pl. infml.)
you, to you (dative) *dir* (sg. infml.), *euch* (pl. infml.), *Ihnen* (sg. fml./pl. fml.)
you, to you (dative) *euch* (pl. infml.)
young *jung*
your *Ihr* (sg. fml./pl. fml.), *dein* (sg. infml.), *euer* (pl. infml.)
yourself *sich* (sg. fml.), *dich* (sg. infml.)
yourselves *sich* (pl. fml.), *euch* (pl. infml.)

Z

zero *null*